Research Methods in Language Learning

CAMBRIDGE LANGUAGE TEACHING LIBRARY
A series covering central issues in language teaching and learning, by authors who have expert knowledge in their field.

In this series:

Research Methods in Language Learning

David Nunan

National Centre for English Language Teaching and Research
Macquarie University

CAMBRIDGE
UNIVERSITY PRESS

PUBLISHED BY THE PRESS SYNDICATE OF THE UNIVERSITY OF CAMBRIDGE
The Pitt Building, Trumpington Street, Cambridge, United Kingdom

CAMBRIDGE UNIVERSITY PRESS
The Edinburgh Building, Cambridge CB2 2RU, UK   http://www.cup.cam.ac.uk
40 West 20th Street, New York, NY 10011–4211, USA   http://www.cup.org
10 Stamford Road, Oakleigh, Melbourne 3166, Australia
Ruiz de Alarcón 13, 28014 Madrid, Spain

First published 1992
Eighth printing 1999

Printed in the United States of America

Typeset in Sabon

Library of Congress Cataloging-in-Publication Data

Nunan, David
Research methods in language learning / David Nunan.
Bibliography: p.
p. cm. – (Cambridge language teaching library)
Includes bibliographical references and index.
ISBN 0-521-41937-9 (hardback) ISBN 0-521-42968-4 (paperback)
1. Language and languages – Study and teaching – Research –
Methodology. I. Title. II. Series.
P53.N87   1992
418'.007-dc20   91-44022
                                              CIP

A catalog record for this book is available from the British Library

ISBN 0-521-41937-9 hardback
ISBN 0-521-42968-4 paperback

To my colleagues in the School of English and Linguistics and the National Centre for English Language Teaching and Research, Macquarie University, this book is affectionately dedicated.

Contents

Contents

Preface

Over the last few years, two phenomena of major significance for this book have emerged. The first of these is the strengthening of a research orientation to language learning and teaching. The second is a broadening of the research enterprise to embrace the collaborative involvement of teachers themselves in research.

Within the language teaching literature there are numerous works containing, at worst, wish lists for teacher action and, at best, powerful rhetorical prescriptions for practice. In both cases, the precepts tend to be couched in the form of received wisdom – in other words, exhortations for one line of action rather than another are argued logico-deductively rather than on the basis of empirical evidence about what teachers and learners actually do, inside and outside the classroom, as they teach, learn, and use language.

Over the last ten years, this picture has begun to change, the change itself prompted, at least in part, by practitioners who have grown tired of the swings and roundabouts of pedagogic fashion. While position papers and logico-deductive argumentation have not disappeared from the scene (and I am not suggesting for a moment that they should), they are counterbalanced by empirical approaches to inquiry. I believe that these days, when confronted by pedagogical questions and problems, researchers and teachers are more likely than was the case ten or fifteen years ago to seek relevant data, either through their own research, or through the research of others. Research activity has increased to the point where those who favour logico-deductive solutions to pedagogic problems are beginning to argue that there is too much research.

If teachers are to benefit from the research of others, and if they are to contextualise research outcomes against the reality of their own classrooms, they need to be able to read the research reports of others in an informed and critical way. Unfortunately, published research is all too often presented in neat, unproblematic packages, and critical skills are needed to get beneath the surface and evaluate the reliability and validity of research outcomes. A major function of this book, in addition to providing a contemporary account of the 'what' and the 'how' of research, is to help nonresearchers develop the critical, analytical skills which will enable them to read and evaluate research reports in an informed and knowledgeable way.

Two alternative conceptions of the nature of research provide a point of tension within the book. The first view is that external truths exist 'out there' somewhere. According to this view, the function of research is to uncover these truths. The second view is that truth is a negotiable commodity contingent upon the historical context within which phenomena are observed and interpreted. Further, research 'standards are subject to change in the light of practice [which] would seem to indicate that the search for a substantive universal, ahistorical methodology is futile' (Chalmers 1990: 21).

While I shall strive to provide a balanced introduction to these alternative traditions, I must declare myself at the outset for the second. Accordingly, in the book I shall urge the reader to exercise caution in applying research outcomes derived in one context to other contexts removed in time and space.

This second, 'context-bound' attitude to research entails a rather different role for the classroom practitioner than the first. If knowledge is tentative and contingent upon context, rather than absolute, then I believe that practitioners, rather than being consumers of other people's research, should adopt a research orientation to their own classrooms. There is evidence that the teacher-researcher movement is alive and well and gathering strength. However, if the momentum which has gathered is not to falter, and if the teacher-researcher movement is not to become yet another fad, then significant numbers of teachers, graduate students, and others will need skills in planning, implementing, and evaluating research. Accordingly, a second aim of this book is to assist the reader to develop relevant research skills. At the end of the book, readers should be able to formulate realistic research questions, adopt appropriate procedures for collecting and analysing data, and present the fruits of their research in a form accessible to others.

I should like to thank all those individuals who assisted in the development of the ideas in this book. While these researchers, teachers, learners, and graduate students are too numerous to mention, I trust that they will recognise the contributions which they have made. One person who deserves explicit acknowledgment is Geoff Brindley, who provided many useful references and who helped to synthesise the ideas set out in Chapter 7. Thanks are also due to the anonymous reviewers, whose thoughtful and detailed comments were enormously helpful. Finally, grateful thanks go to Ellen Shaw from Cambridge University Press, who provided criticism and encouragement in appropriate measure and at just the right time. Thanks also to Suzette André, and especially to Sandy Graham, who is quite simply the best editor any author could wish for. Needless to say, such shortcomings as remain are mine alone.

1 An introduction to research methods and traditions

Scientists should not be ashamed to admit . . . that hypotheses appear in their minds along uncharted byways of thought; that they are imaginative and inspirational in character; that they are indeed adventures of the mind.

> (Peter Medawar, 1963, "Is the Scientific Paper a Fraud?" BBC Presentation)

This book is essentially practical in nature. It is intended as an introduction to research methods in applied linguistics, and does not assume specialist knowledge of the field. It is written in order to help you to develop a range of skills, but more particularly to discuss and critique a wide range of research methods, including formal experiments and quasi-experiments; elicitation instruments; interviews and questionnaires; observation instruments and schedules; introspective methods, including diaries, logs, journals, protocol analysis, and stimulated recall; interaction and transcript analysis; ethnography and case studies. Having read the book, you should have a detailed appreciation of the basic principles of research design, and you should be able to read and critique published studies in applied linguistics. In relation to your own teaching, you should be better able to develop strategies for formulating questions, and for collecting and analysing data relating to those questions.

The purpose of this initial chapter is to introduce you to research methods and traditions in applied linguistics. The chapter sets the scene for the rest of the book, and highlights the central themes underpinning the book. This chapter deals with the following questions:

- What is the difference between *quantitative* and *qualitative research?*
- What do we mean by 'the status of knowledge', and why is this of particular significance to an understanding of research traditions?
- What is meant by the terms *reliability* and *validity*, and why are they considered important in research?
- What is *action research?*

Research traditions in applied linguistics

The very term *research* is a pejorative one to many practitioners, conjuring up images of white-coated scientists plying their arcane trade in laboratories filled with mysterious equipment. While research, and the conduct of

1

research, involves rigour and the application of specialist knowledge and skills, this rather forbidding image is certainly not one I wish to present here.

I recently asked a group of graduate students who were just beginning a research methods course to complete the following statements: 'Research is . . .' and 'Research is carried out in order to . . .' Here are some of their responses.

Research is:
- about inquiry. It has two components: process and product. The process is about an area of inquiry and how it is pursued. The product is the knowledge generated from the process as well as the initial area to be presented.
- a process which involves (a) defining a problem, (b) stating an objective, and (c) formulating an hypothesis. It involves gathering information, classification, analysis, and interpretation to see to what extent the initial objective has been achieved.
- undertaking structured investigation which hopefully results in greater understanding of the chosen interest area. Ultimately, this investigation becomes accessible to the 'public'.
- an activity which analyses and critically evaluates some problem.
- to collect and analyse the data in a specific field with the purpose of proving your theory.
- evaluation, asking questions, investigations, analysis, confirming hypotheses, overview, gathering and analysing data in a specific field according to certain predetermined methods.

Research is carried out in order to:
- get a result with scientific methods objectively, not subjectively.
- solve problems, verify the application of theories, and lead on to new insights.
- enlighten both researcher and any interested readers.
- prove/disprove new or existing ideas, to characterise phenomena (i.e., the language characteristics of a particular population), and to achieve personal and community aims. That is, to satisfy the individual's quest but also to improve community welfare.
- prove or disprove, demystify, carry out what is planned, to support the point of view, to uncover what is not known, satisfy inquiry. To discover the cause of a problem, to find the solution to a problem, etc.

Certain key terms commonly associated with research appear in these characterisations. These include: inquiry, knowledge, hypothesis, information, classification, analysis, interpretation, structured investigation, understanding, problem, prove, theory, evaluation, asking questions, analysing data, scientific method, insight, prove/disprove, characterise phenomena, demystify, uncover, satisfy inquiry, solution. The terms, taken together, suggest that research is a process of formulating questions, problems, or hypotheses; collecting data or evidence relevant to these questions/problems/hypotheses; and analysing or interpreting these data. The minimal definition to which I shall adhere in these pages is that *research* is a systematic process of inquiry consisting of three elements or components: (1) a question, problem, or hypothesis, (2) data, (3) analysis and interpretation of data. Any activity which lacks one of these elements (for example, data) I shall classify as something other than research. (A short definition of key terms printed in italic can be found in the glossary at the end of the book.)

Traditionally, writers on research traditions have made a binary distinction between qualitative and quantitative research, although more recently it has been argued that the distinction is simplistic and naive. Reichardt and Cook (cited in Chaudron 1988), for example, argue that in practical terms, qualitative and quantitative research are in many respects indistinguishable, and that 'researchers in no way follow the principles of a supposed paradigm without simultaneously assuming methods and values of the alternative paradigms' (Reichardt and Cook 1979: 232). Those who draw a distinction suggest that quantitative research is obtrusive and controlled, objective, generalisable, outcome oriented, and assumes the existence of 'facts' which are somehow external to and independent of the observer or researcher. Qualitative research, on the other hand, assumes that all knowledge is relative, that there is a subjective element to all knowledge and research, and that holistic, ungeneralisable studies are justifiable (an ungeneralisable study is one in which the insights and outcomes generated by the research cannot be applied to contexts or situations beyond those in which the data were collected). In metaphorical terms, quantitative research is 'hard' while qualitative research is 'soft'. Terms (sometimes used in approbation, sometimes as abuse) commonly associated with the two paradigms are set out in Figure 1.1.

In an attempt to go beyond the binary distinction between qualitative and quantitative research, Chaudron (1988) argues that there are four research traditions in applied linguistics. These are the psychometric tradition, interaction analysis, discourse analysis, and ethnography. Typically, *psychometric* investigations seek to determine language gains from different methods and materials through the use of the 'experimental method' (to be dealt with in detail in Chapter 2). *Interaction analysis* in classroom settings investigates such relationships as the extent to which learner behaviour is a function of teacher-determined interaction, and utilises various observation systems and schedules for coding classroom interactions. *Discourse analysis* analyses classroom discourse in linguistic terms through the study of classroom transcripts which typically assign utterances to predetermined categories. Finally, *ethnography* seeks to obtain insights into the classroom as a cultural system through naturalistic, 'uncontrolled' observation and description (we shall deal with ethnography in Chapter 3). While Chaudron's aim of attempting to transcend the traditional binary distinction is a worthy one, it could be argued that discourse analysis and interaction analysis are methods of data

Qualitative research	Quantitative research
Advocates use of qualitative methods	Advocates use of quantitative methods
Concerned with understanding human behaviour from the actor's own frame of reference	Seeks facts or causes of social phenomena without regard to the subjective states of the individuals
Naturalistic and uncontrolled observation	Obtrusive and controlled measurement
Subjective	Objective
Close to the data: the 'insider' perpsective	Removed from the data: the 'outsider' perspective
Grounded, discovery-oriented, exploratory, expansionist, descriptive, and inductive	Ungrounded, verification-oriented, confirmatory, reductionist, inferential, and hypothetical-deductive
Process-oriented	Outcome-oriented
Valid: 'real', 'rich', and 'deep' data	Reliable: 'hard' and replicable data
Ungeneralisable: single case studies	Generalisable: multiple case studies
Assumes a dynamic reality	Assumes a stable reality

Figure 1.1   Terms commonly associated with quantitative and qualitative approaches to research (adapted from Reichardt and Cook 1979)

collection rather than distinct research traditions in their own right. In fact these methods can be (and have been) utilised by researchers working in both the psychometric and ethnographic traditions. For example, ethnographers can use interaction analysis checklists to supplement their naturalistic observations, while psychometric research can use similar schemes to identify and measure distinctions between different classrooms, teaching methods, approaches, and teachers (the studies reported by Spada 1990 are excellent examples of such research).

Grotjahn (1987) provides an insightful analysis of research traditions in applied linguistics. He argues that the qualitative-quantitative distinction is an oversimplification and that, in analysing actual research studies, it is necessary to take into consideration the method of data collection (whether the data have been collected experimentally or non-experimentally); the type of data yielded by the investigation (qualitative or quantitative); and the type of analysis conducted on the data (whether statistical or interpretive). Mixing and matching these variables provides us with two 'pure' research paradigms. Paradigm 1 is the 'exploratory-interpretive' one which utilises a non-experimental method, yields qualitative data, and provides an interpretive analysis of that data. The second, or 'analytical-nomological' paradigm, is one in which the data are collected through an experiment, and yields quantitative data which are subjected to statistical analysis. In addition to these 'pure' forms, there are six 'mixed' paradigms which mix and match the three variables in different ways. For example, there is an 'experimental-qualitative-interpretive' paradigm which utilises an experiment but yields qualitative data, which are analysed interpretively. The different research paradigms resulting from mixing and matching these variables are set out in Figure 1.2. (It should be pointed out that, while all of these various 'hybrid' forms are theoretically possible, some are of extremely unlikely occurrence. For example, it would be unusual for a researcher to go to the trouble of setting up a formal experiment yielding quantitative data which are analysed interpretively.)

While I accept Grotjahn's assertion that in the execution of research the qualitative-quantitative distinction is relatively crude, I still believe that the distinction is a real, not an ostensible one, and that the two 'pure' paradigms are underpinned by quite different conceptions of the nature and status of knowledge. Before turning to a discussion of this issue, however, I should like to outline a model developed by van Lier (1988; 1990) for characterising applied linguistic research.

Van Lier argues that applied linguistic research can be analysed in terms of two parameters: an interventionist parameter and a selectivity parameter. Research is placed on the interventionist parameter according to the extent to which the researcher intervenes in the environment. A formal experiment which takes place under laboratory conditions would be placed at one end of the interventionist continuum/parameter, while a naturalistic study of a classroom in action would be placed at the other end of the continuum. The other parameter places research according to the degree to which the researcher prespecifies the phenomena to be investigated. Once again, a formal experiment, in which the researcher prespecifies the variables being focused on, would be placed at one end of the continuum, while an ethnographic 'portrait' of a classroom in action would occur at the other end of the continuum. Figure 1.3 illustrates the relationship between these two parameters.

The intersection of these two parameters creates four 'semantic spaces': a 'controlling' space, a 'measuring' space, an 'asking/doing' space, and a 'watching ' space. The controlling space, which is characterised by a high degree of intervention and a high degree of control, contains studies in which the experimenters focus their attention on a limited number of variables and attempt to control these in some way. For example, in an investigation into the effect of cultural knowledge on reading comprehension, the investigator may set up an experiment in which subjects from different cultural backgrounds read texts in which the content is derived from their own and other cultures. In such an experiment, the focus is on a single variable (cultural background) which is controlled through the reading texts administered to the subjects.

The measuring space encloses those research methods involving a high degree of selection but a low degree of control. 'One selects certain features, operationally defines them, and quantifies their occurrence, in order to establish a relationship between features, or between features and other things,

PURE FORMS

Paradigm 1: exploratory-interpretive

1 non-experimental design
2 qualitative data
3 interpretive analysis

Paradigm 2: analytical-nomological

1 experimental or quasi-experimental design
2 quantitative data
3 statistical analysis

MIXED FORMS

Paradigm 3: experimental-qualitative-interpretative

1 experimental or quasi-experimental design
2 qualitative data
3 interpretive analysis

Paradigm 4: experimental-qualitative-statistical

1 experimental or quasi-experimental design
2 qualitative data
3 statistical analysis

Paradigm 5: exploratory-qualitative-statistical

1 non-experimental design
2 qualitative data
3 statistical analysis

Paradigm 6: exploratory-quantitative-statistical

1 non-experimental design
2 quantitative data
3 statistical analysis

Paradigm 7: exploratory-quantitative-interpretive

1 non-experimental design
2 quantitative data
3 interpretive analysis

Paradigm 8: experimental-quantitative-interpretive

1 experimental or quasi-experimental design
2 quantitative data
3 interpretive analysis

Figure 1.2   Types of research design (from Grotjahn 1987: 59–60)

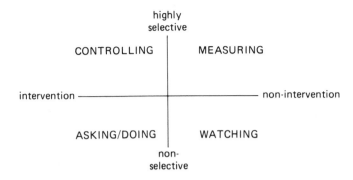

Figure 1.3   Parameters in research design (after van Lier 1988)

such as educational outcomes' (van Lier 1990: 34). For example, the researcher may be interested in the effect of teacher questions on student responses. Armed with a taxonomy of teacher questions, the researcher observes a series of classes, documenting the types of questions asked and the length and complexity of the responses. Here the researcher is highly selective in what he or she chooses to look at or for, but does not attempt to control the behaviour of either the teacher or the students.

The asking/doing space contains studies in which there is a high degree of intervention, but a low degree of control. 'One investigates certain problem areas by probing, trying out minor changes, asking for participants' views and concerns, and so on. After a while it may be possible to pinpoint the problem so precisely that a controlled environment can be created in order to conduct an experiment, thus moving from [asking/doing] through watching to controlling. On the other hand, increased understanding through interpretation can also make experimentation unnecessary' (van Lier 1990: 34–35).

The final semantic space, watching, is characterised by a lack of selectivity and a lack of intervention. The researcher observes and records what happens without attempting to interfere with the environment. Additionally, the researcher does not decide which variables are of interest or of potential significance before engaging in the research. While some form of quantification or measurement may be used, it is seen as no more than one tool among many, and not inherently superior to any other way of analysing data. An example of a study fitting into this final semantic space would be one in which the researcher wishes to provide a descriptive and interpretive portrait of a school community as its members go about their business of living and learning together.

I find van Lier's model of types of research a useful one, although, as van Lier himself points out, it is a simplification of what really happens when research is carried out. In reality, a particular piece of research may well transcend its initial 'semantic space'. An investigation may well begin in the 'watching' space, and then, as issues emerge, the focus may become narrower. The researcher may then decide to establish a formal experiment to test an hypothesised relationship between two or more variables. In this instance, the research will have moved from the 'watching' space to the 'controlling' space. Regardless of the fact that it is a simplification, it does serve to highlight two of the most important questions researchers must confront at the beginning of their research, namely:

- To what extent should I attempt to prespecify the phenomena under investigation?
- To what extent should I attempt to isolate and control the phenomena under investigation?

Brown (1988) provides a very different introduction to research from van Lier, being principally concerned with quantitative research. In his framework for analysing types of research, he draws a distinction between primary and secondary research. Secondary research consists of reviewing the literature in a given area, and synthesising the research carried out by others. Normally, this is a necessary prerequisite to primary research, which 'differs from secondary research in that it is derived from the primary sources of information (e.g., a group of students who are learning a language), rather than from secondary sources (e.g., books about students who are learning a language)' (1988: 1). Hence, it has the advantage of being closer to the primary source of information. Primary research is subdivided into case studies and statistical studies. Case studies centre on a single individual or limited number of individuals, documenting some aspect of their language development, usually over an extended period of time. Statistical studies, on the other hand, are basically cross-sectional in nature, considering 'a group of people as a cross section of possible behaviors at a particular point or at several distinct points in time. In addition, statistical analyses are used in this approach to estimate the probability, or likelihood, that the results did not occur by chance alone' (p. 3). In Brown's model, statistical studies are further subdivided into survey studies and experimental studies. Survey studies investigate a group's attitudes, opinions, or characteristics, often through some form of questionnaire. Experimental studies, on the other hand, control the conditions under which the behaviour under investigation is observed.

For instance, a researcher might wish to study the effects of being male or female on students' performance on a language placement test. Such research might involve administering the test to the students, then separating their scores into two groups according to gender, and finally studying the similarities and differences in behavior between the two groups. Another type of experimental study might examine the relationship between students' scores on a language aptitude test and their actual

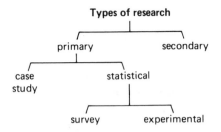

Figure 1.4   Types of research (after Brown 1988)

performance in language classes, as measured by course grades. Experimental studies, then, can be varied in the types of questions being asked . . . (p. 3)

Brown's characterisation of types of research is set out in Figure 1.4.

According to Brown, experimental research should exhibit several key characteristics. It should be systematic, logical, tangible, replicable, and reductive, and one should be cautious of any study not exhibiting these characteristics. A study is *systematic* if it follows clear procedural rules for the design of the study, for guarding against the various threats to the internal and external validity of the study, and for the selection and application of statistical procedures. A study should also exhibit *logic* in the step-by-step progression of the study. *Tangible* research is based on the collection of data from the real world. 'The types of data are numerous, but they are all similar in that they must be *quantifiable,* that is, each datum must be a number that represents some well-defined quantity, rank, or category' (p. 4). *Replicability* refers to the ability of an independent researcher to reproduce the study under similar conditions and obtain the same results. In order for a reader to evaluate the replicability of a study, it should be presented clearly and explicitly. *Reductivity* is explained in the following way: '. . . statistical research can reduce the confusion of facts that language and language teaching frequently present, sometimes on a daily basis. Through doing or reading such studies, you may discover new patterns in the facts. Or through these investigations and the eventual agreement among many researchers, general patterns and relationships may emerge that clarify the field as a whole' (p. 5). Most of these characteristics can ultimately be related to issues of validity and reliability, and we shall look in detail at these critical concepts later in the chapter. Table 1.1 summarises the key characteristics of good experimental research according to Brown.

In this section I have reviewed the recent literature on research traditions in applied linguistics. My main point here is that, while most commentators reject the traditional distinction between qualitative and quantitative research as being simplistic and naive, particularly when it comes to the anal-

TABLE 1.1 CHARACTERISTICS OF GOOD EXPERIMENTAL RESEARCH

Characteristic	Key question
Systematic	Does the study follow clear procedural rules?
Logical	Does the study proceed in a clear step-by-step fashion, from question formation to data collection and analysis?
Tangible	Are data collected from the real world?
Replicable	Could an independent researcher reproduce the study?
Reductive	Does the research establish patterns and relationships among individual variables, facts, and observable phenomena?

Source: Based on Brown (1988).

ysis of published research, the distinction between the research traditions persists. Ultimately, most researchers will admit to subscribing to one tradition rather than another. How, then, are we to account for the persistence of a distinction which has been so widely criticised?

The status of knowledge

One reason for the persistence of the distinction between quantitative and qualitative research is that the two approaches represent different ways of thinking about and understanding the world around us. Underlying the development of different research traditions and methods is a debate on the nature of knowledge and the status of assertions about the world, and the debate itself is ultimately a philosophical one. It is commonly assumed that the function of research is to add to our knowledge of the world and to demonstrate the 'truth' of the commonsense notions we have about the world. (You might recall the statements made by students of research methods, some of which are reproduced at the beginning of this chapter.) In developing one's own philosophy on research, it is important to determine how the notion of 'truth' relates to research. What is truth? (Even more basically, do we accept that there is such a thing as 'truth'?) What is evidence? Can we ever 'prove' anything? What evidence would compel us to accept the truth of an assertion or proposition? These are questions which need to be borne in mind constantly as one reads and evaluates research.

In a recent television advertising campaign, the following claim was made about a popular brand of toothpaste: 'University tests prove that Brand X toothpaste removes 40% more plaque'. (The question of 40% more than what is not addressed.) By invoking the authority of 'university tests' the manufacturers are trying to invest their claim with a status it might otherwise lack. There is the implication that claims based on research carried out in universities are somehow more 'scientific' and therefore believable than claims made on the basis of anecdotes, the experience of the layperson, or the in-house research of the manufacturers themselves. According to Winograd and Flores (1986), the status of research based on 'scientific' experiments and, indeed, the rationalist orientation which underlies it, is based on the success of modern science.

The rationalist orientation . . . is also regarded, perhaps because of the prestige and success that modern science enjoys, as the very paradigm of what it means to think and be intelligent. . . . It is scarcely surprising, then, that the rationalistic orientation pervades not only artificial intelligence and the rest of computer science, but also much of linguistics, management theory, and cognitive science . . . rationalistic styles of discourse and thinking have determined the questions that have been asked and the theories, methodologies, and assumptions that have been adopted. (p. 16)

The following assertions have all been made publicly. You might like to consider these, and the evidence on which they are based, and reflect on which deserve to be taken seriously on the balance of the evidence provided.

ASSERTION 1

Second language learners who identify with the target culture will master the language more quickly than those who do not. (Evidence: A case study of an unsuccessful language learner.)

ASSERTION 2

Schoolchildren are taught by their teachers they they need not obey their parents. (Evidence: A statement by a parent on a radio talk-back program.)

ASSERTION 3

Immigrants are more law abiding than native-born citizens. (Evidence: An analysis of district court records.)

ASSERTION 4

Deaf children are more successful in school if their parents do not succumb to a sense of powerlessness when they experience difficulty communicating with their children. (Evidence: A study based on data from 40 deaf and 20 hearing children.)

ASSERTION 5

Affective relationships between teacher and students influence proficiency gains. (Evidence: A longitudinal ethnographic study of an inner city high school class.)

ASSERTION 6

Students who are taught formal grammar develop greater proficiency than students who are taught through 'immersion' programs. (Evidence: A formal experiment in which one group of students was taught through immersion and another group was taught formal grammar.)

In actual fact, all of these assertions can be challenged on the basis of the evidence advanced to support them. Some critics would reject assertions 1, 2, and 5 on the grounds that they are based on a single instance (in the case of 1 and 2 on the instance of a single individual, and in the case of 5 on the instance of a single classroom). Such critics would argue that the selection of a different individual or classroom might have yielded a very different, even contradictory, response. (We shall return to the issues of 'representativeness' and 'typicality' of data again in later chapters, particularly Chapter 3 on ethnography, and Chapter 4 on case study.) Assertion 3 could be challenged on the grounds that the causal relationship between fewer court convictions and demographic data has not been demonstrated. (It might simply be, for example, that criminals from immigrant communities are smarter, and therefore less likely to be caught than native-born criminals.) The problem with this study is that we can account for the outcomes through explanations other than the one offered by the researchers. Someone versed in research methods would say that the study has poor internal validity. (We shall look at the question of validity in the next section.) Assertion 4 might be criticised on the grounds that 'power' and 'powerlessness' have not been adequately defined. Such a criticism is aimed at the construct validity of the study. (We shall also look at issues related to constructs and construct validity in the next section.) The final assertion can be challenged on the grounds that the two groups might not have been equal to begin with.

In the final analysis, the extent to which one is prepared to accept or reject particular methods of inquiry and the studies utilising these methods will depend on one's view of the world, and the nature of knowledge. For some people the notion that there are external truths 'out there' which are independent of the observer is self-evident. For others, this notion, which underlies the quantitative approach to research, is questionable (see, for example, Winograd and Flores 1986).

Some key concepts in research

In this section, we shall look in greater detail at some key concepts which have to this point only been touched on in passing. We shall look in particular at the concepts of reliability and validity. First, however, I should like briefly to discuss two other terms. These are *deductivism* and *inductivism*.

Two procedures open to researchers are inductivism and deductivism. *Deductive research* begins with an hypothesis or theory and then searches for evidence either to support or refute that hypothesis or theory. *Inductivism* seeks to derive general principles, theories, or 'truths' from an investigation and documentation of single instances. Numerous commentators have criticised what is called naive inductivism (see Chalmers 1982), which is the belief that we can arrive at the 'truth' by documenting instances of the phenomenon under investigation. Popper (1968, 1972) illustrated the naivety of inductivism with his celebrated swan example. He pointed out that we are never entitled to make the claim that 'All swans are white', regardless of the number of sightings of white swans. Though we may have sighted one thousand white swans, there is nothing to say that the one thousand and first sighting will not be a black swan. This led Popper to advance his falsificationist principle. This principle states that while we can never conclusively demonstrate truth through induction, we can in fact falsify an assertion through the documentation of a single disconfirming instance (as in the case of the black swan). According to Popper, all hypotheses should therefore be formulated in a way which enables them to be falsified through a single disconfirming instance. Taken to its logical conclusion, this view would have it that all knowledge is tentative and that, in fact, 'absolute truth' is an ideal which can never be attained.

Chalmers (1982) introduces the falsificationist's position in the following manner:

> According to falsificationism, some theories can be shown to be false by an appeal to the results of observation and experiment. I have already indicated in Chapter 2 that, even if we assume that true observational statements are available to us in some way, it is never possible to arrive at universal laws and theories by logical deductions on that basis alone. On the other hand, it is possible to perform logical deductions starting from singular observation statements as premises, to arrive at the falsity of universal laws and theories by logical deduction. . . . The falsificationist sees science as a set of hypotheses that are tentatively proposed with the aim of accurately describing or accounting for the behaviour of some aspect of the world or universe. However, not any hypothesis will do. There is one fundamental condition that any hypothesis or system of hypotheses must satisfy if it is to be granted the status of a scientific law or theory. If it is to form part of science, an hypothesis must be falsifiable. (pp. 38–39)

The argument that progress in applied linguistics should be through the formulation and testing of hypotheses which are falsifiable has been advanced by numerous researchers. Pienemann and Johnston (1987) mount a vigorous attack on a major and influential research program in applied linguistics on the basis that it is not falsifiable. McLaughlin (1987) also argues that falsifiability or disconfirmation is the most important means to achieving scientific progress in applied linguistics.

13

In any scientific endeavour the number of potentially positive hypotheses very greatly exceeds the number of hypotheses that in the long run will prove to be compatible with observations. As hypotheses are rejected, the theory is either disconfirmed or escapes from being disconfirmed. The results of observation 'probe' but do not 'prove' a theory. An adequate hypothesis is one that has repeatedly survived such probing – but it may always be displaced by a new probe.
(McLaughlin 1987: 17)

In reality, comparatively few hypotheses in applied linguistics can be demolished by a single disconfirming instance. In most cases we are interested in general trends and statistical tendencies rather than universal statements. Even researchers who claim their research is falsifiable have ways of protecting their theories from attack. For example, some second language acquisition researchers (see, for example, Pienemann and Johnston 1987) claim that the morphosyntax of all learners of English as a second language passes through certain developmental stages. These stages are defined in terms of the morphosyntactic items that learners are able to control at a particular stage, which in turn are governed by speech-processing constraints. According to the researchers, it is impossible for learners to 'skip' a stage, and if a single learner were to be found who had mastered, say, a stage 4 grammatical item while still at stage 2, then the developmental hypothesis would have been falsified. In fact, when such instances occur, it may be claimed that the learners in question have not really internalised the item but are using it as a formulaic utterance. Given the difficulty in determining with certainty whether or not an item is or is not a formulaic utterance, it is highly unlikely that the theory will ever be falsified.

Two terms of central importance to research are *reliability* and *validity*, and I shall return to these repeatedly in the course of this book. *Reliability* refers to the consistency of the results obtained from a piece of research. *Validity*, on the other hand, has to do with the extent to which a piece of research actually investigates what the researcher purports to investigate. It is customary to distinguish between internal and external reliability and validity, and I shall deal with each of these briefly in this section. The description and analysis provided here is developed and extended in subsequent chapters.

Reliability refers to the consistency and replicability of research. *Internal reliability* refers to the consistency of data collection, analysis, and interpretation. *External reliability* refers to the extent to which independent researchers can reproduce a study and obtain results similar to those obtained in the original study. In a recent investigation into classroom interaction, one of my graduate students coded the interactions of three teachers and their students using an observation schedule developed for that purpose. I also coded a sample of the interactions independently. When the student and I compared the categories to which we had assigned interactions, we found that we were in agreement in 95% of the cases. We took this high level of agreement as an indication that this aspect of the study had high internal reliability. If a second graduate student were to conduct the study a second time and obtain the same results, we could claim that the study was externally reliable. (This 'inter-rater reliability' procedure is but one way of guarding against threats to the internal reliability of a study. We shall consider alternative procedures in Chapter 3.)

There are two types of validity: internal validity and external validity. *Internal validity* refers to the interpretability of research. In experimental research, it is concerned with the question: Can any differences which are found actually be ascribed to the treatments under scrutiny? *External validity* refers to the extent to which the results can be generalised from samples to populations. Researchers must constantly be alive to the potential and actual threats to the validity and reliability of their work. Table 1.2 provides two sample studies which illustrate the threats to validity posed by poor research design.

One of the problems confronting the researcher who wishes to guard against threats to external and internal validity is that measures to strengthen internal validity may weaken external validity and vice versa, as Beretta has shown.

Internal validity has to do with factors which may directly affect outcomes, while external validity is concerned with generalisability. If all variables, such as treatments and sampling of subjects, are controlled, then we might say that laboratory conditions pertain and that the experiment is more likely to be internally valid. However, what occurs under such conditions may not occur in typical circumstances, and the question arises as to how far we may generalise from the results. (Beretta 1986a: 297)

However, if the researcher carried out the study in context, this may increase the external validity but weaken the internal validity.

In addition to internal and external validity, researchers need to pay close attention to *construct validity*. A construct is a psychological quality, such as intelligence, proficiency, motivation, or aptitude, that we cannot directly observe but that we assume to exist in order to explain behaviour we can observe (such as speaking ability, or the ability to solve problems). It is extremely important for researchers to define the constructs they are investigating in a way which makes them accessible to the outside observer. In other words, they need to describe the characteristics of the constructs in a way which would enable an outsider to identify these characteristics if they came across them. If researchers fail to provide specific definitions, then we need to read between the lines. For example, if a study investigates 'listening comprehension', and the dependent variable is a written cloze test, then the default definition of 'listening comprehension' is 'the ability to complete a written cloze passage'. If we were to find such a definition unacceptable, we would be questioning the *construct validity* of the study. Construct validity

TABLE 1.2 THREATS TO INTERNAL AND EXTERNAL VALIDITY POSED BY POOR
RESEARCH DESIGN: SAMPLE STUDIES

Example	Critique
Internal validity under threat	
In an investigation of three different methods of teaching grammatical structure, three teachers in three different schools are each trained in one of the methods and apply it to their classes. One teacher has three mixed ability classes, another has four mixed ability classes, and the third has two homogeneous groups of fast track learners. At the end of the term, each group is administered a test devised by their teacher. Group means for each group are computed and compared.	In this investigation, the results are uninterpretable. It is impossible to say whether the results are due to the method, the proficiency of the students, the skill of the teacher, or the ease of the test.
External validity under threat	
(Adapted from Wiersma 1986) A study investigates the effect of length of visual exposure on the ability to memorise and recall nonsense words. Subjects are ten postgraduate students who are undertaking a master of arts program in psychology. There are five different lengths of exposure, so five groups of two volunteers each receive different lengths of exposure. A volunteer participates in the study by being exposed to 20 nonsense words individually. After each exposure, the volunteer is to reproduce the nonsense word.	Assuming that the performance scores generally increase with increased length of exposure, the question remains: To which populations and conditions can the results be generalised? Can they be generalised to primary and secondary students learning meaningful material? Can they be generalised to young adults working on meaningful tasks in a highly structured situation? The answer to both questions is no. The results may not even be generalisable to the graduate student population, since the participants were volunteers.

has to do with the question: Is the study actually investigating what it is supposed to be investigating? Brown characterises the notion of a psychological
construct in the following way:

A psychological construct is a theoretical label that is given to some human
attribute or ability that cannot be seen or touched because it goes on in the
brain. . . .

It is through tests that . . . constructs are measured indirectly. But researchers
cannot take the constructs out and show that the tests are measuring them.

TABLE 1.3 QUESTIONS FOR ESTABLISHING THE RELIABILITY AND VALIDITY OF A
STUDY

Type	Key question
Internal reliability	Would an independent researcher, on reanalysing the data, come to the same conclusion?
External reliability	Would an independent researcher, on replicating the study, come to the same conclusion?
Internal validity	Is the research design such that we can confidently claim that the outcomes are a result of the experimental treatment?
External validity	Is the research design such that we can generalise beyond the subjects under investigation to a wider population?

Therefore, they do the next best thing: They try to demonstrate experimentally that a given test is measuring a certain construct. . . . The experiment may take numerous forms but, most commonly, it is in the form of a differential-group or intervention experiment. A *differential-group experiment* might compare the performance of two groups on a test: one group that obviously has the particular construct and another group that clearly does not. . . .

There are numerous ways to go about establishing the construct validity of a test, but the basic strategy is always the same. The test developer sets up an experiment to demonstrate that a given test is indeed testing the construct that it claims to be testing. (Brown 1988: 103–104)

The central concepts of validity and reliability are extremely important in language research (as indeed they are in all other types of research), as we shall see in the succeeding chapters of this book. I have summarised the discussion in this section by setting out, in Table 1.3, the key questions one needs to ask in relation to reliability and validity.

Action research

A form of research which is becoming increasingly significant in language education is *action research*. This research has been defined in a number of different ways. Kemmis and McTaggart (1988), for example, argue that the three defining characteristics of action research are that it is carried out by practitioners (for our purposes, classroom teachers) rather than outside researchers; secondly, that it is collaborative; and thirdly, that it is aimed at changing things. 'A distinctive feature of action research is that those affected by planned changes have the primary responsibility for deciding on courses of critically informed action which seem likely to lead to improvement, and for evaluating the results of strategies tried out in practice. *Action research is a group activity*' (Kemmis and McTaggart 1988: 6). A piece of descriptive research carried out by a teacher in his or her own classroom, without the involvement of others, which is aimed at increasing our understanding rather than changing the phenomenon under investigation, would not be considered by these commentators to be 'action research'. For Kemmis and McTaggart, the essential impetus for carrying out action research is to change the system.

Cohen and Manion (1985) offer a similar set of characteristics. They argue that action research is first and foremost situational, being concerned with the identification and solution of problems in a specific context. They also identify collaboration as an important feature of this type of research, and state that the aim of action research is to improve the current state of affairs within the educational context in which the research is being carried out.

While collaboration is highly desirable, I do not believe that it should be seen as a defining characteristic of action research. Many teachers who are interested in exploring processes of teaching and learning in their own context are either unable, for practical reasons, or unwilling, for personal reasons, to do collaborative research. The work that such people carry out should not necessarily be excluded as action research. I would also dispute the claim that action research must necessarily be concerned with change. A descriptive case study of a particular classroom, group of learners, or even a single learner counts as action research if it is initiated by a question, is supported by data and interpretation, and is carried out by a practitioner investigating aspects of his or her own context and situation. That said, I know of few such studies which have not resulted in change of some sort.

Figure 1.5 illustrates the scope of action research and the various stages involved. Several points are worth noting from this example. In the first place, the research is initiatied by the practitioner and is derived from a real problem in the classroom which needs to be confronted. Secondly, the research is collaborative – not, in this instance, between colleagues, but between a teacher and a university-based researcher. Thirdly, the teacher collects objective data in the form of classroom interactions and learner language. Fourthly, the results are disseminated. Finally, the project takes the form of an ongoing cycle (Kemmis and McTaggart speak of the 'action research spiral') in which the teacher reflects on, returns to, and extends the initial inquiry.

Is this activity research? I would argue that it is, in that it fits my minimalist definition, containing a question/issue, data, and interpretative analysis. Others may argue that such activity can only lay claims to being research if the teacher has taken steps to guard against threats to the reliability and validity of the research. I believe that care needs to be taken over the reliability of all forms of inquiry, but that for action research there is not the same imperative to deal with external validity. In many cases practitioners are less con-

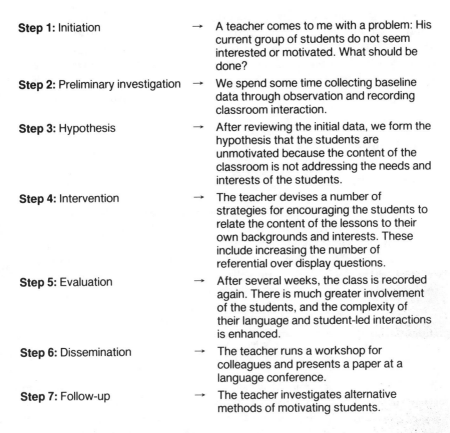

Step 1: Initiation	→	A teacher comes to me with a problem: His current group of students do not seem interested or motivated. What should be done?
Step 2: Preliminary investigation	→	We spend some time collecting baseline data through observation and recording classroom interaction.
Step 3: Hypothesis	→	After reviewing the initial data, we form the hypothesis that the students are unmotivated because the content of the classroom is not addressing the needs and interests of the students.
Step 4: Intervention	→	The teacher devises a number of strategies for encouraging the students to relate the content of the lessons to their own backgrounds and interests. These include increasing the number of referential over display questions.
Step 5: Evaluation	→	After several weeks, the class is recorded again. There is much greater involvement of the students, and the complexity of their language and student-led interactions is enhanced.
Step 6: Dissemination	→	The teacher runs a workshop for colleagues and presents a paper at a language conference.
Step 7: Follow-up	→	The teacher investigates alternative methods of motivating students.

Figure 1.5   Steps in the action research cycle

cerned with generating generalisable knowledge than with solving pressing problems associated with their own particular workplace. (Allwright 1991 prefers the term 'puzzle' to 'problem', in that it avoids the possible negative connotations of 'problem'.) While such activities therefore fulfil a professional development function, I still believe that if they address questions of interest to other practitioners, if they generate data, and if they contain analysis and interpretation, then they qualify as research. In the sample study summarised in Figure 1.5, extreme caution needs to be exercised in making strong claims about the research outcomes. While the reliability of the research was strengthened by the involvement of an outside researcher, the internal validity of the research is particularly problematic, and it would be extremely unwise for the teacher (or anyone else) to claim that improvements in the students' language were a result of interventions such as the increased use of referential questions. Numerous competing explanations suggest themselves.

For example, because the class was in progress for several weeks between steps 4 and 5, it could be argued that improvements were simply due to maturation, and that progress would have been recorded regardless of the types of questions asked by the teacher. Despite these problems, I still believe that the investigation was worth carrying out and reporting, particularly as it is the sort of investigation which can be replicated rather easily by other teachers.

Conclusion

In this chapter, I have dealt with some of the central themes and issues associated with research into language learning and use. I have argued that, while the distinction between qualitative and quantitative research is simplistic in many ways, it does represent a real, not an ostensible, distinction. However, the distinction is a philosophical one which is not always reflected in the actual conduct of empirical investigation. Underpinning quantitative research is the positivistic notion that the basic function of research is to uncover facts and truths which are independent of the researcher. Qualitative researchers question the notion of an objective reality. As Rist asserts:

Ultimately, the issue is not research strategies, per se. Rather, the adherence to one paradigm as opposed to another predisposes one to view the world and the events within it in profoundly different ways. (1977: 43)

In the chapters which follow, we shall take up and explore these issues in greater detail. Chapter 2 provides an introduction to the use of the experimental method. We shall also look at the use of statistics and the logic of inferential statistics, which enables us to make generalizations beyond the subjects we have studied to a wider population. Issues associated with descriptive and interpretive research are taken up in Chapter 3, which looks at ethnography, and Chapter 4, which deals with case study methodology, including single case research. Chapter 5 looks at aims, issues, and methods in classroom observation. In Chapter 6, the focus of concern is introspection and the use of introspective methods in research, including think-aloud techniques, diaries, and retrospection. The focus of Chapter 7 is the collection and analysis of speech data collected in naturally occurring interactions. The theme of Chapter 8 is elicitation, and the chapter deals with a number of different methods, such as the interview and questionnaire, which are designed to elicit data from language learners and users. Chapter 9 looks at some of the theoretical and practical issues involved in program evaluation, and raises the question of whether or not program evaluation is a form of research. In the final chapter, practical questions associated with the formulation of a research question or hypothesis, the selection of an appropriate research design, and the analysis and presentation of data are taken up.

Questions and tasks

1. Complete the following statements

Research is . . .
Research is carried out in order to . . .

2. Here is a list of questions which have been addressed in the research literature. (a) What are the key constructs associated with each question? (b) Which do you think might best be investigated through some form of experiment, and which might best be investigated through naturalistic investigation? (c) Can you find any studies which might be investigated *either* through an experiment or a naturalistic study?

- Are authentic materials more effective in bringing about learning than materials written specifically for the classroom?
- Does learning a second language involve the same psycholinguistic processes as learning a first language?
- Are there significant differences in the ways in which people interact with members of the same / opposite sex?
- Do learners from the same ethnic background share learning strategy preferences?
- In classrooms containing both first (L1) and second (L2) language learners, should teachers use different language and interactional patterns with L1 and L2 speakers?
- Do learners who have grammatical rules explained to them learn more effectively than those who learn inductively?
- What happens when teachers share decision-making with their learners?
- Is there a positive correlation between the language addressed to a child in its preschool years by the primary caregiver and ultimate academic attainment?
- Is the difficulty of a listening text influenced by the listener's background knowledge of the subject in question?
- How do people keep casual conversations going?
- Is there a 'critical period' for language acquisition, after which it is much more difficult to acquire a second language?
- Do children consciously try and work out rules as they acquire their first language, or is it a subconscious process?
- How are power relationships in the multilingual workplace linguistically marked?
- Are doctors who are trained in the language and culture of patients from different ethnic backgrounds able to diagnose more effectively?
- Do first language learners learn to do discourse before they learn grammar?
- How do parents help their children acquire language?

21

3. Which of the following statements from Chalmers (1982) are falsifiable and which are not?

a. It never rains on Wednesdays.
b. All substances expand when heated.
c. All points on a Euclidean circle are equidistant from the centre.
d. Heavy objects, such as a brick, when released near the surface of the Earth fall straight downwards if not impeded.
e. When a ray of light is reflected from a plane mirror, the angle of incidence is equal to the angle of reflection.
f. Luck is possible in sporting speculation.

There are some types of applied linguistic research in which a single disconfirming instance is sufficient to invalidate the claim, hypothesis, or theory under investigation. Which of the following statements would you accept as being invalidated by the existence of a single disconfirming instance?

- Learners will acquire the ability to form questions through inversion before they acquire Wh- questions formed through 'do' insertion.
- Authentic listening materials are more effective than materials specially written for the classroom.
- Parents of hearing and hearing-impaired children will code-switch to accommodate the hearing status of the child.
- The degree to which a learner acculturates to the target language group will control the degree to which he or she acquires a second language.

(In the first part of the preceding task, assertions c and f are not falsifiable. Assertion c is a definition and therefore a necessary truth. Assertion f is quoted from a newspaper horoscope, and, as Chalmers (1982: 40) says: 'It typifies the fortune-teller's devious strategy. The assertion is unfalsifiable. It amounts to telling the reader that if he has a bet today he might win, which remains true whether he bets or not, and if he does, whether he wins or not.')
4. Review one or more studies concerned with some aspects of language learning and use which has been published in a language journal such as *Language Learning, Modern Language Journal, Applied Linguistics, TESOL Quarterly, Canadian Modern Language Review, JALT Journal*, or *Studies in Second Language Acquisition*. Make a note of the functions of the following components of the report – in other words, what is the author trying to do in each of these sections? (Not all reports will necessarily contain all of these elements, which is why you may need to look at several.)

Abstract
Introduction
Rationale
Literature review
Hypothesis or research questions

Data collection instruments or methods
Research procedure
Subjects
Data analysis
Results
Discussion
Conclusions

5. What do you see as the potential threats to the validity and reliability of the action research project described in Figure 1.5? What steps might be taken to guard against these threats?
6. What are some of the questions, issues, or problems from your own professional context which might be investigated through action research?

Further reading

Chalmers (1982) provides a detailed introduction to the nature and philosophy of scientific research. He deals at some length with the problems of deduction, induction, and falsifiability.

Nunan (1989) is intended as a practical introduction to action research for those classroom practitioners interested in carrying out such research in their own classrooms. A useful collection of papers on action research can be found in Lomax (1989).

Chaudron (1988) provides an extremely detailed and comprehensive introduction to issues in second language classroom research. Although the emphasis in the book tends to be towards quantitative rather than qualitative research, both are dealt with.

For an introduction to the ethnography of classroom research, see van Lier (1988). Key studies in classroom research are published with a critical commentary in Allwright (1988).

2 The experimental method

Thomas Gradgrind, sir. . . . A man of facts and calculations. A man who proceeds upon the principle that two and two are four, and nothing over, and who is not to be talked into allowing for anything over. Thomas Gradgrind, sir – peremptorily Thomas – Thomas Gradgrind. With a rule and a pair of scales, and the multiplication table always in his pocket, sir, ready to weigh and measure any parcel of human nature, and tell you exactly what it comes to.

(Charles Dickens, *Hard Times*)

One popular image of research is that it is concerned with formal experiments of various types (recall the statements of students at the beginning of Chapter 1). In this book we shall see that although experiments are important, they are by no means the only way in which research can or should be conducted. In this chapter, we shall consider what is meant by *the experimental method*. We shall also consider the use of *statistics* in research, and look at some of the more commonly employed statistical tools in applied linguistics. I should make clear at the outset that this chapter is not intended to teach the reader how to 'do' statistics. Rather, it is intended as a guide to the basic concepts needed to read with some understanding research reports utilizing statistics, and to appreciate the logic behind the use of statistical inference. For a more detailed introduction to statistics in applied linguistic research, see the references cited in the 'Further Reading' section at the end of this chapter.

This chapter addresses the following questions:

- What are *variables, samples,* and *populations,* and why are they important in research?
- What are the basic principles of sound experimental design?
- What do we mean by *inferential statistics?*
- When is it appropriate to use the following statistical procedures: *t-test analysis of variance, correlation, chi-square?*
- What is the difference between *true experiments, quasi-experiments,* and *pre-experiments?*

The context of experimentation

What are the contexts in which an experiment is the appropriate method for collecting and analysing data? Generally speaking, experiments are carried

TABLE 2.I   TYPES OF VARIABLES USED IN LANGUAGE RESEARCH

Type	Example
Nominal	L1 background: e.g., Arabic, Spanish, etc.
Ordinal	Rank on a test of grammar: e.g., first, second, third, etc.
Interval	Numerical score on standardised language test

out in order to explore the strength of relationships between variables. A variable, as the term itself suggests, is anything which does not remain constant. In our case, it includes language proficiency, aptitude, motivation, and so on. Language researchers often want to look at the relationship between a variable such as a teaching method and a second variable, such as test scores on a formal test of *language proficiency*. In such a case it is customary to distinguish between the two variables by giving them different labels. The label given to the variable that the experimenter expects to influence the other is called the *independent variable*. In our case this would be the teaching method. The variable upon which the independent variable is acting is called the *dependent variable* – in our case, the test scores.

Variables can also be classified according to the type of scale on which they are measured (see Table 2.1). A *nominal scale* measures mutually exclusive characteristics, such as sex and eye colour. (A subject cannot simultaneously belong to the category 'male' and the category 'female', or the category 'blue-eyed' and the category 'brown-eyed'.) *Ordinal scales* are for those variables which can be given a ranking, such as first, second, third, but in which the actual score itself is not given. An *interval scale* not only provides information on the rankings of scores, as does an ordinal scale, but also indicates the distance between the scores. Most test score data are of this type. A final type of scale for measuring variables is the *ratio scale,* which measures absolute values, such as temperature. Ratio scales are of little interest in applied linguistics, because variables such as language proficiency do not exist as absolute quantities; therefore, ratio scales will not be dealt with further here.

Let us consider an example of a situation in which an experiment might be an appropriate way of gathering data. Imagine that you have developed some innovative listening materials for low level learners. You have used these materials with a range of classes, and believe that they are significantly superior to the traditional materials which are used in your school. However, your colleagues are sceptical. How can you convince them that your materials are more effective than the traditional ones? There are many ways in which you could collect evidence. You could survey the students through interviews and questionnaires, and obtain their subjective impressions. You could ask a sympathetic colleague to become a participant observer in your classroom and make an ethnographic record of the teaching and learning going on. These measures, however, are unlikely to sway your sceptical colleagues, who will be convinced only by test score data obtained through standardized tests.

You might be tempted to test your students at the end of the semester and present the results (assuming they are favourable) to your colleagues. However, you come across the following attack on such an approach (which is rather contemptuously dismissed as 'one-shot research'):

Much research in education today conforms to a design in which a single group is studied only once, subsequent to some agent or treatment presumed to cause change. Such studies might be diagramed as follows:

$$XO$$

[X = the treatment administered to the subjects, and O = the observation.] [Unfortunately] . . . such studies have such a total absence of control as to be of almost no scientific value. . . . It seems well-nigh unethical . . . to allow, as theses or dissertations in education, case studies of this nature (i.e., involving a single group observed at one time only). (Campbell and Stanley 1963: 176–177)

Convinced by this argument, your next inclination is to test two groups, one which has used the innovative materials and one which has not. However, you quickly realize that it is no good simply testing the students at the end of the semester and comparing their scores with those obtained from another class at the same year level, because the groups might not have been at the same level to begin with. Fine, you might think, we can test both groups at the beginning of the term as well as the end. Then, if the group which has had the benefit of the innovative materials does better than the group that has used the traditional materials, we can presumably ascribe the superior performance to the materials.

While your research design is becoming more rigorous, it is still not rigorous enough to allow you to claim that there is a causal relationship between the independent variable (your innovative materials) and the dependent variable (the students' test scores). There is always the possibility that some factor other than the experimental materials has brought about the observed differences in the scores. For example, you may have happened to select a group of fast track or high aptitude students as the recipient of the experimental materials, and a group of slow learners as the 'traditional' group. In order to guard against such 'contamination', sound experimental design suggests that you should randomly assign students to either the control group, which uses the traditional materials, or the experimental group, which uses the innovative materials. You are then in a better position to argue that any differences on the end-of-term test are due to the experimental treatment (i.e., the innovative materials), because you can assume that other variables which might have an effect (such as intelligence or aptitude) exist in equal quantities in both the control and experimental groups, and therefore cancel one another out. You should also test both groups of students before the experiment just to make sure that the groups really are the same.

If you carry out the procedures already described, that is, randomly assigning your subjects to either the control or experimental group, and administering a pre- and post-treatment test, then you could reasonably claim to have carried out what is known as a 'true' experiment. If you have not carried out these procedures, then the internal validity of your experiment is under threat (recall the discussion on reliability and validity in Chapter 1), because some variable you have not controlled may be affecting the dependent variable. Recalling van Lier's model (see Figure 1.3), you can see from this description why the formal experiment belongs to the highly controlled/highly selective quadrant of the diagram.

Unfortunately, it is not always practicable to rearrange students into different groups or classes at will. There are times when, if we are to carry out an experiment at all, it will have to be with intact groups of subjects, that is, subjects who have been grouped together for reasons other than the carrying out of an experiment. In these situations, while the internal validity of the experiment is weakened, it may still be thought desirable to proceed with the study. In instances such as this, researchers speak of quasi- or pre-experiments rather than true experiments. We shall look a littler further at these different types of experiments later in this chapter.

For argument's sake, let us imagine that you have been able to randomly assign sixty final-year secondary school students to control and experimental groups, and that a pre-test shows the two groups to be at the same level of proficiency. You teach both groups for a term, using the innovative materials with the experimental group and the traditional materials with the control group. At the end of the term, the groups are retested, and you obtain the scores for each student. You work out the *mean*, or average, for each group and obtain the following:

Control group: 58
Experimental group: 62

The experimental group has, on average, outscored the control group. Are you therefore in a position to claim that the innovative materials are superior to the traditional materials? Not yet. You have selected a sample, or subset, of all the possible students in the final year of secondary school who are studying your subject. If you tested them again tomorrow, or if you selected a second group of subjects and tested them, you would get different scores. Therefore, you need to use 'statistical inference' to work out whether the scores you obtained resulted from students' really being different, as suggested by the test scores, or whether the difference came about by chance or sampling variation. If all the students do share common, observable characteristics which differentiate them from other students, we say they represent a different *population*. A subset of individuals from a given population is a *sample*.

In order to illustrate the logic of inferential statistics, we need to go back a step or two and consider a number of basic concepts. This we shall do in the next section.

The logic of statistical inference

The aim of this section is to introduce you to the logic of statistical inference. While the information in the section will not necessarily provide you with the skills needed to carry out statistically based research, it should help you to understand the logic behind experimental research in which the researcher makes claims about an entire population based on data obtained from a subset or sample of that population.

In most research, it is not possible to collect data from the entire population of individuals in which one is interested. Consider an investigation of the listening proficiency of first-year secondary school French students. It would be extremely time consuming, although not impossible, to obtain data on all such students. Normally, someone wishing to carry out such an investigation would select a sample (say 30, 50, 100, 200) from the population and test these. However, a problem immediately arises: To what extent are the sample data representative of the population as a whole? Fortunately, certain procedures exist which enable us to determine the probability that the sample does represent the population from which it is drawn. In order to appreciate the logic behind these procedures, one must be familiar with the following statistical concepts: *mean, standard deviation, normal distribution,* and *standard error.*

From a statistical point of view, when studying numerical data of various sorts, the two things we will be most interested in are the extent to which the data are similar and the degree to which the data differ. The most frequently employed measure of similarity is the *mean* (symbolised by $\overline{X}$) which is simply the average of a set of scores (obtained by adding the individual scores together and dividing by the total number of scores). It gives us information about the central tendency of the scores. The *standard deviation* (SD), on the other hand, is the most important measure of dispersion, giving us information on the extent to which a set of scores varies in relation to the mean. It is calculated by deducting the mean from each individual score, squaring the resulting figures to get rid of the minus signs, adding these together, and dividing by the number of scores minus one. (Dividing by one less than the number of scores is a correction for the fact that the variability of scores for a single group of subjects tends to be less than the variability for all possible scores.) This gives us the *variance.* By obtaining the square root of this figure we arrive at the standard deviation. A simple example is set out in Table 2.2 to demonstrate the procedures involved.

From Table 2.2, we see that the variance for these scores is 5.111, and the

TABLE 2.2 CALCULATING THE STANDARD
DEVIATION: A WORKED EXAMPLE

Score	Score − mean[a]	Squares of figures in 2nd column
2	−2	4
8	4	16
5	1	1
3	−1	1
4	0	0
1	−3	9
2	−2	4
3	−1	1
5	1	1
7	3	9
40		46

The sum of the squares/(no. of scores minus 1):
$46/(10 - 1) = 5.111$

Variance = 5.111

Standard deviation (i.e., square root of variance) = 2.26

[a]The mean = 4. This is calculated by dividing the sum
of the scores (40) by the total number of individual scores
(10).

square root of the variance is 2.26. Thus, the standardised amount by which these scores deviate from the mean is 2.26.

As we shall see, in order to determine the probability that scores from two different samples come from two different populations, it is crucial that we have information on the central tendency (in the form of mean scores) and dispersion of the scores (in the form of standard deviations). While it is clear that two sets of scores with widely differing means will have come from samples from different populations, it is also the case that scores with widely differing standard deviations would also indicate that they are from different populations. We need both types of information because scores can have very similar means, but quite different standard deviations, which would indicate that they come from different populations.

Let us imagine that the following scores were obtained from some of the students in our experimental listening group:

62	62	61	62	60	62
63	61	65	60	64	63
60	63	59	63	58	61
64	59	62			

There are several things to note about the scores. Firstly, and most obviously, the scores vary. Less obvious is the fact that the variation is systematic. In fact, if we plot them as a *frequency distribution,* they are close to what is known as a *normal distribution.* This is demonstrated in Figure 2.1. Not all sets of data are normally distributed. However, if we have a set of data that are normally distributed, then we can use the special characteristics of the distribution to do a number of interesting things, including determining the probability that our sample is representative of the population from which it was drawn. For our purposes, one of the most important facts about the normal distribution is that a predictable number of scores from the sample will be within limits established by the mean and standard deviation (see Figure 2.2). We can see from the figure that in any set of normally distributed scores, 68% of those scores will be within 1 SD of the mean, 95% of the scores will be within 2 SDs of the mean, and over 99% of the scores will be within 3 SDs of the mean.

Let us return to our listening example. I have calculated the mean and SD of scores from the fifty subjects making up the experimental group to be 62 and 3.8, respectively. Plotting these on the figure showing the normal distribution provides us with Figure 2.3. We can use this information to make numerous observations. For example, we know that 95% of all scores will fall within the range 54.4–69.6, and that 97.5% of scores will fall below 69.6. Therefore, a student scoring 70 or better will be in the top 2.5% of the group.

Armed with information about means and standard deviations, we can analyse and compare numerical data in ways which are not possible with raw scores. (Raw scores are the actual scores obtained on tests, etc.) We can, for instance, compare scores which have been derived from different sources. Consider the case of a student who obtained a raw score of 90 in Japanese and 80 in Chinese. We might be tempted to conclude that the student is better at Japanese than Chinese. However, raw scores do not allow us to come to such conclusions. If we know the mean and SD of the sample, we can draw conclusions. In this student's case, the mean and SD on the test of Japanese were 60 and 15, and on the Chinese test, 65 and 5. Knowing this, we can say that the student did comparatively better in Chinese than Japanese. Why? Well, we know from the characteristics of the normal distribution (ND) that a score of 90 in Japanese is 2 SDs above the mean, putting the student in the top 2.5% of the sample. However, the score of 80 in Chinese is 3 SDs above the mean, putting the student in the top 1% for that subject.

In doing research in which the data are obtained from formal experiments, it is usually only feasible to test a sample of the population, for reasons outlined earlier. The problem for the researcher is to decide whether the data obtained from the sample are representative of the population as a whole. Imagine you are presented with the score of a single subject from our listening experiment. This student obtained a score of 58 on the listening test. Given

```
                        X
                X       X       X
                X       X       X
        X       X       X       X       X
    X   X       X       X       X       X       X
58     59      60      61      62      63      64      65
```

Figure 2.1   Distribution of scores from hypothetical listening test

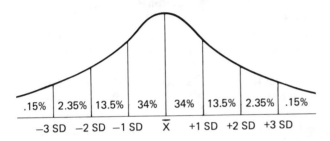

Figure 2.2   Percentage of scores falling within 1, 2, and 3 standard deviations of the mean

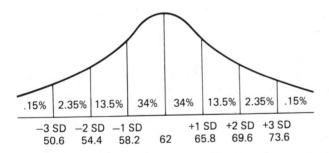

Figure 2.3   Scores falling within 1, 2, and 3 standard deviations of the mean: an example

what we already know about the percentage of students falling within 1, 2, and 3 SDs of the mean, which of the following statistics would be more likely to represent the entire population from which this single subject has been drawn?

	A	B	C
$\overline{X}$	50	60	70
SD	2	3	5

The A statistics would imply that the student is more than 3 SDs above the mean, which would place him or her in the top .15%. The C statistics would place the student more than 2 SDs below the mean, and therefore in the lowest 2.5%. The B statistics would place the student within 1 SD below the mean, and therefore much closer to the hypothesised mean than either the A or C statistics. It is therefore most likely that the B statistics represent the population as a whole for the simple reason that the further a score is from the overall population mean, the less likely it is to occur.

The problem, of course, is in determining the critical statistics of mean and SD for the population. While we can never be certain of these data without testing the entire population (which we have already seen is generally not feasible), we can estimate them from sample data. Imagine we obtain the following scores from several more students: 61, 60, 64, 57. We can now revise our estimation of the population mean, which, if reflected by our sample of 5, would be 60, and the standard deviation, which would be around 2.75. The additional information enables us to modify our predictions about the population as a whole. We can see that the B statistics are now confirmed as most likely to represent the population from which the sample was drawn. This example demonstrates two points. Firstly, the more information we have, the more confident we can be about the accuracy of our predictions, and secondly, we can make predictions based on relatively small amounts of information.

If we selected another five students from the population and tested them, we would probably obtain different scores, with a different mean and standard deviation – say, 61.5 and 3.1, respectively (possibly, we would even obtain different scores from the same students if we tested them on another occasion). If we kept selecting samples, calculating the means, and plotting these as a frequency distribution, we would find that they are normally distributed, that their standard deviation is smaller than that of the individual samples, and that their mean is equal to the population mean. (It stands to reason that the means will have less variability than the individual scores.) Given the fact that the sample means are normally distributed, we know that 68% of all sample means will be within one standard deviation of the mean, that 95% of scores will be within 2 SDs of the mean, and that over 99% of sample means will be within 3 SDs of the mean.

The standard deviation of sample means is known as the *standard error*. We can use this information to place a single sample mean in relation to the population mean from which it is drawn. For simplicity's sake, suppose that the mean of the sampling distribution in our current example is 61 and the standard error is 1. We know that 68% of all sample means will be within

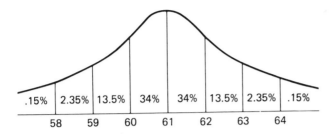

Figure 2.4   Distribution of sample means

the range 60–62, that 95% of sample means will be within the range 59–63, and that 99% of the sample means will be within the range 58–64. This means that if we drew 100 samples from the population, the mean for only one of these is likely to lie outside the range 58–64 (see Figure 2.4).

The problem of course is that, as it is not a practical proposition to extract many samples from our population to test, we do not know the mean and standard error of the sampling distribution. However, we can estimate the standard error from a single sample by dividing the standard deviation of the sample by the square root of the number of observations in the sample (N); that is, the standard error equals the standard deviation divided by the square root of N.

From the formula presented in the preceding paragraph, we can see that the standard error will be affected by the size of the sample and the standard deviation of the sample. If we increase our sample size, the standard error will be reduced. If the standard deviation of the sample were larger than 3.8, then the standard error would also be larger.

Thus far, we have studied a procedure for determining the extent to which we can say that a single sample mean is representative of the mean of the population from which it has been drawn. However, in most experimental research, we are interested not in a single mean, but in two or more means. Let us return to our listening example. With 100 subjects at our disposal, we have run a classical experiment and have done all the right things. For example, we have ensured that our subjects are randomly assigned to experimental and control groups, and we have excluded a group of subjects who are judged to be fast learners. At the end of the experimental period we test both groups and obtain the data in Table 2.3.

Although there is a difference between the mean scores of the two groups, we are not yet entitled to say that the difference indicates that the samples have been drawn from two different populations. As we have already seen, variation between samples is to be expected. The question we need to settle statistically is the balance of probability that the two samples have been drawn from two different populations or from the same population. Another way

TABLE 2.3 MEANS AND STANDARD
DEVIATIONS FOR EXPERIMENTAL AND
CONTROL GROUPS

	Experimental	Control
Mean	62.0	58.0
SD	3.8	4.2

of putting this is to ask whether, by exposing students to the innovative materials, we have 'created' another population, a population which is defined as 'those students of a foreign language who have been exposed to authentic listening materials'.

We settle the issue statistically in the following manner. First we calculate the standard error for both groups by dividing the SD for each group by the square root of the number of subjects. Since there are 50 students in each group, and the square root of 50 is about 7, then we divide 3.8 and 4.2 by 7 to obtain the standard errors (SE) for the experimental and control groups. This gives us the following:

	Experimental	Control
SE	.5428	.6

Knowing these figures, we work out how close our sample means are likely to be to the population mean from which they were drawn. We know that we can be 95% confident that the true population mean will be within two standard errors of the sample means. In the case of the experimental group this will be 62 plus or minus (.5428 × 2), which yields a range of 60.9 to 63.085. For the control group, this is 58 plus or minus (.6 × 2), which yields a range of 56.8 to 59.2. This is represented in tabular form in Table 2.4. Figure 2.5 provides a visual representation of these estimates.

From these data, it looks as though, at the 95% level of confidence, we can be reasonably confident that the samples have been drawn from different populations. It must be kept in mind, however, that there is still a 5% chance in the case of both the experimental and the control groups that the true population mean will lie outside the range we have established.

I have worked through the examples in this section in some detail to give you an idea of the logic behind inferential statistics ('inferential' because we are 'inferring' from samples to populations). Doing statistical calculations by hand is tedious, time consuming, and likely to result in error. Fortunately, computer software is now available for taking the pain out of such work. However, when doing such calculations, or when reading published studies employing statistics, it is important to understand the logic behind them.

TABLE 2.4 ESTIMATING POPULATION MEAN

Group	Mean	Population mean (95% level of confidence)
Experimental	62	between 60.9 and 63.085
Control	58	between 56.8 and 59.2

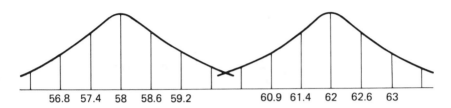

Figure 2.5 Standard error estimates for experimental and control groups

When comparing two means, as we have done in this section, the appropriate test is a *t*-test, which carries out the sorts of analytical procedures we have just examined. The great disadvantage of the *t*-test is that it can compare only two groups. When comparing more than two means, or more than two groups, the appropriate test is the *F*-test, which is based on a procedure called *analysis of variance* (ANOVA). In order to illustrate the procedure, consider the following study. In this study, we are interested in the reading comprehension of first and second language learners when they are dealing with academic texts. In particular, we are investigating the effect of memory constraints on the ability of first and second language learners to integrate information within and beyond sentences in a text. There are three groups of subjects: Group A = native speakers; Group B = second language learners; and Group C = foreign language learners. Each group is administered a test consisting of a reading passage followed by two sets of comprehension questions. One set of questions requires the subjects to comprehend information within individual *sentences* in the test passage (we shall call this 'S-level' information), while the other set of questions requires the subjects to synthesise information located in different parts of the *text* (we shall call this 'T-level' information). Means and standard deviations for the three groups are calculated. The mean scores are represented diagrammatically in Figure 2.6.

From the data in Figure 2.6 it can be seen that, as might be expected, the first language group scored higher than the second language and foreign language groups on both sentence level and text level questions, and that the second language group scored higher than the foreign language group. We can also see that all groups did better on the S-level questions than the T-level

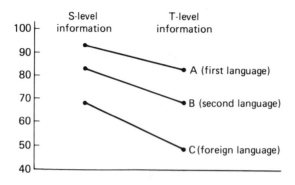

Figure 2.6 Comparison of mean scores for S- and T-level information for three language groups

questions. Further, the second and foreign language groups also seem to have done comparatively worse on the T-level questions than on the S-level questions. However, are these differences significant? An analysis of variance can help us answer this question.

We have already seen that any set of scores from a given group of subjects will vary, as will the score from one group to another. Basically, the analysis of variance compares the variability of scores within groups with that between groups. First of all, the different language groups are compared, then the different question types are compared, and then the interaction between the groups and the question types are compared. The computations result in an *F*-ratio, which we can use to consult a set of tables to determine whether the differences are significant. Table 2.5 shows what an ANOVA summary table looks like.

The analysis of variance presented in Table 2.5 reveals that the difference between the means of the language groups is significant at the 0.05 level of confidence (that is, we can be 95% confident that the difference is significant). It can also be seen that the difference between means of the two different question types is significant. Finally, it shows that the interaction between subjects and question type is significant. This ability of ANOVA to test the significance of interactions between different variables is its great strength. In our example, it would seem to indicate that second and foreign language learners have comparatively more difficulty than native speakers in integrating information from different sources within a text. Pedagogically, this would suggest that teachers should develop strategies which help non-native speakers comprehend beyond the level of the sentence. (Note that in the last sentence or two, I have gone beyond the evidence provided by the statistical data to an interpretation of the results.)

TABLE 2.5 ANALYSIS OF VARIANCE BETWEEN LANGUAGE GROUPS FOR S-LEVEL
AND T-LEVEL QUESTIONS

Source	SS	df	MS	F	Sig.
Between subjects					
Language groups (A)	39557.44	2	19778.7	21.07	0.05
Error between	137984.03	147	938.67		
Within subjects					
Question types (B)	22654.83	1	22654.83	380.71	0.05
Interaction (AB)	1069.20	2	534.60	8.98	0.05
Error 2	8747.47	147	59.51		

Key:
SS = sum of squares
df   = degrees of freedom
MS = mean squares
F   = the *F*-ratio
Sig. = the significance level of the *F*-ratio
Note: For further explanation of the terms used in this table, see Hatch and Lazaraton
(1991).

Additional statistical tools

In the preceding section, the logic of statistical inference was illustrated with
statistical tools for comparing means. While comparing means is one of the
most common tasks confronting the language researcher, it is by no means
the only task. Language researchers also want to do such things as compare
the frequency with which certain events occur, and determine the extent to
which one event is correlated with another. In this section we shall look at
some of the tools that enable researchers to carry out these tasks.

Experiments are very often concerned with the frequency with which
events occur, rather than with the comparison of mean scores. For example,
a researcher might be interested in testing the hypothesis that 'on task' behaviour by second language learners is higher in withdrawal classes ('withdrawal'
or 'pullout' classes are those in which the second language learners are seg-
regated from the native speakers) than in mixed classrooms, which contain
both first and second language learners. In testing this hypothesis, an independent observer might observe a number of integrated and withdrawal classrooms (either live or on video), noting each time that predefined on-task and
off-task behaviours occur. (Students are 'on-task' when they are actively
engaged in the pedagogic work of the day. They are 'off-task' when doing
other things such as talking to friends, walking about the room, etc.)

TABLE 2.6 FREQUENCY OF OFF-TASK AND ON-TASK
BEHAVIOURS IN INTEGRATED AND WITHDRAWAL
CLASSES

	Integrated	Withdrawal	Total
Off-task behaviours	140	60	200
On-task behaviours	100	100	200
Total	240	160	400

Note: This is called a 2 × 2 table because it shows the
relationship between two variables with two levels.

Such observations might result in a 2 × 2 table of the type set out in
Table 2.6.

We can deduce very little from such figures as they stand, apart from a few
rather obvious facts (for example, that there is more on-task behaviour in the
withdrawal classroom). We know from the discussion in the preceding section that it is highly unlikely that the observations will be identical. What we
want to know is whether the difference is significant. The appropriate statistical tool for determining the significance or otherwise of such frequency
counts is the chi-square test. I shall not go through the logic behind this test
in the same detail as for the test of significance of the difference between two
means, because it is similar to that behind the *t*-test and ANOVA. What follows is an explanation of the procedure.

If there is no association between the variables in our 2 × 2 tables (i.e.,
between type of class and type of behaviour), we would expect the same proportions to hold in each instance. Chi-square calculates the difference
between the expected frequencies, if the proportions were the same, and compares these with the actual frequencies. It is then possible to determine
whether or not these differences occurred by chance or whether there is a
probability that the differences are significant. If there is no association
between the variables, we would expect to obtain the following data. (These
data are obtained by multiplying the individual totals and dividing by the
grand total.)

Table 2.7 shows us the frequencies we should expect if there is no association between type of class and task behaviour. The next step is to compare
the expected values with the observed values, shown in Table 2.8. The bigger
the discrepancy between expected and observed frequencies, the less likely it
is that they have been derived from the same population. (A fully worked
example of chi-square can be found in Nunan 1989.)

Another important family of statistical tests in applied linguistics belongs
to the area known as *correlation*. These tests estimate the degree of association between two variables. For example we may wish to investigate the rela-

TABLE 2.7 EXPECTED FREQUENCIES

	Integrated	Withdrawal	Total
Off-task behaviours	120	80	200
On-task behaviours	120	80	200
Total	240	160	400

TABLE 2.8 EXPECTED (E) VERSUS OBSERVED (O)
FREQUENCIES

	Integrated	Withdrawal	Total
Off-task behaviours	120 (E)	80 (E)	200
	140 (O)	60 (O)	
On-task behaviours	120 (E)	80(E)	200
	100 (O)	100 (O)	
Total	240	160	400

tionship between speaking ability and reading ability in a foreign language. Or we might want to determine whether completing a cloze test taps the same underlying ability as completing a dictation test. We would carry out such studies by administering to a group of subjects tests which were assumed to tap the skills we were investigating, and then apply a statistical procedure to determine the extent to which a high score on one test tended to go with a high score on the other test, a mid-level score on one test went with a mid-level score on the other test, and so on. If the person obtaining the top score on one test also obtained the top score on the second test and the person scoring second on one test scored second on the second test, and so on, all the way through the subjects, then we would have a case of perfect positive correlation. If the reverse were the case (the person obtaining the top score on one test obtained the lowest score on the second test, and so on) we would have a perfect negative correlation. Of course it is extremely rare for researchers to obtain perfect correlations. The extent of correlation is measured by a figure between -1 and 1. Perfect positive correlation would result in a score of 1. Perfect negative correlation would result in a score of -1. The procedure you are most likely to encounter in published research is the 'Pearson product-moment correlation'.

In this section, and the one which preceded it, we have looked briefly at the most commonly employed types of statistical analysis: the *t*-test and ANOVA, which are used to compare means; chi-square, for computing frequencies; and correlation, which enables us to examine the degree of association between scores. In the next section, we look at types of experiments.

Types of experiments

Earlier in the chapter, I pointed out that it was not always feasible to carry out a true experiment – that circumstances such as the impossibility of randomly assigning subjects to experimental and control groups sometimes dictated that a quasi- or pre-experiment rather than a true experiment be conducted. (Of course, it is also possible that a quasi- or pre-experiment is carried out because of ignorance on matters of research design on the part of the researchers.) In this section, I shall describe the differences between these three types of experiments. The different designs are illustrated by Cohen and Manion (1985), who describe and critique three experiments reported in the literature: the New Zealand Book Flood Experiment, the Bradford Book Flood Experiment, and the Understanding of Electrical Circuits Experiment. (I shall only describe the first of these studies. For an account and critique of the other two studies, see Cohen and Manion 1985.)

The New Zealand Book Flood Experiment was established to examine the effects of extensive reading and the wide availability of books on the reading habits and skills of primary school children. The two schools which took part in the study contained large numbers of Maori (New Zealand aboriginal) children who were believed to have limited access to books. The children were given sets of pre-experimental attitudinal, vocabulary and reading tests. They were then 'flooded' with books selected by teachers and librarians. Data included scores on posttests administered six months after the initiation of the project, as well as qualitative data on the reading habits of five children from each group. Informal reading inventories were also used to obtain information on the reading behaviours of the subjects. Dependent variables included the quantity of reading undertaken and the skills, interests, and attitudes of the subjects. Subjects showed significant improvements on all of these measures. The experiment is summarised in Table 2.9.

This study is an example of a one-group pretest posttest design. (In fact, Cohen and Manion call it a pre-experiment.) Such studies have weak internal validity because it is almost impossible to state with any confidence that the dependent variables, that is, postintervention improvements in reading, were due to the independent variable, that is, the book 'flood'. Many other reasons for improvements could be advanced, including the effect of taking part in an educational innovation, the fact that the children matured during the course of the experiment, the effect of other variables which have not been controlled, and so on.

The internal validity of this study would have been greatly improved by

TABLE 2.9 SUMMARY OF NEW ZEALAND BOOK FLOOD EXPERIMENT

Rationale	To examine possible correlations between extensive reading/wide availability of books and reading habits and skills
Experimental subjects	Maori children in two schools
Control subjects	None
Independent variable	Wide access to books
Dependent variables	Scores on reading tests Qualitative information on reading habits
Outcome	Significant improvement in reading scores

TABLE 2.10 CONTRASTING PRE-EXPERIMENTS, QUASI-EXPERIMENTS, TRUE EXPERIMENTS

Type	*Characteristics*
Pre-experiment	May have pre- and posttreatment tests, but lacks a control group
Quasi-experiment	Has both pre- and posttests and experimental and control groups, but no random assignment of subjects
True experiment	Has both pre- and posttests, experimental and control groups, and random assignment of subjects

the addition of one or more control groups. Given the fact that it was not feasible to assign subjects at random to experimental and control schools, it would be important for the researchers to match the schools in terms of size, background, organisation, teaching methods, and background abilities of learners. The research design would also be strengthened by providing subjects with carefully selected pre- and posttreatment tests. Finally, it would be highly desirable to collect qualitative data on reading habits, classroom teaching procedures, and so on, in both experimental and control classrooms. Such qualitative information is often crucial for the interpretation of quantitative data, as Spada (1990) has shown. The major differences between pre-experiments, quasi-experiments, and true experiments are set out in Table 2.10.

The psychometric study: an example

In this section, I shall illustrate the characteristics of psychometric research by taking you in some detail through a research report based on such a study.

The study is an investigation by Chaudron and Richards (1986) into the effect of discourse markers on the comprehension of lectures by non-native speaking university students. I have chosen this study because it exemplifies some of the central points which have been discussed in the chapter.

RESEARCH AREA

The general research area investigated by Chaudron and Richards was the comprehension of university lectures by non-English speaking background students.

AIM

The aim of the study was to investigate the effects of discourse signals and markers on the comprehension of lectures by second langauge learners.

QUESTIONS/HYPOTHESES

Two research questions were posed by the researchers:

1. What is the effect on L2 learners' comprehension of lectures of the use of discourse markers which indicate the overall organisation of lectures – that is, macro markers, which signal the macro structure of a lecture through highlighting the major information in the lecture and the sequencing or importance of that information?
2. What is the effect on L2 learners' comprehension of lectures of the use of micro markers, which indicate links between sentences within the lecture or function as fillers?

These two questions were formulated as three research hypotheses:

Hypothesis 1: L2 learners would comprehend a lecture better when micro markers were added than when no markers were added.
Hypothesis 2: L2 learners would comprehend the lecture with macro markers better than the lecture with only micro markers.
Hypothesis 3: L2 learners would comprehend best the lecture with both micro and macro markers.

In other words, the researchers were suggesting (1) that the comprehension of lectures would be enhanced if the lecturer used different types of signals; (2) that lectures in which both the overall structure and organisation, as well as between-sentence links, are explicitly signalled will be more comprehensible than lectures in which there are no signals, or in which only one type of signal is present, and (3) that signalling overall structure and organisation will result in greater comprehension than signalling relationships between sentences only.

JUSTIFICATION (WHY THE QUESTION IS WORTH INVESTIGATING)

The researchers justified the research on the grounds that, with greater numbers of non-native speakers of English entering universities around the world in which English is the medium of instruction, there is a need for research into the processes underlying performance in a second or foreign language within a university environment. Such research can provide guidance for teacher education, instructional materials, and curriculum development.

In their literature review, the researchers contrast bottom-up and top-down comprehension strategies. Bottom-up strategies begin with the processing of individual sounds, then words, then clauses, and then whole messages. Top-down strategies, on the other hand, begin with overall knowledge of the subject matter and structure of the text to be comprehended. For many years there has been an ongoing debate about the relative merits of top-down and bottom-up approaches to language processing. While the debate has dealt principally with reading comprehension, it has also been important in the literature on listening (see, for example, Anderson and Lynch 1988; Rost 1990). The debate, and the research into comprehension processes on which it rests, is important for pedagogy, because the different approaches have clear implications for the design of teaching strategies and classroom materials. The bottom-up approach suggests that we begin by teaching the individual elements which constitute language (that is, phonemes and graphemes), then words and phrases, then sentences, and finally whole texts. The top-down approach, on the other hand, suggests that we begin with whole texts and encourage learners to use their knowledge of text structure and the overall purpose of the speaker/writer to orient them to the text. In recent years, it has been suggested that both bottom-up and top-down strategies are important, and that the good reader/listener is able to employ both appropriately.

Chaudron and Richards argue that both top-down and bottom-up processing are important in understanding lectures, and they cite studies which suggest that both macro markers and micro markers can facilitate this understanding. Macro markers can help learners with the overall organisation of a lecture, as well as assist in comprehending the functional intention of the speaker in relation to subsidiary parts of the lecture. Micro markers, which serve as breathing spaces and which provide learners with opportunities to employ bottom-up processing strategies, should also facilitate the comprehension of lectures.

SUBJECTS

There were two groups of subjects in the study: a pre-university group consisting of 71 ESL (English as a second language) students enrolled in a university language program, and a university group, consisting of 81 ESL students enrolled in university programs. The researchers had placement test and standardised test scores on the subjects.

MATERIALS

Four versions of a lecture on American history were used in the study. The baseline version was a 'natural' version presented to ESL students ('natural' in that it was not altered by the researchers). A macro version contained markers of discourse organisation such as the following:

what I'm going to talk about today . . .
let's go back to the beginning . . .
this brought about new problems . . .

The micro version contained 'filler' phrases and markers of intersentential relations such as the following:

temporal links: then, and, now, after this, at that time
causal links: because, so
contrastive relationships: but, actually
relative emphasis: you see, unbelievably, of course
framing/segmentation: well, OK, all right?

The final version combined versions two and three, and contained both macro and micro markers. The following extracts, taken from the study, show examples of all four versions.

Baseline version:

"The United States came into existence officially in 1783 after eight years of war . . ."
"By 1803, the original thirteen colonies had doubled in size . . ."

Micro version:

"Well, the United States came into existence officially in 1783 after eight years of war . . ."
"And so, by 1803, the original thirteen colonies had doubled in size . . ."

Macro version:

"To begin with, the United States came into existence officially in 1783 after eight years of war . . ."
"What we've come to by now was that by 1803, the original thirteen colonies had doubled in size . . ."

Micro-macro version:

"Well, to begin with, the United States came into existence officially in 1783 after eight years of war . . ."

"And so, what we've come to by now was that by 1803, the original thirteen
  colonies had doubled in size . . ."

PROCEDURE

The four different versions of the lecture were assigned at random to the subjects, who were provided with a set of instructions on how to do cloze, multiple choice, and true/false questions. They were also given two short practice listening passages.

Dependent variable: Scores on cloze, multiple choice, and true/false
  questions.
Independent variable: Micro and macro markers in academic lectures.

TYPE OF DATA

Subjects' scores on the cloze, multiple choice, and true/false tests. Subjects' placement scores.

(Before proceeding, you might like to pause and think about the statistical tools the experimenters might use to analyse their data. Are the researchers interested in comparing means, in comparing frequencies, or in investigating the extent to which two or more events correlate?)

TYPE OF ANALYSIS

The data were analysed using the following statistical procedures: Pearson product-moment correlations were calculated between the listening comprehension and the various placement test scores. (As we saw earlier, correlation is used to test the strength of association between sets of scores – in this instance, the strength of association between listening comprehension and placement scores. In essence, the researchers were asking, 'Does a student who scored well on the placement test also score well on the listening comprehension?')

Possible differences in the mean scores on the different versions of the lecture were tested by means of an analysis of covariance (ANCOVA). (This performs a similar analytical task as analysis of variance, but takes into account differences in the learners' proficiency levels.)

CONCLUSIONS

The researchers found that macro markers (that is, the higher-order discourse markers which indicate the overall organisation of a text) were more conducive to successful recall of the lecture than micro markers (that is, the lower-order markers of segmentation and intersentential markers). They point out that this is in line with the top-down theory of comprehension,

45

which suggests that explicitly signalled guidance on the organisation of major ideas in the discourse will help listeners construct appropriate schematic models of the lecture.

Another finding was that the micro markers did not facilitate comprehension. They account for this by suggesting that these markers probably do not add enough content to make the subsequent information more comprehensible, that the markers may actually make the lecture less comprehensible by distracting the listeners, and that the baseline version may already have been slow enough to allow learners to obtain the maximum comprehensible input without the aid of further pauses and built-in redundancy.

Another surprising finding was that the combined micro-macro version was actually inferior to the macro version. The researchers attempt to account for this finding by suggesting that the insertion of the micro markers increased the listening load on the subjects without adding information which might have facilitated their overall comprehension, and that this detracted from the effect of the macro markers alone.

CRITIQUE

This study is a carefully conceived and conducted investigation into the listening comprehension of NESB university and pre-university students which illustrates some important characteristics of the experimental method. The researchers derive a number of questions/hypotheses from their review of the empirical and theoretical literature on the subject at hand. They suggest relationships between variables, and test these out through the exposure of randomly assigned subjects to control and experimental groups. The data yielded by the experiment are then subjected to statistical analysis, which enables the researchers to assess the probability that the independent variable did have an effect on the dependent variable.

The study is particularly interesting to students of research methods, because the researchers do not attempt to gloss over or minimize the practical difficulties which emerged in the course of the study, nor the interpretive problems associated with the unexpected outcomes of the study. The fact that placement and standardised test data were used, rather than a listening pretest, means that we should probably view this study as a quasi-experiment rather than a true experiment. In their paper, the researchers acknowledge the complications that the use of these test data occasioned – for example, some of the subjects were tested several months after the others, which made their pretest scores highly suspect, and these subjects were subsequently excluded from the research. Ideally, the researchers should have constructed a test to operationalise the construct 'listening comprehension' and used this test, or versions of it, for both pre- and posttesting purposes.

I have already discussed the importance of constructs in research and the need for researchers to operationalise their constructs. As we have seen, constructs are unobservable qualities which are assumed to underlie observable behaviour. Operationalising a construct means defining it in terms of observable behaviour. In the case of Chaudron and Richards, the key construct is 'listening comprehension', and the researchers operationalise the construct in terms of the ability to answer true/false, multiple choice, and cloze questions about the listening text. While the use of such tests has been criticised as inadequate as a measure of overall comprehension (see, for example, Aslanian 1985), this type of experimental research must necessarily rest on such measures. In defence of Chaudron and Richards, it should be pointed out that they attempted to strengthen the internal validity of the research by using not one but three measures of comprehension. The internal validity may have been strengthened further by supplementing the quantitative data with qualitative data, such as follow-up interview data of the type employed by Aslanian.

The other noteworthy aspect of the study is the way in which the researchers dealt with the unexpected finding that the combined micro-macro version was inferior to the macro version. The researchers considered and dismissed the notion that the groups hearing these passages were less proficient, and also the possibility that the quality of the recording for that particular version was inferior. The only explanation they could come up with was that adding the micro markers increased the listeners' attention requirements without adding semantic information, and that this detracted from the effect of the macro markers. While this explanation may not be particularly convincing, it is the researchers' best guess at the probable cause. Research, even when carried out in controlled settings, often results in some outcomes which are counter-intuitive in the light of other outcomes and therefore difficult to account for. This is one such finding. It underlines the fact that experimental researchers, no less than those engaged in naturalistic, interpretive inquiry, have to interpret and account for their data. With hindsight, it might have been wise to conduct a pilot study. Such a study could have revealed some of the problems which emerged (such as problems with the micro version), and thereby enabled the researchers to strengthen their major investigation.

Conclusion

The formal experiment and its variants, the pre-experiment and quasi-experiment, are important research tools in language study, and they have added significantly to our knowledge of language learning, teaching, and use. Experiments are designed to collect data in such a way that threats to the reliability and validity of the research are minimised. Experimental researchers are particularly concerned with the issue of external validity, and the formal experiment is specifically designed to enable the researcher to extrapolate the outcomes of the research from the sample to the broader population. In order to appreciate the reasoning which lies behind such extrapolations, it is necessary to understand the logic of inferential statistics and some of the more commonly employed statistical tools. These have been the focus of this chapter.

In the chapters to come, we shall see that experiments are by no means the only tool available to the applied linguistic researcher, and that for some types of research, the tool is inappropriate. In the next chapter, we turn to ethnography, which is based on a very different logic from the formal experiment, and which seeks to answer quite different questions about the nature of language learning and use. These two methods, experiments and ethnography, form extreme points on a methodological continuum, and so they will provide us with several signposts from which we can take our bearings in the rest of the book.

Questions and tasks

1. Write out your own definitions of the following terms: construct, frequency table, central tendency, variable, variability, mean, variance, standard deviation, population, sample.

2. Imagine that you are about to carry out a detailed investigation of the foreign reading skills of a group of high school (or secondary school) students. The school has provided you with a great deal of information on each student, including the following. For each of the variables listed identify the most likely type of scale it would represent.

Potential variable	*Most likely type of scale*
a. Sex	_____
b. Age	_____
c. Class rank	_____
d. Nationality	_____
e. First language	_____
f. Scores on proficiency test	_____
g. Rank on class test	_____
h. Amt. of time spent studying French	_____
i. Whether parents are native speakers of the language	_____

3. Which statistical procedure would you employ for the following situations? Indicate the appropriate procedure by placing a number in the bracket.

1 – *t*-test (tests differences between two means)
2 – ANOVA (tests differences between multiple means, and tests for possible interaction between means)

3 – correlation (tests strength of association between variables)
4 – chi-square (tests association between frequencies)

a. This study investigated the relationship between scores on a traditional standardised test of oral proficiency and a new test of communicative speaking ability. The investigators wanted to determine whether subjects who scored well on the traditional test did well on the innovative test and vice versa. [   ]

b. This study examined the effect of content familiarity on the reading comprehension of secondary level second language learners. Subjects were given two test passages to read, and their comprehension was tested on a multiple choice test. The test passages were analysed using the Lix readability formula, which showed they were both at the same level of linguistic difficulty. However, one passage was on a topic familiar to the students while the other was on an unfamiliar topic. [   ]

c. In this investigation, the researcher wanted to find out whether the native-like production of word-final consonants and consonant clusters varied according to the type of communicative task in which the learner is engaged. She collected data from a single subject as he took part in three different tasks – free conversation, oral reading of continuous text, and elicited imitation of words and short phrases. [   ]

d. A study was established to test the hypothesis that field-dependent learners would benefit more from learning grammar inductively, while field-independent learners would benefit from learning deductively. One group of field-dependent subjects and one group of field-independent subjects were taught inductively. A second group of field-dependent subjects and a second group of field-independent subjects were taught deductively. Pre- and posttreatment scores on a standardised test of grammar were administered. [   ]

4. The following hypothetical study is presented by Brown (1988: 18–19). Read the study and identify the independent and dependent variables.

Jas Menbrow noticed that people do not always perform in their native languages with equal ability. It occurred to him that there might be some relationship between the native language ability of his American students and their proficiency in French after three years of high school study. To investigate this possibility, he administered the verbal subtest of the Scholastic Aptitude Test (to measure proficiency in native English) and his school district's French Proficiency Test to all 132 students who were finishing their third year of study. He was concerned that differences between the sexes should not interfere with the results, so he eliminated all males from his analysis. Thus 89 female students were left. In addition, he wanted to determine what differences there might be between the women in the college-bound track (44 students) and those in the accelerated track (45 students). So he considered the two groups separately on this basis.

49

5. The effect of randomisation can be demonstrated by carrying out the following experiment devised by Pilliner and reported by Cohen and Manion (1985: 191).

Select twenty cards from a pack, ten red and ten black. Shuffle and deal into two ten-card piles. Now count the number of red cards and black cards in either pile and record the results. Repeat the whole sequence many times, recording the results each time. You will soon convince yourself that the most likely distribution of reds and blacks in a pile is five in each; the next most likely, six red (or black) and four black (or red); and so on. You will be lucky (or unlucky for the purposes of the demonstration!) to achieve one pile of red and the other entirely of black cards. The probability of this happening is 1 in 92,378! On the other hand, the probability of obtaining a 'mix' not more than 6 of one colour and 4 of the other is about 82 in 100.

If you imagine the red cards to stand for the 'better' ten children and the black cards to stand for the 'poorer' ten children in a class of twenty, you will conclude that the operation of the laws of chance alone will almost probably give you close equivalent 'mixes' of 'better' and 'poorer' children in the experimental and control groups.

Replicate this experiment yourself.

Look at the reported conclusion of this experiment (the last line in the preceding extract). Based on your experiment, do you concur with this conclusion?

6. Examine the following research summary adapted from Cohen and Manion (1985: 172). What type of study is it? What criticisms, if any, would you make of it?

Out of 802 students who began their studies at the University of Bradford in 1966, 102 dropped out at the end of their first year. On entry to the university, the entire freshman intake had provided academic and personal information about their backgrounds, their interests, their motivations and their values.

In an investigation of factors associated with failure at university, comparisons were made between dropouts and non-dropouts.

In line with previous studies, university failure was found to relate (1) to inferior educational qualifications on entry; (2) to less certainty about choice of career; (3) to a greater degree of worry over abilities to pursue a university course of study; and (4) to feelings of being overwhelmed by the academic work demanded.

7. Design one of the following: (1) a follow-up investigation to the Chaudron and Richards study, or (b) an alternative to the study (this can either be an alternative way of investigating the phenomenon of discourse markers and comprehension or an investigation of some other aspect of language learning and use which employs a similar research design). Include the following:

question/hypothesis   subjects
elicitation procedure   type of data
type of analysis   anticipated problems/difficulties

Further reading

A number of books on statistics in linguistics and applied linguistics have appeared in recent years. The best of these is by J. D. Brown (1988), who provides an introduction to the subject which is generally sensible and readable, although there are several conceptual leaps in the book that could make it difficult going, at times, for the naive reader. A detailed treatment of statistics and experimental research, as well as an introduction to general principles of research, is to be found in Hatch and Lazaraton (1991).

For those with no knowledge of linguistics, Rowntree (1981) provides a useful introduction. Although this book is not written specifically for the language teacher or applied linguist, it is, like most of Rowntree's books, sensible, easy to read, and witty. Another excellent publication is Robson (1973). This provides 'recipes' for calculating various statistics by hand.

3 Ethnography

Educators should not look here for experiments, controlled conditions, and systematic score keeping on the academic gains and losses of specific children. Nor should psycholinguists look here for data taped at periodic intervals under similar conditions over a predesignated period of time. What this book does do is record the natural flow of community and classroom life over nearly a decade. The descriptions here [are] of the actual processes, activities, and attitudes involved in the enculturation of children.

(Shirley Brice Heath, 1983, *Ways with Words*)

Ethnography contrasts markedly with the experimental method in its assumptions, methods, and attitudes to evidence. In principle there is no reason why research programs should not integrate psychometric and ethnographic methods of investigation, and, indeed, several calls have already been made for such integration. In practice, however, integrated approaches seem to be almost non-existent. I have already argued that this reflects the fact that the two approaches are underpinned by very different conceptions of social reality – 'truth' and the nature of evidence. It also reflects the fact that both traditions are seeking to answer different types of questions.

The different conceptions of 'truth', 'reality' and 'evidence' held by some language researchers is one reason for the growing attention being paid to the use of ethnographic techniques for gathering and analysing language data. Interest in finding alternatives to formal experiments has also been stimulated by a scepticism over the ability of psychometry to 'produce the definitive answers that some researchers expect' (Ellis 1990a: 67). Ellis advances two reasons for this scepticism. In the first place, the relationship between instruction and learning is extremely complex. It is not a linear relationship, and there is no one-to-one relationship between teaching and learning. Experimental research can therefore only provide us with an understanding of individual pieces of the language learning jigsaw, but not the whole puzzle. Secondly, according to Ellis, classrooms do not exist simply to provide cannon-fodder for research. The relationship between findings from a formal experiment, conducted under laboratory conditions, and classroom practice is complex and indirect.

Innovation in the classroom can never be just a question of implementing a recommendation derived from research. It is always a process of negotiation, involving the teacher's overall educational ideology, the learner's expectations and preferences and local constraints that determine what is feasible. There is no single pedagogical solution which is applicable to all classrooms. (Ellis 1990a: 68)

In this chapter, I shall define ethnography and describe its central character-istics and principles. I shall also look at the key research concepts of reliability and validity as they relate to ethnography, and will discuss the importance of context to ethnographic inquiry. In the final part of the chapter, I shall high-light some of the central concerns of this chapter and the preceding one, by contrasting psychometry and ethnography. The chapter seeks to address the following questions:

- What do we mean by *ethnography?*
- What are the key principles guiding ethnographic research?
- How might one deal with threats to the reliability and validity of this type of research?
- Why is context important to ethnographic research?
- In what ways does ethnography contrast with psychometric research?

Principles of ethnographic research

Ethnography has suffered somewhat from being applied rather loosely to any research that is not a formal experiment, giving rise, in some quarters, to the suspicion that the tradition and its practitioners lack rigour. However, as Chaudron (1988) and others have pointed out, true ethnography demands as much training, skill, and dedication as psychometric research.

Wilson (1982) identifies the roots of ethnography in anthropology and soci-ology, although there is also a strong tradition in research into animal behav-iour (see, for example, Martin and Bateson 1986). Wilson relates the tradition to two sets of hypotheses about human behaviour. These are the *naturalistic-ecological hypothesis* and the *qualitative-phenomenological hypothesis*.

The naturalistic-ecological perspective has, as its central tenet, the belief that the context in which behaviour occurs has a significant influence on that behaviour. It follows that if we want to find out about behaviour, we need to investigate it in the natural contexts in which it occurs, rather than in the experimental laboratory. Arguments in favour of field research as opposed to laboratory research are supported by studies of particular phenomena which come up with different findings according to whether the research is con-ducted in a laboratory or in the field. For example, Bellack, Hersen, and Tur-ner (1978) found that subjects performed in a role-play situation very differ-ently from the way they performed in real-life social situations where the same behaviours were observed. It has also been observed that parents and pupils respond differently to questions according to whether they are posed in school or at home.

It would seem to be a matter of commonsense that if one wants to generalise one's findings beyond the laboratory to the real world, then the research should be carried out in contexts which resemble those to which the researcher wishes to generalise. The dilemma, as we saw in Chapter 1, is that in dealing with the problem of generalisability (an issue of external validity) and placing the research in the field, one increases the possibility of a threat to the internal validity of the research, because intervening variables may make it impossible to ascribe a causal relationship between the variables under investigation. However, not all ethnography is out to ascribe such causal relationships, and so the problems which beset the quantitative researcher in a field setting become unimportant.

The second hypothesis identified by Wilson is the qualitative-phenomenological hypothesis. This principle also throws ethnography into stark contrast with psychometry because it questions the belief that there is an objective reality which is independent of the subjective perceptions of researchers and their subjects. Rather than subscribing to a belief in external 'truth', ethnographers believe that human behaviour cannot be understood without incorporating into the research the subjective perceptions and belief systems of those involved in the research, both as researchers and subjects. According to Wilson, the ramifications of this hypothesis are far reaching, because it implies that the traditional stance of the researcher as 'objective' observer is inadequate, and the procedures of the experimental method of framing hypotheses and operationalising constructs before engaging in any data collection or analysis are at best inappropriate and at worst irrelevant.

The psychometrician's belief that the task of research is to identify, describe, and explain external, objective reality has been imported into the social sciences from the natural sciences. Most people accept the notion of external reality and objective facts in relation to the natural world – we can see seeds germinating, flowers growing, day following night. For those brought up in a Western educational tradition, it also seems reasonable to assume that there are mechanisms and principles that similarly govern human behaviour, and that it is the task of the researcher to identify those principles. It can therefore come as something of a shock to encounter writers such as Wilson questioning the idea of an objective reality, and suggesting that the methods, procedures, and assumptions governing the physical sciences may not be appropriate for investigating human behaviour. (It is interesting to note that at present in physics, the hardest of the hard sciences, the notion of objective reality is being questioned by some researchers.)

Watson-Gegeo and Ulichny (1988) identify similar defining characteristics as Wilson, that is, the importance of context and subjective perception to the research enterprise. They highlight in particular the contextual characteristic which focuses the research in real situations and settings where people actually live and work rather than in laboratory or simulated settings. Within this context, the research focuses on the cultural meanings revealed by the behaviour of the subjects under study.

Van Lier (1988) also identifies cultural description as a central characteristic of ethnography. He presents two views on ethnography, the 'weak' view and the 'strong' view. The weak view, which according to van Lier is currently prevalent in applied linguistics, sees ethnography as essentially inferior to psychometry, as it consists of unstructured and unsystematic observation. The principal virtue of ethnography, according to the weak view, is that it may throw up questions or hypotheses which can subsequently be tested in a formal experiment. In other words, it is essentially a 'ground-clearing' operation rather than a valid tradition in its own right. The strong view, to which van Lier himself subscribes, sees ethnography as a valid research paradigm in its own right: '. . . ethnography is theory-building, and thus the core of a humanistic approach to social science. In this sense it can be traced back to naturalistic approaches to social science . . .' (van Lier 1988: 54). Ultimately, whether one subscribes to a strong or weak interpretation of ethnography will depend on one's views on the status of knowledge, the nature of 'truth', and what one accepts as legitimate evidence.

Despite differences of emphasis, these different statements all agree that ethnography involves the study of the culture/characteristics of a group in real-world rather than laboratory settings. The researcher makes no attempt to isolate or manipulate the phenomena under investigation, and insights and generalisations emerge from close contact with the data rather than from a theory of language learning and use. The principles are exemplified in an influential educational ethnographic study carried out in the sixties by Smith and Geoffrey (1968). The purpose of the study was to describe what goes on in the contemporary urban classroom. The data collection procedure for this study was deceptively simple – Smith, a university-based researcher who was trained as a psychologist, spent a term sitting in Geoffrey's classroom as a participant observer. His database consisted of extensive field notes of what he observed, as well as interviews with the teacher and students. These data were used to construct a rich descriptive and interpretive picture of the complexities of an urban classroom in the sixties.

In language teaching, a similar investigation was carried out by Freeman (1992). Freeman became a participant observer in a French as a foreign language classroom, and his database included lesson transcripts, fieldnotes, and interviews with the teacher and students. The analysis consists of discursive and interpretive work on the database. Freeman concludes from his investigation that:

The process of evolving a shared understanding of what to learn and how to learn it is at the heart of what makes [the teacher's] classes work. It takes place against the backdrop of constant social interaction . . . and is intimately tied to sharing authority and control. [The teacher] has been able to make public the process of creating and internalizing the language precisely because she allows the talk and activity in her class to be largely self-regulated. Students come to control themselves in their interactions; that control goes hand-in-hand with authority over the

TABLE 3.1 CHARACTERISTICS OF ETHNOGRAPHIC RESEARCH

Characteristic	Gloss
Contextual	The research is carried out in the context in which the subjects normally live and work.
Unobtrusive	The researcher avoids manipulating the phenomena under investigation.
Longitudinal	The research is relatively long-term.
Collaborative	The research involves the participation of stakeholders other than the researcher.
Interpretive	The researcher carries out interpretive analyses of the data.
Organic	There is interaction between questions/hypotheses and data collection/interpretation.

language. Both involve the responsibility to an inner sense of rightness for appropriate behaviour and for accurate language use. This responsibility is individual and collective. [The teacher] is a resource for the language and a source for criteria and explanations of correctness. Likewise she is the source of activity in the classroom and a resource for successful accomplishment of that activity.

These examples share several characteristics. In the first place, the research takes place in context, with an attempt to minimize the disruption caused by the researcher's intrusion. The researcher does not attempt to control or manipulate the phenomena under investigation. The research is relatively long-term, taking place over several weeks, months, or even years. It entails the collaborative involvement of several participants, including the researcher, the teacher, and the learners. Finally, generalisations and hypotheses emerge during the course of the data collection and interpretation, rather than being predetermined by the researcher (these principles are revisited in the extended example presented later in this chapter). Table 3.1 summarises these characteristics.

The principles of ethnographic research differ in important ways from those of psychometry, and result in very different research procedures. Ethnography places great store on the collection and interpretation of data, and, in marked contrast with the experimental method, questions and hypotheses often emerge during the course of the investigation, rather than beforehand. This is anathema to the proponents of experimental approaches to research. It is sometimes suggested that psychometry is an hypothesis in search of data, whereas ethnography is data in search of an hypothesis. While this is something of an exaggeration, in that ethnographers often begin with questions, if not formal hypotheses, it does highlight one important characteristic of ethnography: the fact that there is often an interaction between questions and data. During the course of their investigations, ethnographers may obtain data which do not support their original questions or hypotheses but are suggestive of others. They may therefore end up answering questions other than those with which they began, thus violating Brown's (1988) principle of logicality. In fact, while it is considered unacceptable for psychometricians to begin with one set of questions and conclude by answering others, the literature is littered with experiments which do just this. Notwithstanding these violations, many of these studies provide important insights into language learning and use, which suggests that perhaps the principles of formal experimentation could well be revised.

The practice of deriving theory from data rather than the other way round is known as *grounded theory*. This 'data first' approach is criticised by Long (1986) and Gregg (1989), who argue that a 'theory then data' rather than 'data then theory' approach is more efficient and rational. This approach to research sits more comfortably with a weak view of ethnography and, indeed, in a later paper Long (1990) argues that the primary purpose of educational ethnography is to describe classroom processes so that they may later be subjected to experimental manipulation. 'It would be premature and unwarranted to make causal claims on the basis of descriptive studies or to offer anything more than hypotheses as to potential explanations of the findings' (Long 1990: 7). While it is true that there are dangers in making strong causal claims on the basis of description, I do not believe that this leaves ethnography in a position which is subservient to experimentation. Ethnography is a valid tradition in its own right, and should not be considered simply as an hypothesis-generating device for experimental research.

Numerous writers have set out principles to define and guide ethnographic research. LeCompte and Goetz (1928) argue that ethnography is defined by the use of participant and non-participant observation, a focus on natural settings, use of the subjective views and belief systems of the participants in the research process to structure that research, and an avoidance by the investigator of manipulating the study variables. Watson-Gegeo and Ulichny (1988) identify several key principles of ethnographic research. These include the adoption of a grounded approach to data, the use of 'thick' explanation, and going beyond description to analysis, interpretation, and explanation. They point out that ethnography involves interpretation, analysis, and explanation – not just description. 'Explanation takes the form of "grounded" theory, which, as we have seen, is theory based in and derived from data, and arrived at through a systematic process of induction' (p. 76). (The most complete treatment of grounded theory is to be found in Glaser and Strauss 1967.) Their two other key principles are 'holism' and 'thick' explanation. Holistic research must take into account both the behaviour of the individuals and/or groups under investigation and the context in which the behaviour occurs, which has a major influence on the behaviour. There are two dimensions to this type of analysis, a horizontal dimension and a vertical dimension. The horizontal, or historical, dimension refers to the description of events and behaviours as they evolve over time. The vertical dimension refers to the factors which influence behaviours and interactions at the time at which they occur. The principle of 'thick' explanation refers to the importance of taking into account all of the factors which may have an effect on the phenomena under investigation. Of course, deciding what is or is not relevant and salient is a subjective and relativistic matter, which is why ethnographers generally insist on 'thick' description, that is, the collection of data on all of the factors which might impinge on the phenomena under investigation.

The need to go beyond description to explanation and analysis is taken up by Goodson and Walker (1983), who argue that educational research should focus strongly on 'portrayal', even if this is at the expense of analysis and explanation. They point out that the choice of a research methodology is more than a technical issue: It is political and moral as well, and they propose a new research genre which is separate from either ethnography or case study, which they call 'story telling'. While admitting anxiety at the threats to objectivity, reliability, and validity posed by their approach, they claim that rich, descriptive accounts seem to offer 'a kind of intermediate technology of research adapted to the study of practical problems in realistic time scales without the prospect of ten years' initiation among dwindling (and probably best left) tribes of Primitives' (p. 29). We shall look in greater detail at their proposals in the next chapter, when we consider case study methodology.

As we saw in Chapter 1, Chaudron (1988) identifies ethnography as one of the four major traditions in applied linguistic research, although he does not devote a great deal of his book to research carried out within this tradition. He characterises ethnographic research as a qualitative, process-oriented approach to the investigation of interaction, and points out that it is a rigorous tradition in its own right, involving 'considerable training, continuous record keeping, extensive participatory involvement of the researcher in the classroom, and careful interpretation of the usually multifaceted data' (p. 46).

The reliability and validity of ethnography

The major criticisms leveled at ethnography by proponents of quantitative research concern the reliability and validity of such research. Most of these criticisms stem from the fact that ethnographies are based on the detailed description and analysis of a particular context or situation. Because of the quantity of data yielded in these studies, it is generally impossible to include anything but a small amount of the data in a published account of the research. This makes it difficult for outsiders either to analyse the data themselves (and thereby establish the internal reliability of the study) or to replicate the study (thereby establishing its external reliability). Whether or not internal and external validity are problematic will depend on the scope of the research, and the researcher's purposes. If the researcher is not attempting to establish a causal relationship between variables, the issue of internal validity will be less problematic than if such a relationship is being sought. The essential consideration in relation to external validity is to what extent the findings from a study carried out in a particular site can be generalised to other sites. If the researcher is not concerned with the issue of generalisation, then the issue of external validity is not a concern. A detailed and considered analysis of problems associated with reliability and validity in ethnographic research is provided by LeCompte and Goetz (1982). They use 'ethnography' as a shorthand term to encompass a range of qualitative methods, including case study research, field research, and anthropological research.

LeCompte and Goetz deal firstly with reliability, which they define as the extent to which studies can be replicated. They argue that at first blush ethnography may 'baffle attempts at replication', in comparison with laboratory experiments. Given the naturalistic setting, the fact that the researcher may be attempting to record processes of change over time, and the possible uniqueness of the situation and setting, the use of standardised controls may be impossible. In reporting the research, constraints of time and space may preclude the presentation of data in a way which would enable other researchers to reanalyse these and draw similar conclusions.

External reliability, that is, the replication of the research by others, can be enhanced if the ethnographer is explicit about five key aspects of the research. These are: the status of the researcher, the choice of informants, the social situations and conditions, the analytic constructs and premises, and the methods of data collection and analysis.

Attending to researcher status position requires researchers to be explicit about the social position they hold within the group being investigated. LeCompte and Goetz make the point that in one sense, no ethnographer can exactly replicate the finding of another because, even if an exactly parallel context could be found, the second researcher is unlikely to hold exactly the same status in the second social situation. A related problem is that of finding parallel informants in the second research context. This is a potential problem of major proportions when it is considered that 'the extent to which knowledge is gathered is a function of who gives it' (LeCompte and Goetz 1982: 38). It is therefore imperative for researchers to describe their informants extremely carefully. The social situation and conditions which obtain also need to be described explicitly. (LeCompte and Goetz document a study of education in an ethnic neighbourhood in which parents provided discrepant information in the school setting and in the neighbourhood setting.) Explicit definitions of constructs and premises are also crucial.

Even if a researcher reconstructs the relationships and duplicates the informants and social contexts of a prior study, replication may remain impossible if the constructs, definitions, or units of analysis which informed the original research are idiosyncratic or poorly delineated. Replication requires explicit identification of the assumptions and metatheories that underlly choice of terminology and methods of anlysis. (p. 39)

Finally, ethnographers need to present their methods so explicitly that their report can be used as a procedural manual by those wishing to replicate the research.

A study has internal reliability if independent researchers, on analysing the primary data, come to the same conclusions as the original investigators. Many of the safeguards identified in relation to external reliability are pertinent here, the key difference being that external reliability refers to the replication of the original study, while internal reliability concerns the reanalysis of the original data by independent researchers. Such reanalysis is complicated by the fact that ethnographers rarely use standardised instruments such as observation schedules. Strategies identified by LeCompte and Goetz for guarding against threats to internal reliability include the use of low inference descriptors, multiple researchers, participant researchers, peer examination, and mechanically recorded data.

LOW INFERENCE DESCRIPTORS

A low inference descriptor describes behaviour on which it is easy for independent observers to agree. For example in classrooms, 'wait time' (the time a teacher waits between asking a question and then following up, for example by answering the question) and use of factual questions would be examples of low inference behaviours. High inference behaviours, on the other hand, are those requiring the observer to make inferences about the observed behaviour. A high inference descriptor would be 'student lacks interest in activity' because it requires the observer to infer unobservable mental states from observable behaviour. The problem here is that it is the high inference behaviours that are often of most interest.

MULTIPLE RESEARCHERS/PARTICIPANT RESEARCHERS

The most effective way of guarding against threats to internal reliability is through the use of multiple researchers. In much research this is not feasible, because a research team consisting of several members can be extremely expensive, particularly given the extended nature of much ethnographic research. An alternative is to enlist the aid of local informants to validate the interpretations of the ethnographer. For example, an ethnographic study of a school could involve teachers in reviewing and validating the researcher's data and conclusions.

TABLE 3.2 GUARDING AGAINST THREATS TO THE RELIABILITY OF
ETHNOGRAPHIC RESEARCH

Type	*Questions*
Internal reliability	Does the research utilise low inference descriptors? Does it employ more than one researcher/collaborator? Does the researcher invite peer examination or cross-site corroboration? Are data mechanically recorded?
External reliability	Is the status of the researcher made explicit? Does the researcher provide a detailed description of subjects? Does the researcher provide a detailed description of the context and conditions under which the research was carried out? Are constructs and premises explicitly defined? Are data collection and analysis methods presented in detail?

PEER EXAMINATION

Peer examination involves the corroboration by other researchers working in similar settings. According to LeCompte and Goetz, this can proceed in three ways. Firstly, researchers may utilise outcomes and findings from other field-workers in their report. Secondly, findings from studies carried out concurrently may be integrated into the report. This provides a form of cross-site validation. Finally, provided sufficient primary data are included in the published report, these may be used for reanalysis by the researcher's colleagues.

MECHANICALLY RECORDED DATA

The final strategy researchers can employ to guard against threats in internal reliability is the use of mechanically recorded data (for example, in the form of audio or video recordings). This strategy allows for the preservation of the primary data. However, it must be remembered that these devices do not preserve all of the data, but only those data selected by the researcher for preservation.

The five key strategies which I have just outlined, and which are designed to protect a study from threats to internal reliability, are summarised as a series of questions in Table 3.2.

While the foregoing strategies are valuable, they may not all be practical for someone carrying out an ethnographic investigation with limited time and resources. The use of multiple sites and researchers in particular could prove to be extremely expensive. As I have already indicated, the use of low inference descriptors is also a problem, because high inference behaviours and constructs are often of greatest interest. (Ethnographies in language classrooms have investigated phenomena such as motivation, interest, power, authority, and control, all of which are high inference behaviours.) The overall thrust of LeCompte and Goetz's suggestions for guarding against threats to reliability can be summarised in two words – care and explicitness. Basically, what they are suggesting is that if one is careful in the collection and analysis of one's data, and if one is explicit about the way the data were collected and analysed, then one can reasonably claim reliability for one's investigation.

I shall now look at problems associated with the internal and external validity of ethnographic research, once again following the analysis of LeCompte and Goetz, who argue that internal validity is one of the strengths of ethnographic research (a view questioned by a number of other researchers, including Beretta 1986a). Internal validity, you will recall, relates to the extent to which an investigation is actually measuring what it purports to measure. External validity, on the other hand, poses the question: To what extent can research outcomes be extended to other groups? Dealing with threats to the external validity of their research can be the most difficult methodological task confronting ethnographers.

LeCompte and Goetz argue that the claim of ethnography to high internal validity derives from the data collection and analysis techniques employed:

First, the ethnographer's common practice of living among participants and collecting data from long periods provides opportunities for continual data analysis and comparison to refine constructs and to ensure the match between scientific categories and participant reality. Second, informant interviewing, a major ethnographic data source, necessarily is phrased more closely to the empirical categories of participants and is formed less abstractly than instruments used in other research designs. Third, participant observation, the ethnographer's second key source of data, is conducted in natural settings that reflect the reality of the life experiences of participants more accurately than do contrived settings. Finally, ethnographic analysis incorporates a process of researcher self-monitoring . . . that exposes all phases of the research activity to continual questioning and reevaluation. (p. 43)

For the researcher wishing to generalise beyond the context in which the data were collected, external validity is particularly problematic, as the procedures we discussed in the previous chapter (such as the use of subjects randomly assigned to experimental and controlled conditions) are generally irrelevant. The external validity of ethnographic research is threatened by effects that reduce its comparability. The researcher can guard against this threat by

TABLE 3.3   GUARDING AGAINST THREATS TO THE VALIDITY OF ETHNOGRAPHIC
RESEARCH

Type	Questions
Internal validity	Is it likely that maturational changes occurring during the course of the research will affect outcomes? Is there bias in the selection of informants? Is the growth or attrition of informants over time likely to affect outcomes? Have alternative explanations for phenomena been rigorously examined and excluded?
External validity	Are some phenomena unique to a particular group or site and therefore non-comparable? Are outcomes due in part to the presence of the researcher? Are cross-group comparisons invalidated by unique historical experiences of particular groups? To what extent are abstract terms and constructs shared across different groups and research sites?

describing phenomena so explicitly that they can be compared with other studies, or by carrying out multiple-site investigations. LeCompte and Goetz argue that the credibility of cross-group comparisons can be affected by four particular factors: selection effects, setting effects, history effects, and construct effects.

Selection effects can have a bearing on the external validity of an ethnography if the constructs under investigation are specific to a single group, or because there has been a mismatch between the chosen group and the constructs for investigation. In discussing setting effects, LeCompte and Goetz point out that the very act of investigating a group, culture, or setting may have an effect which renders cross-group comparisons invalid. Their discussion brings to mind Labov's (1972) 'observer's paradox' (Labov pointed out that the aim of sociolinguistic research is to find out how people behave when they are not being systematically observed, but the data can be obtained only through systematic observation). Cross-group comparisons may also be rendered invalid by the unique historical experiences of groups and cultures. Finally, construct effects can refer either to the extent to which abstract terms and concepts are shared across different populations, or to the extent to which explanations are regarded as valid across groups. A summary of these points is provided in Table 3.3.

In this section I have drawn principally upon the work of LeCompte and Goetz to address the various factors which may threaten the internal and external reliability and validity of ethnographic research. While the adoption of an ethnographic approach to research can pose formidable problems of reliability and validity, these problems are not insurmountable, and there are practical steps one can take to guard against them, although these may involve additional time and resources. In the next section, I shall contextualise and illustrate the operation of these factors with reference to a major investigation of language learning and use.

The importance of context in ethnographic inquiry

In this section, I shall attempt to expand on and exemplify some of the principal features of ethnography by analysing a major study carried out by Heath (1983). I have chosen this study because it is arguably the major contemporary ethnographic investigation of language development to have been published since the early sixties.

RESEARCH AREA

The acquisition of a first language at school and at home.

CONTEXT

Over a ten-year period, Heath carried out an extensive ethnographic investigation of children learning to use language at home and at school in two communities only a few miles apart in the southeastern United States. 'Roadville' is a white working-class community of families who have worked in the local mills for generations. 'Trackton' is a black working-class community in which there is a transition between the older generation, who worked as farm labourers, and the current generation, who work in the mills.

JUSTIFICATION

The justification for the research came in the form of legislation mandating school desegregation. The massive shift in students brought about by desegregation created a need to investigate how children talk when they come to school and what educators should know and do about oral and written language.

RESEARCH QUESTION

Heath's investigative question, which formed the point of departure for her research, was formulated in the following way: What are the effects of home and community environments on the learning of the language structures and functions needed to succeed at school and at work?

SUBJECTS

The subjects were children from two culturally different communities in the Carolinas who were learning to use language at home and in their communities. Heath also worked with teachers, showing them how a knowledge of the ways children learn and use language outside the classroom can enrich classroom learning. She also trained them to be their own ethnographers.

RESEARCH PROCEDURE

Heath spent several years living among the communities who provided the subjects and database for her research. Her role was therefore one of participant researcher. As we know from the preceding section, this close involvement enchances the internal validity of the research, as the researcher is very close to the communities and the phenomena she investigates. Her intimate involvement in the community is revealed in the following quote:

I spent many hours cooking, chopping wood, gardening, sewing, and minding children by the rules of the communities. For example, in the early years of interaction in the communities, audio and video recorders were unfamiliar to community residents; therefore, I did no taping of any kind then. By the mid-1970s, cassette players were becoming popular gifts, and community members used them to record music, church services, and sometimes special performances in the community. When such recordings became a common community-initiated practice, I audiotaped, but only in accordance with community practices. Often I was able to write in a field notebook while minding children, tending food, or watching television with families; otherwise, I wrote fieldnotes as soon as possible afterwards when I left the community on an errand or to go to school. In the classrooms, I often audiotaped; we sometimes videotaped; and both the teachers and I took fieldnotes as a matter of course on many days of each year. (Heath 1983: 8–9)

Heath thus took care to ensure that the demands of data collecting should not alter the normal daily habits of her subjects. In this way she attempted to overcome Labov's (1972) 'observer's paradox'. Despite the stringent research rules she set herself, she developed an extensive and extremely rich database consisting of fieldnotes, recordings and transcriptions, environmental language (such as street signs and notices), children's songs and rhymes, and various kinds of written language.

As I have already observed, ethnographic research is data rich. Studies such as the one by Heath, which was carried out over a decade, yield such huge quantities of data that only a small fraction can be presented in the written report. This makes it impossible to investigate the internal reliability of the research through peer review and other means recommended by LeCompte and Goetz. To a large extent, one has to take Heath's interpretations and conclusions on trust.

TYPE OF DATA AND ANALYSIS

The data provided by Heath in the published account of her research include, in addition to the rich descriptive accounts which form the bulk of the text, photographs, maps, figures, tables, texts, and transcriptions. The four figures in the book illustrate preschool concepts of print and examples of arithmetic problems. The tables quantify types of questions asked of preschool children, uses of reading and writing, the structure of children's narratives, and the like. Table 3.4 illustrates the translation of the social reality of the familiar community domain into the unfamiliar school domain. I have reproduced the table because it illustrates the way in which Heath reduced and reformulated a huge quantity of descriptive data into an interpretive schema. It also highlights one of the themes of her research – the tension between the contextualised, personal knowledge of the home, and the depersonalised, decontextualised knowledge of the school. One of Heath's theses is that educational success is, in large measure, dependent on mastering this decontextualised knowledge.

Only nineteen short texts from Roadville and Trackton are included in the written account of the research. The following extract (Heath 1983: 126) is from a ten minute exchange in which the mother, Martha, is trying to keep her sick child, Wendy, quiet.

Martha: */pointing to a picture of Wendy's dog in the baby book/* Who's that?
Wendy: Nuf [the dog's name was Snuffy]
Martha: Let's see if we can find another picture of Nuffie.
     //Wendy points to the same picture//
     /pointing to another picture/ Here he is, he's had a bath with daddy.
     There he is, this is Nuffie.
Wendy: All wet.
Martha: Nuffie got daddy all wet too.
Wendy: Where's daddy?
Martha: Daddy's gone to work. */seeing Wendy look at the picture/* Oh, he's not in
     the picture.
Wendy: Where Nuf
Martha: Nuffie's over to gran'ma's, he dug under the fence again.
Wendy: Bad dog, Nuf, bad dog.
Martha: That's right, Nuffie *is* a bad dog, now let's find another picture of Nuffie
     /turns pages of book/
Wendy: Nana, nana */pointing to a picture of Mrs. Dee/*
Martha: Yes, that's nana, where's Nuffie?
Wendy: I don't wanna */pushes book away/*
Martha: But look, there's daddy fixin' to give Nuffie a bath.
Wendy: No. */trying to get down off her bed/*
Martha: No, let's stay up here, */holding Wendy around the waist/* we'll find
     another Nuffie.

TABLE 3.4 TRANSLATING KNOWLEDGE AND LANGUAGE FROM THE COMMUNITY DOMAIN TO THE SCHOOL DOMAIN

Familiar community domain features	Translation process	Unfamiliar school domain features
Personalized, contextualized verbal knowledge – chiefly oral opinions narratives with evaluations sayings, proverbs recipes, newspaper items	identify and define folk terms, folk concepts specify elements and processes from folk domain which have parallels in unfamiliar domains identify gaps in information between two domains formulate specific questions for obtaining missing information determine methods of testing occurrence of events against known principles of operation	Depersonalized, decontextualized verbal knowledge – largely written statements of fact written accounts of principles as borne out in experiments, demonstrations, third person objective narratives without evaluation from a personal perspective explanation and demonstration of scientific method defense of scientific method need for testing of hypotheses, facilitating replication, etc.
Personalized nonverbal knowledge observation of others trial and error attempts repeated participation without articulation of processes	specify sequenced steps of stages of activity segment continuum into episodes if process does not work, specify trouble sources and conditions in environment which could aggravate problems identify in unfamiliar domain possible explanations of problems identify in unfamiliar domain principles which may help predict outcomes under different conditions	Depersonalized behavioral knowledge pictorial illustration, instructor demonstration according to formalized procedures written accounts of trial and error of others narrative biographical accounts of individual scientists, groups, or institutions involved in scientific research

Source: Reprinted with permission from Heath (1983: 322–3).

> See, look here, who's thát with Núffie?
> //*Wendy struggles and begins to cry*//

Heath provides the following interpretive gloss on this interaction:

Here, Martha, in spite of Wendy's wandering interest and struggles to change first the topic and then the activity, persists in looking for pictures of Snuffy. Once Wendy responded to her request for that label, Martha continued it as the topic, and did not take up Wendy's possible suggestion of Nana (or the finding of pictures of other persons) as new topic. Thus throughout the conversation, Nuffie is the topic, both with reference to the pictures in the book and to the here and now. (Heath 1983: 127)

CONCLUSION

The general conclusion drawn by Heath is that adults help children focus their attention on the names and features of particular items or events. She also ascribes to her subjects the belief that teaching children to attend, listen, and behave develops both language skills and learning skills. She goes on to assert that Roadville parents believe that preschool age children need to develop the ability to communicate their needs and desires, and that they must learn 'to be communicative partners in a certain mold' (p. 127). She supports this assertion with a brief comment from one of the mothers:

"I figure it's up to me to give 'im a good start. I reckon there's just some things I know he's gotta learn, you know, what things are, and all that. 'n you just don't happen onto doin' all that right. Now, you take Danny 'n Bobby, we, Betty 'n me, we talk to them kids all the time, like they was grown-up or something, 'n we try to tell 'em 'bout things, 'n books, 'n we buy those educational toys for 'em. (pp. 127–128)

In educational terms, success and failure are dependent on the child's mastering the decontextualised language of the classroom.

Contrasting psychometry and ethnography

In this section, I shall try to bring together the key issues which have emerged over the last three chapters. In Chapter 1 I argued that while some researchers (see, for example, Chaudron 1988) argue for the complementarity of quantitative and qualitative research, it is possible to discern a gap between the two traditions which occasionally widens into a gulf. A major issue here concerns what one accepts as 'truth': that is, whether one should admit the subjective views and perceptions of the researcher and the researched as valid evidence – whether, in fact, one believes that there can ever be such things as objective facts which are external to the individual.

LeCompte and Goetz (1982) argue that ethnography differs from experimentation in that data are gathered before the formulation of hypotheses, and that the subjective experience of the participants in the research process are accepted as valid knowledge.

Ethnographic research differs from positivistic research, and its contributions to scientific progress lie in such differences. These may involve the data gathering that necessarily precedes hypothesis formulation and revision or may focus on descriptive investigation and analysis. By admitting into the research frame the subjective experiences of both participants and investigator, ethnography may provide a depth of understanding lacking in other approaches to investigation. (LeCompte and Goetz 1982: 32)

They expand on this contrast, identifying salient distinctions between the two traditions in the way in which problems are formulated, in the nature of the research goals, and in the application of research results. In formulating a research problem, psychometry attempts to identify causal relationships amongst variables by extracting these variables from their natural setting, and thereby attempting to neutralise or eliminate extraneous variables. Ethnography, in contrast, gives central importance to the context in which the variables occur, and emphasises the interplay amongst them. The second distinction identified by LeCompte and Goetz concerns the nature of the research goals and, in particular, the stage of the research at which theoretical considerations become salient. In psychometric research, the research questions are formulated as hypotheses and the constructs are operationalised in advance of the data collection phase. In ethnography, on the other hand, there is an attempt to remain as open minded as possible, and there is an interaction between questions and data to the extent that it is not uncommon for the questions themselves to change in the course of the research (Freeman 1992), something which is unacceptable to the psychometrician. Although oversimplifying things somewhat, LeCompte and Goetz have captured this distinction rather neatly, suggesting that 'experimental researchers hope to find data to match a theory; ethnographers hope to find a theory that explains their data' (p. 34). The final area of contrast, that of application of results, relates to the issue of external validity, which I have already discussed. Whereas experimental research seeks to generalise from samples to populations, such statistical generalisation is not possible in ethnography, where there has been no random assignment of subjects to experimental and control treatments. Rather than seeking generalisability, ethnographers seek validity in terms of comparability and transferability.

Comparability requires that the ethnographer delineates the characteristics of the group studied or constructs generated so clearly that they can serve as a basis for comparison with other like and unlike groups. . . . Translatability assumes that research methods, analytic categories, and characteristics of phenomena and groups are identified so explicitly that comparisons can be conducted confidently. Assuring

TABLE 3.5 CONTRASTING PSYCHOMETRY AND ETHNOGRAPHY: PRINCIPLES

	Psychometry	*Ethnography*
Formulating a research problem	Identifies causal relationships among variables by extracting from context	Central importance given to context
Nature of goals	Hypothesis then data	Data then hypothesis
Application of results	To generalise from samples to populations	Comparability and translatability

TABLE 3.6 CONTRASTING PSYCHOMETRY AND ETHNOGRAPHY: AN EXAMPLE

	Chaudron and Richards (1986)	*Heath (1983)*
Research question	What is the effect on L2 learners' comprehension of lectures of the use of discourse markers which indicate (a) overall organisation and (b) links between sentences within the lecture?	What are the effects of home and community environments on the learning of those language structures and functions which are needed to succeed at school and at work?
Subjects	Two groups of pre-university/university ESL students	Children belonging to two rural working-class communities in the United States
Method	Experiment	Naturalistic, contextualised data collection
Type of data	Scores on cloze, multiple choice, and true/false tests	Interviews; fieldnotes; transcripts of child–adult child–child interactions; environmental language
Type of analysis	Statistical: correlation, ANCOVA	Interpretive, discursive

comparability and translatability provides the foundation upon which comparisons are made. (LeCompte and Goetz 1982: 34)

Tables 3.5 and 3.6 highlight the main distinctions between the two traditions. Table 3.5 summarises the contrast between the two traditions in terms of problems, goals, and applications. In Table 3.6, the contrast between these two sets of principles is exemplified by a comparative summary of Heath's study, which we looked at in this chapter, and the Chaudron and Richards study, which we examined in Chapter 2.

Conclusion

In this chapter, I have introduced ethnography as an alternative research tradition to psychometry. In the first part of the chapter, I suggested that ethnography was underpinned by very different values and assumptions from those of psychometry. Two beliefs in particular have guided the evolution of this research tradition. These are the importance of context to human behaviour, and the centrality of the subjective belief systems of those involved in research to the processes and outcomes of research.

Ethnographic research has sometimes been criticised for its failure to guard against threats to reliability and validity, and in this chapter I devoted some time to a discussion of the practical steps which can be taken to guard against such threats. While reliability and validity are critical to psychometry, some researchers have argued that they are not necessarily the appropriate criteria against which ethnography should be judged. My own view is that all research needs to be reliable. Internal validity is important in explanatory rather than descriptive research (and is therefore important if one accepts Watson-Gegeo and Ulichny's stricture that ethnography should be explanatory as well as descriptive). External validity is only an issue for researchers wishing to make claims of generality beyond the research sites where their data were collected.

The ethnographic tradition was illustrated by a detailed summary of the research by Heath into language learning and use in rural communities in the United States. In providing this summary, I have tried to provide some idea of the types of questions which ethnographers ask, and the sorts of analyses in which they engage.

In this chapter, as in Chapter 2, I have tried to avoid making normative statements about the two different research traditions. In principle, the research method or methods one employs should be determined by the questions which one wishes to investigate, rather than by any predetermined adherence to one tradition rather than another. In practice, however, I suspect that a preference for one particular tradition determines the types of questions one considers worth asking in the first place. Some of these issues will be revisited in the next chapter on the use of case studies.

Questions and tasks

1. Read the following observations Heath makes on her research methodology. In what ways are Heath's comments and orientation consistent with her research as exemplified in this passage?

For my work on children learning language in the two communities, I focused primarily on the face-to-face network in which each child learns the ways of acting, believing, and valuing of those around him. For the children of Roadville and Trackton, their primary community is geographically and socially their immediate neighborhood. Thus, these ethnographies of communication focus on each of the communities in which the children are socialized as talkers, readers, and writers to describe:

the boundaries of the physical and social community in which communication to or by them is possible;
the limits and features of the situations in which such communication occurs;
the what, how, and why of patterns of choice children can exercise in their uses of language, whether in talking, reading, or writing;
the values or significance these choices of language have for the children's physical and social activities.

Added to all the details of the daily existence of children which the above imply are the history and current ecology of the community. Opportunities, values, motivations, and resources available for communication in each community are influenced by that group's social history as well as by current environmental conditions.

By many standards of judgment, this book also cannot be considered a model piece of educational or child language research. For example, educators should not look here for experiments, controlled conditions, and systematic score-keeping on the academic gains and losses of specific children. Nor should psycholinguists look here for data taped at periodic intervals under similar conditions over a predesignated period of time. What this book does do is record the natural flow of community and classroom life over nearly a decade. The descriptions here of the actual processes, activities, and attitudes involved in the enculturation of children in Roadville and Trackton will allow readers to see these in comparison with those of mainstream homes and institutions.

Often the approaches to research in education have been quantitative, global, sociodemographic, and dependent on large-scale comparisons of many different schools. Terms from business predominate: input, output, accountability, management strategies, etc. Input factors (independent variables) are said to influence, predict, or determine output factors (dependent variables). Pieces of data about social groups, such as number of siblings or time of mother–child interactions in preschool daily experiences, are correlated with the output of students, expressed in terms of test scores, subsequent income, and continued schooling. The effects of formal instruction have been evaluated by correlating these input factors with educational output.

From an ethnographic perspective, the irony of such research is that it ignores the social and cultural context which created the input factors for individuals and groups. Detailed descriptions of what actually happens to children as they learn to use language and form their values about its structures and functions tell us what children do to become and remain acceptable members of their own communities. (pp. 7–8).

2. Select an ethnographic investigation from the literature (for example Au and Jordan 1981; Carrasco 1981; Cleghorn and Genesse 1984). Summarise and critique the study by supplying the following information:

a. Question/hypothesis
b. Significance/value of the study
c. Subjects
d. Procedure
e. Type of data
f. Type of analysis
g. Conclusions
h. Further research
i. Critique

Now, with reference to the questions in Tables 3.2 and 3.3, decide how well the researchers have managed to guard against threats to the reliability and validity of their research.

3. Design one of the following: (a) a follow-up investigation to the Heath study, or (b) an alternative to the Heath study (this can either be an alternative way of investigating the development of language at home and at school, or an investigation of some other aspect of language learning and use which employs a similar research design). Include the following: research question; justification; data collection procedure(s); type of data; type of analysis.
4. What do you see as the potential threats to the reliability and validity of the study you designed?

Further reading

For anyone seriously interested in contextualised research into language learning and use, Heath's (1983) investigation of language and learning is essential reading.

LeCompte and Goetz (1982) provide an articulate and considered analysis of threats to the reliability and validity of ethnographic research, as well as suggestions on ways in which these threats may be overcome.

4 Case study

"A case study is what you call a case, in case, in case you don't have anything else to call it."

(unidentified student cited in Jaeger 1988)

The focus of this chapter is the case study in research on language learning and teaching. Methodologically, the case study is a 'hybrid' in that it generally utilises a range of methods for collecting and analysing data, rather than being restricted to a single procedure. In this chapter, issues and problems associated with the case study will be examined. We shall see that, while there are problems of validity associated with case study research, the potential of the method, particularly for those interested in action-based research, is considerable. The chapter deals with the following questions

- What is a case study?
- What are the characteristics of single case research?
- How are the reliability and validity of case study research to be established?

Defining case studies

Deciding whether a study is or is not a case is not always particularly easy. In fact, the term *case study* is defined in various ways, and it is probably easier to say what a case study is not rather than what it is. While it would seem reasonably clear that the study of an individual language learner is a case, and that the same can be said for the study of an individual classroom, what about an investigation of a whole school, or a complete school district? In an important position paper on the use of case study in education, Adelman, Jenkins, and Kemmis (1976) state that a case study should not be equated with observational studies as this would rule out historical case studies, that case studies are not simply pre-experimental, and that *case study* is not a term for a standard methodological package.

The issue of whether or not case studies are pre-experimental recalls the debate in Chapter 3 over the status of ethnography – whether it is a research tradition in its own right or merely a ground-clearing operation which acts as a preliminary step to experimentation. Adelman et al. state:

Although case studies have often been used to sensitise researchers to significant variables subsequently manipulated or controlled in an experimental design, that is not their only role. The understandings generated by case study are significant in their own right. It is tempting to argue that the accumulation of case studies allows theory-building via tentative hypotheses culled from the accumulation of single instances. But the generalisations produced in case study are no less legitimate when about the instance, rather than the class from which the instance is drawn (i.e. generalising about the case, rather than from it). (Adelman et al. 1976: 140)

In this extract, the authors argue that the investigation of a single instance is a legitimate form of inquiry, and that the case study researcher need not feel bound to report the instance as an exemplar of a class of objects, entities, or events. This view, as we shall see later in the section, is challenged by some researchers.

Having determined what case study is not, Adelman et al. go on to suggest that it is the study of an 'instance in action'. In other words, one selects an instance from the class of objects and phenomena one is investigating (for example, 'a second language learner' or 'a science classroom') and investigates the way this instance functions in context. From this description, there may seem to be little distinguishable difference between ethnography and case study, and, indeed, some researchers appear to see the case study as a limited type of ethnography (see, for example, the contributions to Bartlett, Kemmis, and Gillard 1982). I would agree that the case study resembles ethnography in its philosophy, methods, and concern for studying phenomena in context. However, while the comprehensive case study (for example, of a whole school district) may be indistinguishable from ethnography, for most case studies, the differences are more apparent. In the first place, the case study is generally more limited in scope than an ethnography. Another possible difference is in the focus of the research. Deriving, as it does, from anthropology, ethnography is essentially concerned with the cultural context and cultural interpretation of the phenomena under investigation (Wolcott 1988). This is not necessarily true of case studies. Finally, while the case study, like ethnography, can utilise qualitative field methods, it can also employ quantitative data and statistical methods.

Smith, cited in Stake (1988), admits that the definition of the case study is ambiguous, but states that the term *bounded system* defines the method for him.

The crux of the definition is having some conception of the unity or totality of a system with some kind of outlines or boundaries. For instance, take a child with learning disabilities as the bounded system. You have an individual pupil, in a particular circumstance, with a particular problem. What the researcher looks for are the systematic connections among the observable behaviors, speculations, causes, and treatments. What the study covers depends partly on what you are trying to do. The unity of the system depends partly on what you want to find out. (p. 255)

Adelman et al. suggest that case study research may be initiated in one of two ways. In the first of these, an issue or hypothesis is proposed, and an instance drawn from that class is selected and studied. In the second, a case is selected and studied in its own right (rather than as an exemplar of a class). In both approaches, the case will be a 'bounded system' or 'single instance', such as an individual teacher, a classroom, or even a school district. The instance may even be a construct, such as an innovative teaching program. While it is relatively straightforward to see that the linguistic development of a single individual constitutes a case, there are occasions (e.g., when investigating larger 'bounded systems' such as a school district) when the researcher is forced to confront the question: Has my study ceased to be a case?

Within the literature, a range of definitions and descriptions is offered, as can be seen from the following sample:

1. 'The study of the speech, writing or language use of one person, either at one point in time or over a period of time, e.g. the language acquisition of a child over a period of one year' (Richards, Platt, and Weber 1985: 36).
2. '... it tries to illuminate a decision or set of decisions: why they were taken, how they were implemented, and with what result' (Schramm 1971 cited in Yin 1984: 23).
3. 'A case study is an empirical inquiry that investigates a contemporary phenomenon within its real-life context; when the boundaries between phenomenon and context are not clearly evident; and in which multiple sources of evidence are used' (Yin 1984: 23).
4. 'The most common type of CS [case study] involves the detailed description and analysis of an individual subject, from whom observations, interviews, and (family) histories provide the database (Dobson et al. 1981; Shaughnessy & Zechmeister 1985). CSM [case study methodology] is particularly characteristic of some areas of psychological research, such as clinical psychology, which studies and aims to treat abnormal (e.g., antisocial) behaviour. In principle, though, CSM may involve more than one subject (e.g. a series of CSs, cf. Meisel et al. 1981). It may be based on particular groups (e.g. group dynamics within a classroom); organisations (e.g. a summer intensive language learning program at a university); or events (e.g. a Japanese language tutorial . . . where one could examine the amount of time a teacher speaks in either Japanese or English for class management purposes)' (Duff 1990: 35).
5. 'A longitudinal approach (often called a case study in the SLA field) typically involves observing the development of linguistic performance, usually the spontaneous speech of one subject, when the speech data are collected at periodic intervals over a span of time. . . . The longitudinal approach could easily be characterized by at least three of the qualitative paradigm attributes: naturalistic (use of spontaneous speech), process-oriented (it takes place over time) and ungeneralizable (very few subjects)' (Larsen-Freeman and Long 1991: 11–12).

6. '. . . the qualitative case study can be defined as an intensive, holistic description and analysis of a single entity, phenomenon, or social unit. Case studies are particularistic, descriptive, and heuristic and rely heavily on inductive reasoning in handling multiple data sources' (Merriam 1988: 16).

Unlike the experimenter, who manipulates variables to determine their causal significance, or the surveyor, who asks standardised questions of large, representative samples of individuals, the case study researcher typically observes the characteristics of an individual unit – a child, a clique, a class, a school, or a community. The purpose of such observation is to probe deeply and to analyse the intensity of the multifarious phenomena that constitute the life cycle of the unit with a view to establishing generalisations about the wider population to which the unit belongs (Cohen and Manion 1985: 120). With reference to the research model from van Lier presented in Chapter 1 (see Figure 1.3), the amorphous nature of the case study is reflected in the fact that there are studies in the literature which represent three of the four semantic spaces identified by van Lier (I am not aware of any studies involving formal experiments and statistical inference).

Stenhouse (1983) develops a typology of case studies. The first type he identifies is the *neo-ethnographic,* which is the in-depth investigation of a single case by a participant observer. Next, we have the *evaluative,* which is 'a single case or group of cases studied at such depth as the evaluation of policy or practice will allow (usually condensed fieldwork)'. In contrast with these first two, the *multi-site case study* consists of 'condensed fieldwork undertaken by a team of workers on a number of sites and possibly offering an alternative approach to research to that based on sampling and statistical inference'. Such research probably approaches ethnography, particularly if it attempts to investigate a range of issues and questions. The final type of case study identified by Stenhouse is teacher research. This is 'classroom action research or school case studies undertaken by teachers who use their participant status as a basis on which to build skills of observation and analysis' (Stenhouse 1983: 21). This typology is set out in Table 4.1.

Denny (1978) draws a distinction between ethnography, case study, and 'story telling'. While an ethnography is a complete account of a particular culture, case studies examine a facet or particular aspect of the culture or subculture under investigation. Despite this more limited reach of case studies, many case studies share certain characteristics with ethnographies. Both attempt to provide a portrait of what is going on in a particular setting. Additionally, according to Denny, they must be more than objective accounts of the culture being portrayed – they must encapsulate a point of view (in other words, they must go beyond description). Finally, they must present sufficient data for the reader to draw conclusions other than those presented directly by the writer.

TABLE 4.1 THE CASE STUDY: A TYPOLOGY

Type	Description
Neo-ethnographic	The in-depth investigation of a single case by a participant observer — *Studying your own teaching*
Evaluative	An investigation carried out in order to evaluate policy or practice
Multi-site	A study carried out by several researchers on more than one site
✸Action	An investigation carried out by a classroom practitioner in his or her professional context *test teaching approach*

Source: Based on Stenhouse (1983). *+ dessiminate to others*

Adelman et al. (1976) suggest that there are six principal advantages of adopting the case study as a method of research. In the first place, in contrast with other research methods, it is 'strong in reality' and therefore likely to appeal to practitioners, who will be able to identify with the issues and concerns raised. Secondly, they claim that one can generalise from a case, either about an instance, or from an instance to a class. (We shall consider this particular claim in the next section when we look at issues of reliability and validity.) A third strength of the case study is that it can represent a multiplicity of viewpoints, and can offer support to alternative interpretations. Properly presented, case studies can also provide a database of materials which may be reinterpreted by future researchers. Fifthly, the insights yielded by case studies can be put to immediate use for a variety of purposes, including staff development, within-institution feedback, formative evaluation, and educational policy-making. Finally, case study data are usually more accessible than conventional research reports, and therefore capable of serving multiple audiences. 'It reduces the dependence of the reader upon unstated implicit assumptions (which necessarily underly any type of research) and makes the research process itself accessible. Case studies, therefore, may contribute towards the "democratisation" of decision-making (and knowledge itself)' (Adelman et al. 1976: 149).

In applied linguistics, the case study has been employed principally as a tool to trace the language development of first and second language learners. In the field of first language acquisition, there have been numerous case studies. Roger Brown's (1973) longitudinal investigation of the semantic and grammatical development of three children acquiring their first language is probably the seminal work in the field. Another study which has had considerable influence is Halliday's (1975) study of the language development of his own child. Studies such as these have played an important part in enhancing the status of the case study in applied linguistics.

The case study has also played an important part in the field of second language acquisition. Case studies

have generated very detailed accounts of the processes and/or outcomes of language learning for a variety of subjects, ranging from young children in bilingual home environments, to adolescent immigrants, adult migrant workers, and university-level foreign language learners. . . . Research questions addressed in CSs in SLA have included . . . How do children manage to function with two linguistic systems at a time when most children are attempting to master one? Why do some learners fossilize in their acquisition of a second language (in some or all domains) while others continue to progress? In what ways do the forms and functions of constructions in a learner's interlanguage (IL) differ? What features characterize the prototypical "good language learner"? How do learners react to and/or benefit from different methods of instruction? Is there a critical period for SLA? (Duff 1990:34)

One widely cited study in the second language area is Schumann (1978), who investigated the hypothesis that second language development will be governed by the extent to which the learner identifies with and wishes to acculturate with the target language community. Schumann carried out a longitudinal case study of Alberto, a 33-year-old Costa Rican, who made little progress in learning English despite intensive instruction. Schumann concluded that Alberto's lack of linguistic development could be attributed to his social and psychological distance from the target culture, and the fact that his limited English was sufficient to enable him to fulfil his communicative needs. A more limited and focused case study is Sato's (1985) investigation of the phonological development of an adolescent Vietnamese learner of English as a second language. Later in this chapter we shall look in some detail at a case study by Schmidt (1983), which took Schumann's research as its point of departure.

In this section, I have reviewed a range of definitions and descriptions of the case study as a method of research. We have seen that a case is a single instance of a class of objects or entities, and a case study is the investigation of that single instance in the context in which it occurs. The contextualised nature of the case study, along with the types of data collection methods which are typically used, make it similar in some respects to ethnography, although I have tried to indicate the ways in which the two types of research may differ. A key issue for this type of research is the extent to which the insights generated by the study can be applied to other cases. This and other issues are taken up in the next section.

Reliability and validity of case study research

As case studies are concerned with the documentation and analysis of a single instance, many of the issues we looked at in the preceding section, and in

Chapter 3, will be pertinent. There are two points of view on the issue of validity. On the one hand, there are the researchers who feel that, while internal validity is important, external validity may be irrelevant. On the other hand, other researchers take a different view, arguing that tests of validity should be as stringently applied to the case study as to any other type of research. Stake (1988) represents the first view:

The principal difference between case studies and other research studies is that the focus of attention is the case, not the whole population of cases. In most other studies, researchers search for an understanding that ignores the uniqueness of individual cases and generalizes beyond particular instances. They search for what is common, pervasive, and lawful. In the case study, there may or may not be an ultimate interest in the generalizable. For the time being, the search is for an understanding of the particular case, in its idiosyncrasy, in its complexity. (Stake 1988: 256)

Yin (1984), however, believes that reliability and validity are just as important for case study research as for any other type of research. He suggests that four critical tests confront the case study researcher. These are:

- construct validity (establishing correct operational measures for the concepts being studied)
- internal validity (establishing a causal relationship, whereby certain conditions are shown to lead to other conditions, as distinguished from spurious relationships)
- external validity (establishing the domain or population to which a study's findings can be generalised)
- reliability (demonstrating that the study can be replicated with similar results).

Yin argues that construct validity is especially problematic in case study research. This is due to the frequent failure of case study researchers to develop a sufficiently operational set of measures and because 'subjective' judgments are used to collect the data.

In relation to the internal validity of case study research, Yin claims that this 'is a concern only for causal or explanatory studies, where an investigator is trying to determine whether event x led to event y. If the investigator incorrectly concludes that there is a causal relationship between x and y without knowing that some third factor – z – may actually have caused y, the research design has failed to deal with some threat to internal validity' (1984: 38). Another problem relating to internal validity is the frequent necessity for case study researchers to make inferences (researchers are required to make inferences every time they deal with an event which cannot be directly observed). Thus, an investigator will 'infer' that a particular event resulted from some earlier occurrence, based on interview and documentary evidence collected as part of the case study. Other researchers argue that internal validity is of concern in all types of research, because it deals with the question of whether investigators are really observing what they think they are observing. For Guba and Lincoln (1981), internal validity takes precedence over external validity because without internal validity results are meaningless, and 'there is no point in asking whether meaningless information has any general applicability' (p. 115).

The third test identified by Yin relates to external validity, that is, knowing whether a study's findings can be generalised from the particularities of the immediate case study to a more general context or situation. This problem has been a major stumbling block for the case study researcher because of the obvious difficulty of arguing from the single instance to the general. Yin deals with this potential threat by arguing that it involves a false analogy with survey research.

Such critics are implicitly contrasting the situation to survey research, where a 'sample' (if selected correctly) readily generalizes to a larger universe. *This analogy to samples and universes is incorrect when dealing with case studies.* This is because survey research relies on *statistical* generalization, whereas case studies (as with experiments) rely on *analytical* generalization. (1984: 39)

I must say I find Yin's line of argument on the major threat to case study research (that is, in relation to external validity) a little obscure. As we have seen, a major barrier to doing case studies concerns the extent to which a particular finding can be generalised beyond the case under investigation. The issue of making generalisations from instances is complex, and there is a branch of higher mathematics devoted to the subject. (See also the discussion on statistical inference in Chapter 2.) The thrust of much scientific work is towards 'predictive generalisation' through a process of theory construction and testing (usually through some form of observation). Yin has dealt with this potential threat by claiming that case studies seek to make 'analytic' rather than 'statistical' generalisations. This brings to mind Popper's work on falsifiability (for a discussion on this, see Chapter 1).

It seems to me that Yin is arguing that case studies are appropriate as a tool for falsifying a particular hypothesis or claim on the grounds that a single disconfirming instance is sufficient to refute a given hypothesis or claim (providing, of course, that it is formulated in a way which enables it to be falsified – this is by no means true of all hypotheses). If this is an accurate reading for Yin, it would seem to cast the case study into a rather negative role, one reminiscent of the 'weak' view of ethnography which we looked at in the preceding chapter.

Single case research

Single case research represents a special type of case study, which is why I have chosen to deal with it in a separate section. It shares some characteristics with

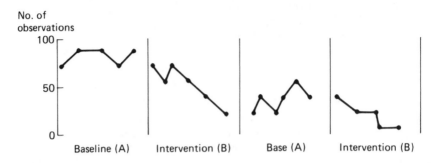

No. of
observations

Figure 4.1   *The four stages in an ABAB single case research design*

the case study as it has been described so far, and also with experimental research. Single case research is similar to experimental research in that some type of intervention usually occurs, that is, the researcher generally does something to the subject being investigated, and measures what happens as a result. The difference between experimental research as described in Chapter 2 and single case research is that experimental studies typically involve comparing two or more groups, while single case research, like the case study, involves a single individual or group, and does not attempt to set up experimental and control groups. In single case research, the behaviour of the subject or subjects is measured at two or more points in time. Single case research has been employed for therapeutic purposes in areas such as psychology and speech pathology. In education, studies have been carried out to alter the classroom behaviour of children who are disruptive or who have specific learning or attitudinal problems.

The basic single case study involves four stages or phases and is known as an ABAB design. Figure 4.1 shows these four stages. The first A phase begins with observations which are carried out in order to establish a baseline against which future behaviour can be evaluated. For example, if the study is being carried out in order to alter the behaviour of a disruptive child, instances of disruptive behaviour would be noted over a period of time. This phase continues until the researcher is satisfied that a stable and reliable measure of the behaviour has been obtained. In the second phase, the researcher or therapist intervenes in some way. For example, the teacher may reward the disruptive child by giving praise whenever the child is observed to be 'on task'. In Figure 4.1, we can see that the disruptive behaviour declines during the intervention phase. (At this point, the researcher needs to be careful not to assume too readily that it is the treatment which has caused the behaviour change. It may be that the child's home circumstances have changed, or the child may simply be growing up. If the researcher were to ascribe the behaviour change to the treatment when in fact it may have been caused by some other factor, we would say that the internal validity of the study was at risk.) In the next phase, the treatment is withdrawn, and the conditions which existed during phase A are restored. The researcher now wants to know whether the behaviour will remain at the (in our example) lower level predicted by the intervention phase. In the final phase, the intervention is restored, and the individual's behaviour is observed once more.

The logic of the ABAB design and its variations consists of making and testing predictions about performance under different conditions. Essentially, data in the separate phases provide information about present performance, predict the probable level of future performance, and test the extent to which predictions of performance from previous phases were accurate. By repeatedly altering experimental conditions in the design, there are several different opportunities to compare phases and to test whether performance is altered by the intervention. If behavior changes when the intervention is introduced, reverts to or near baseline levels after the intervention is withdrawn, and again improves when treatment is reinstated, the pattern of results suggests rather strongly that the intervention was responsible for change. (Kazdin 1982: 113)

In the example I used to describe and exemplify the single case procedure, only a single subject was involved. However, when a researcher carries out an investigation in order to make generalisations, rather than for therapeutic or clinical reasons, it will be necessary to collect data from more than one subject. Barlow and Hersen (1984) point out five difficulties, problems, and objections associated with the use of a single case design for such research purposes. These are ethical objections, practical problems associated with identifying large numbers of subjects (particularly for clinical research), averaging of results over the group, generality of findings, and intersubject variability. These problems are set out in Table 4.2.

The case study: an example   READ THIS

In this section, we shall examine a case study of an adult learner of ESL. The study is from Schmidt (1983).

RESEARCH AREA

Schmidt set out to explore the relationships between social and interactional variables on the acquisition of communicative competence.

JUSTIFICATION

At the beginning of his paper, he points out that most current research is biased towards the acquisition of morphology and syntax, to the virtual exclusion of semantic and pragmatic aspects of second language develop-

TABLE 4.2 PROBLEMS ASSOCIATED WITH SINGLE CASE RESEARCH DESIGN

Problem	Comment
Ethical objections	In clinical research, it may be considered unethical to withhold treatment from subjects during certain phases of the research. Barlow and Hersen (1984) dismiss this objection on the grounds that it assumes the treatment works when, presumably, this is precisely what the research is designed to find out.
Practical problems	The collection of large numbers of subjects with similar characteristics is often extremely difficult, particularly in cases where some form of pathology is involved.
Averaging of results	The averaging of results can be a problem if the researcher is simultaneously trying to derive generalisable results and obtain data on specific subjects for diagnosis or remediation. The averaging of results obscures the performance of individual subjects and, as the over-performance of some subjects can be cancelled out by the under-performance of others, gives a non-significant result.
Generality of findings	This problem is related to averaging. Because results from group studies do not reflect changes in individuals, it is difficult for the researcher, who wants the data for clinical purposes, to determine to what extent any given subject is similar to those in the group who showed improvement.
Intersubject variability	As we have seen, some subjects may improve while others deteriorate or remain stable.

ment. In his literature review he refers to the work of Hatch (1978) and others who maintain that syntactic structures develop out of interaction – that is, the development of syntax is driven by discourse. At the time this work was written, this contrasted with the prevailing view that one first learns structures, and then 'chains' these structures together to produce discourse. Also reviewed are studies testing the relative claims of informal interaction versus formal instruction for language acquisition. Finally, several studies are cited, including Schumann (1978), which suggest that there are affective and social variables which lie behind and determine the amount and quality of interaction, and that these may determine the amount of acquisition. Schmidt concludes from his review that 'there is an assumption that if communicative needs were greater, and social distance less, much greater control of the grammatical structures of the target language could have been acquired without formal instruction' (p. 139).

BACKGROUND

In this case study, Schmidt sought evidence for the acculturation model by carrying out a case study over a three-year period of a learner with low social and psychological distance from the target culture who was acquiring the language naturalistically, that is, without formal instruction. The subject, Wes, was a native speaker of Japanese whose positive attitudes to the target culture were predicted to facilitate second language acquisition. Schmidt made this assessment by examining factors such as attitude, culture shock, and empathy, although he points out that such psychological factors are extremely difficult to operationalise or evaluate, and that they are all subjective, some highly so. For example, on personality variables, Schmidt says, 'All observers agree that Wes is an extremely extroverted and socially outgoing person, with high self-esteem and self-confidence, low anxiety and inhibition. He is highly perceptive of the feelings and thoughts of others, intuitive, rather impulsive, and not at all afraid of making mistakes or appearing foolish in his use of English' (p. 142). While such highly subjective observations cast doubt on the internal validity of the study, it is difficult to see how they might have been obtained in any other way.

The theoretical construct for the study is provided by Canale's (1981) four-component model of communicative competence. This model specifies grammatical, sociolinguistic, discourse, and strategic competence as the basic elements constituting a user's overall competence in any given language. Grammatical competence is glossed as the elements and rules of the target language, including word formation, sentence structure, semantics, pronunciation, and spelling. Because of Wes's limited competence, Schmidt only looks at pronunciation and grammar. Someone who is sociolinguistically competent in a language is able to produce and comprehend utterances which are appropriate to the context in which they are used. This appropriateness can relate to either meaning or form. While grammatical and sociolinguistic competence relate to language at the sentence level, discourse competence refers to mastery of the ways in which forms and meanings combine to achieve unified spoken or written texts. As Wes was unable to write, it was only possible to study the development of his spoken discourse competence. The final component of Canale's model, strategic competence, refers to the verbal and nonverbal strategies which are called into play in order to repair conversational breakdowns, and otherwise keep an interaction going.

TYPE OF DATA AND ANALYSIS

In common with many case studies, Schmidt draws on several data sources, including taped monologues and dialogues, fieldnotes, tables of morphosyntactic items, and interviews. Grammatical competence was investigated by studying the development of pronunciation and the mastery of eleven grammatical morphemes. Schmidt claims that Wes's pronunciation is 'better than that of the average Japanese student I have encountered', although no evidence is provided to support this claim, and the reader must therefore take it on trust. In contrast, data are provided to support Schmidt's claim that there was little progress in the acquisition of nine grammatical morphemes. Using the criterion of 90% accurate suppliance in obligatory contexts, Schmidt claims that over the period of the study (almost a year and a half) no morphemes moved from unacquired to acquired status. Three morphemes – copula *be,* progressive *-ing,* and auxiliary *be* – seemed, on the surface, to have been acquired at the beginning of the study, being supplied in most cases when they were required. However, Schmidt questions whether the progressive and the auxiliary have really been acquired. In order to probe Wes's metalinguistic knowledge, Schmidt asks him the difference between 'paint' and 'painting' to which Wes replies:

Wes: Well if I go to exhibition, I saw 'paint', but 'I'm start painting' means I do it, not finish.
RS: Yeah, OK, sort of, so what's the difference between 'think' and 'thinking'?
Wes: 'I'm think' means now. 'I'm thinking' means later.

(p. 147)

If we accept the validity of introspection, then there would seem to be pretty clear evidence here that Wes has not sorted out the distinction between the two verb forms, at least on a metalinguistic level.

Wes's sociolinguistic competence was evaluated through a discursive analysis of his utterances as recorded in Schmidt's fieldnotes. Schmidt focuses on Wes's use of directives (that is, getting others to do things at his behest) and claims that in the early stages Wes was reliant on a limited number of formulaic utterances, but that there is evidence of development over time. He argues that Wes's improvement in the area of sociolinguistic competence reflects his high motivation to engage in interaction, and his desire to acculturate with the target society.

Discourse competence, that is, the ability to produce coherent texts, is Wes's greatest strength and the area where the greatest improvement is evidenced over the duration of the study. The database for this aspect of development is a series of taped conversations and monologues. The type of data collected by Schmidt, and the interpretive analysis to which he subjects it, is exemplified in the following extract and commentary. Schmidt claims that the extract demonstrates Wes's skill at conversational small talk. In the extract, he is chatting with a married couple whom he has only just met at a hotel garden brunch.

M: I would like eggs benedict (to waitress) / that's the speciality (to Wes)
Waitress: how about you?
Wes: here eggs benedict is good?
M: | yeah
G: | it's the speciality
Wes: yeah? / OK / I have it (waitress leaves)
M: you never ate before?
Wes: no, I ate before / but not this hotel
M: it's very good over here
Wes: but only just English muffin / turkey / ham and egg / right?
G: right
Wes: so how different? / how special?
M: because it's very good here / maybe it's the hollandaise / I don't know
G: maybe it's just the atmosphere
Wes: yeah / I think so / eggs benedict is eggs benedict / just your imagination is different / so / this restaurant is belong to hotel?
G: No / not exactly

(Schmidt 1983: 159–160)

Schmidt comments:

The good-natured, teasing type of humor of this passage (unfortunately and inevitably less obvious from a transcript than from the recording, which preserves tone of voice) is typical of Wes's conversations, as is his skill in listening to what people say and picking up topics for further development. Wes is not a passive conversationalist but nominates topics frequently. Moreover, the topics he nominates are almost always relevant to previous topics. I have never observed any instances of conversation coming to a halt because Wes has raised a topic (or commented on a topic already on the floor) in a way that indicated he had not understood what the previous speaker had said or had made an unfathomable connection to a new topic. In this respect he is quite unlike the majority of nonnative speakers of comparable linguistic level whom I have observed. (p. 160)

The final component of communicative competence in Canale's model is strategic competence: the ability to use verbal and nonverbal communication strategies to compensate for breakdowns in communication. In examining this aspect of Wes's competence, Schmidt draws principally on conversation tapes and fieldnotes. He claims that given Wes's limited grammatical competence, communication breakdowns are not uncommon, but that Wes is almost always able to repair these breakdowns. Personality variables such as confidence, persistence, and willingness to communicate seem to Schmidt to go a long way towards compensating for grammatical shortcomings. In the case study, short conversational extracts are presented, along with an interpretive commentary. In the following example, Schmidt suggests that Wes pays a great deal of attention to signals from native speakers which indicate that they have not understood. In this example, Wes repairs the breakdown by explaining what he means by 'dream', and 'after your life', and also by giving a specific example of what he means.

Wes: Doug / you have dream after your life?
NS: whaddya mean?
Wes: OK / everybody have some dream / what doing / what you want / after your life / you have it?
NS: you mean after I die?
Wes: no no / means next couple years or long time / OK / before I have big dream / I move to States / now I have it / this kind you have it?
NS: security I suppose / not necessarily financial / although that looms large at the present time

(p. 165)

CONCLUSIONS

Having provided selective extracts from his various sources of data and commented on these, Schmidt draws his conclusions. He states that whether or not one considers Wes to be a good or poor language learner will depend on one's definitions. He cites anecdotal evidence to the effect that 'several sociolinguists' believe that Wes is a superior learner, while grammar teachers 'generally consider him a disaster'. Based on his data, Schmidt rejects the hypothesis that there is a causal relationship between the degree of acculturation and grammatical development.

Assuming that the conclusions he has come to are accurate (and Schmidt himself voices some reservations), Schmidt's study demonstrates an important function for the case study – that is, falsifying a previously established hypothesis. Having found a single highly acculturated learner whose grammatical development shows little evidence of development over a significant period of time, Schmidt is able to call into question the acculturation hypothesis: 'The idea that if affective factors are positive then cognitive processes will function automatically, effortlessly, and unconsciously to put together conclusions about grammar is overly optimistic' (p. 173). There are numerous other implications of the study, including the insight that the development of a second language involves more than the acquisition of morphosyntax and that this should be reflected in the research literature.

Conclusion

Despite possible problems of validity and reliability, the case study has a great deal of potential as a research method in applied linguistics, and has already established itself in the area of second language acquisition. A major strength is its suitability to small-scale investigations of the type often carried out by graduate students and/or classroom practitioners. I have found that case studies are particularly suited to the types of action-oriented research projects described in Chapter 1 where the purpose is, in the first instance, to help practitioners enhance their understanding of, and solve problems related to, their own professional workplace, and where the problem of external validity is less significant than in other types of research. In particular, one can learn a great deal about one's own students in general through a detailed study of one particular student, in the same way as insights into language classrooms in general can be derived from the intensive analysis of a single classroom.

Questions and tasks

1. How convincing do you find the following discussion on the external validity of case study research?

Many people criticise case study research because there is too little indication of the degree to which the case is representative of other cases. Usually it is left to the reader to decide. Of course it is easy to argue that a sample of 'size one' is never typical of anything, except itself.

For some research purposes, it will be essential that the 'cases examined' be representative of some population of cases. Presumably, a case could be so unique that it might be unwise to consider any finding as true of other cases. However ... the unique case helps us understand the more typical cases.

Whether or not a case should be representative of other cases depends on the purposes of the research. It would be presumptuous to dismiss all findings as invalid because the case was not demonstrably representative. Some findings – for the purposes some readers have – do not depend on the notion of generalizing to a population of cases.

... A case study is valid to the reader to whom it gives an accurate and useful representation of the bounded system. Accuracy of observing and reporting is not a matter of everyone seeing and reporting the same thing. Observers have different vantage points. .... Readers have different uses for research reports. One reader expects an exact facsimile of the 'real thing'. Another reader is attending to a new type of problem that had not previously been apparent. The validity of the report is different for each, according to the meaning the reader gives to it. (Stake 1988: 261–263)

Can you think of any studies in which representativeness might be unimportant?
What is your reaction to the notion that validity is in the eye of the beholder?

2. Design a study using the single case research design described in the section 'Single Case Research' in this chapter.
3. Make a list of the threats to the internal/external reliability/validity of the Schmidt study. How would you guard against these threats in a replication of the study?
4. Select a case study from the literature (for example, Schmidt 1983; Schu-

mann 1978). Summarise and critique the study by supplying the following information:

a. Question/hypothesis
b. Significance/value of the study
c. Subjects
d. Procedure
e. Type of data
f. Type of analysis
g. Conclusions
h. Further research
i. Critique

5. Carry out a detailed case study of one particular student over a period of time (if possible, over a semester or term). Keep fieldnotes, interviews, transcriptions of interactions between the student and yourself/others, samples of written work, and, if possible, get the student to keep a journal or diary. Some of the questions to address might include the following:

- Is there any evidence of language development over the course of investigation?
- What affective factors seem to facilitate or impede language development?
- How much target language use does the learner engage in inside/outside the classroom?
- What factors in the learner's home environment seem to have an effect on the learner's language development and attitude towards language learning?

Further reading

One of the best books on case study research in education is Merriam (1988), who manages to provide a practical guide while at the same time dealing with theoretical and conceptual concerns surrounding the reliability and validity of case studies. Another book length treatment of the case study as a research method is Yin (1984), who is somewhat more theoretical. However, some of his arguments and lines of reasoning are rather hard to follow. (In the body of the chapter, I dealt with Yin's rather idiosyncratic approach to the threats to external validity posed by case studies.)

The study by Schmidt (1983) is worth looking at as an example of a detailed investigation of the language development of a single learner. Finally, some interesting case studies into language learning and deafness can be found in Strong (1988).

5 Classroom observation and research

The secret of good observation is to create the unusual from out of the commonplace.

(R. Walker, cited in Stenhouse 1975: 150)

As language classrooms are specifically constituted to bring about learning, it is not unreasonable to collect data about what goes on there as a means of adding to our knowledge of language learning and use. In this chapter, we shall review the substantial, and growing, body of literature relating to research on and about language classrooms, keeping in mind as we do so Stenhouse's (1975) stricture that there is no telling it as it is.

This chapter is rather different from the others in the book in that it focuses on a research context, the classroom, rather than on a particular method. Most of the methods dealt with in other chapters, from formal experiments through case studies to interaction analyses and ethnographies, could be utilized in investigating processes of teaching and learning in the classroom. The chapter is principally concerned with the following questions:

- What is the place of the formal experiment in classroom research?
- What is 'stimulated recall', and how is it employed in classroom research?
- In what ways can observation schemes facilitate classroom observation and research?
- How has interaction analysis been used in classroom research?
- What are the strengths and weaknesses of current classroom research?

Methods of classroom observation and research

In this section, I shall look briefly at a range of methods before focusing in some detail on the use of observation instruments. The methods I have chosen to look at are the formal experiment, stimulated recall, observation schemes, and interaction analysis.

The formal experiment

While formal experiments and quasi-experiments have been widely used as a means of collecting evidence on language learning and use, they are comparatively rare in classroom research where the data have been collected in genuine classrooms (by 'genuine' I mean classrooms which have been specifically constituted for teaching purposes, not for the purpose of collecting data for research). Later in the chapter, I shall describe a survey of recent research in which it was found that of fifty classroom-oriented investigations, only fifteen actually took place in genuine classrooms. Of these, only two took the form of experiments as described in Chapter 2.

This state of affairs is hardly surprising. One of the major reasons for carrying out formal experiments is to control those variables which may intervene between the independent and dependent variables and thus render the results uninterpretable or, at the very least, make it extremely difficult to guard against threats to the internal validity of the research. Such control is extremely difficult to achieve in most classroom settings.

Probably the best-known classroom studies employing experimental methods are the so-called methods comparison studies, which seek to evaluate the relative claims of different methods by randomly assigning students to two different groups and providing differential instruction to these groups. At the end of the research period, all students are tested to determine which of the two competing methods is the more effective.

One of the earliest studies of this type was the Pennsylvania Project, which sought to establish whether or not audiolingual instruction was superior to 'traditional' language instruction. In fact, the researchers set out to establish that audiolingualism was, in fact, superior to traditional instruction (Clark 1969). Subjects in this study were beginning and intermediate level high school learners of French and German who were allocated to one of three instructional conditions: 'traditional', 'audiolingual', and 'audiolingual plus grammar'. The scale of the study was enormous, involving over two thousand subjects in fifty-eight high schools. The researchers were aware of the importance of collecting data on what actually went on in the classrooms, and built into the study systematic classroom observation procedures. To the surprise and disappointment of the researchers, this large-scale, expensive study concluded that, after two years of instruction, there were no significant differences between the methods in the areas of listening comprehension, speaking, and writing, although the 'traditional' group was slightly superior in reading. In attempting to account for the inconclusive findings, Clark criticised the classroom observation component of the research. Observers visited the classrooms at random and noted, on a five-point scale, the extent to which teachers conformed to the method they were supposed to be teaching. Unfortunately, different rating scales were used for different methods, and this made detailed comparisons impossible, as there was no provision for an observer to note the use of audiolingual techniques in traditional classrooms, and vice versa. Clark suggests that there was a lack of adherence to the assigned methods, and that this contaminated the results of the study. In other words, for whatever reason, the teachers simply did not do what they were supposed to do.

TABLE 5.1 EMPIRICAL RESEARCH OF L2 CLASSROOMS

Category	Goal	Principal research methods
1. Classroom process research	The understanding of how the 'social events' of the language classroom are enacted	The detailed, ethnographic observation of classroom behaviours
2. The study of classroom interaction and L2 acquisition	To test a number of hypotheses relating to how interaction in the classroom contributes to L2 acquisition and to explore which types of interaction best facilitate acquisition	Controlled experimental studies; ethnographic studies of interaction
3. The study of instruction and L2 acquisition	To discover whether formal instruction results in the acquisition of new L2 knowledge and the constraints that govern whether formal instruction is successful	Linguistic comparisons of L2 acquisition by classroom and naturalistic learners; the experimental studies of the effects of formal instruction

Source: Based on Ellis (1990b).

In his overview of observation in language research, Allwright (1988: 10) suggests that perhaps the wrong question was being asked:

[This research was conducted] on the assumption that it made sense to ask 'Which is the best method for modern language teaching?', and that presumably on the additional assumption that once the answer was determined it would then make sense to simply prescribe the 'winning' method for general adoption.

Following the failure of studies such as the Pennsylvania Project, both these assumptions were questioned. According to Allwright, it was felt that the inconclusiveness of the results indicated that perhaps the method variable was less important than had been thought and that it was therefore meaningless to ask which method was superior (see also Swaffar, Arens, and Morgan 1982). The Pennsylvania Project also showed that prescribing a method and expecting it to be faithfully followed was simplistic and naive.

The time was ripe, then, for an alternative approach to classroom language learning research, an approach that would no longer see the language teaching world in terms of major rival 'methods', and one that would be more respectful of the complexities of the language teacher's task. (Allwright 1988: 10)

Similarly, Ellis (1990b) identifies dissatisfaction with global method comparisons as the impetus for a closer focus on the classroom itself as the locus of research. He suggests that there have emerged three different categories of empirical research, each with its own goal and principal research methods. These are reproduced in Table 5.1.

The fact that language classrooms are complicated places makes life difficult for the researcher who wants to carry out a formal experiment to establish a relationship between the dependent variable of language proficiency and independent variables such as innovative methods and materials. This is not to say that the task is impossible – later in the chapter we shall look at some interesting Canadian research which has attempted to link classroom action and learning outcomes. However, the experience of the methods comparison studies of the sixties alerted researchers to the need for detailed and precise records of what actually goes on in the classrooms under investigation.

Stimulated recall

Stimulated recall is a technique in which the researcher records and transcribes parts of a lesson and then gets the teacher (and, where possible, the students) to comment on what was happening at the time that the teaching and learning took place. Such a technique can yield insights into processes of teaching and learning which would be difficult to obtain by other means. It is a particularly useful technique in collaborative research because it enables teachers and students as well as the researcher to present their various interpretations of what is going on in the classroom, and for these interpretations to be linked explicitly to the points in the lesson which gave rise to them. Two recent investigations of teachers' decision-making have employed this technique. In the first of these, Woods (1989) investigated the decision-making of eight ESL teachers. He used three data collection methods: 'ethnographic' interviews, ethnographic observation over time, and stimulated recall. This third method is described in the following way:

[Stimulated recall] elicited teachers' comments about the options considered, decisions made and actions taken in the classroom. . . . A lesson was videotaped and subsequently viewed and commented upon by the teacher. By pressing a remote pause button to freeze the video and then making a comment (captured on a composite videotape as a voice-over), the teacher provided commentary about the lesson, the students or about what s/he was trying to do as the lesson transpired. The composite videotape containing the lesson and the superimposed comments was analyzed to determine the processes and bases of decisions made during the lesson. (Woods 1989: 110)

The stimulated recall technique, along with follow-up interviews, enabled Woods to draw some interesting conclusions about processes of classroom interaction, including the following:

1. The overall process of decision-making within the classroom context is incredibly complex, not only in terms of the number and types of decisions to be made, but also because of the multiplicity of factors impinging on them.

2. In terms of procedures for course planning, the most surprising finding was the tentativeness of teachers' advance planning – 'lessons were sketched out only in very vague terms and detailed planning occurred at most a couple of lessons in advance even by the most organized of the teachers' (p. 116).

3. Based on an analysis of the teacher interviews, Woods concluded that each teacher's course was internally coherent. He cites as an example one of the teachers whose decision-making was driven by her desire to develop the independence of the students as learners.

4. The final major point to emerge was the fact that different teachers had quite different approaches, criteria for success, and so on, and that different teachers could take identical materials and use them in class in very different ways.

In the second investigation, I looked at a number of different aspects of language pedagogy, including teachers' decision-making (Nunan 1991a). Five experienced (4 to 15 years' experience) and four inexperienced (less than one year's experience) teachers took part in the study. Their lessons were observed, audiotaped, and transcribed. Following the lesson, the teachers were interviewed and invited to comment on any aspect of the lesson they liked. After the transcriptions were completed, they were returned to the teachers for comment.

The following extract from the study is taken from a listening lesson. The lesson was based on a tape recording of a series of authentic interviews. In the classroom extract, the teacher focuses on the questions used by the interviewer and requires the students to use 'proper' or 'full' question forms.

Classroom extract:

T: OK, before we start, I want you to ask the proper questions. So please don't just look and copy. What you have to do is . . . OK, Keith. First question. What's the first question? What . . . (hours) hours does he work? Interests. What's the question?

S: What are his interests.

T: What . . .

Ss: . . . . are

T: . . . . his interests. Again.

Ss: What are his interests?

T: What are his interests. Next question. What's the question? What . . .?

S: What kind of books . . .

T: What kind of books – does he read? – Smokes?

Ss: Do you smoke?

T: Keith. Does he smoke

Ss: Does he smoke?

T: Next question.

S: Does he drink?

T: Does he drink? – Church?

Ss: Does he go to church?
T: Does he go to church? So remember, for Keith you say he, for Sue you say . . .?
Ss: She.
T: She. No 'yous'. Please don't say do you. He or she, OK? Go! You've got five
   minutes.

Stimulated recall:

R: . . . I'm wondering if it's too heavy a load to have the twin aims, the listening
   for key information aim, and also the focus on questions aims – whether it's
   better to separate those out and look at the questions in a separate lesson?
T: What, the question forms . . . Well when I first looked at the material, I thought
   it was quite a straightforward listening, so therefore if I give them a split
   listening, it'll make it more challenging for them. I took the decision to do that
   and I don't regret that. I mean, question forms are always difficult things to do,
   they're always difficult to slot in unless you do a whole lesson on question forms
   so to throw them in now and again like that is quite valid – so to give the both
   focuses I thought was fine.

This technique of inviting the teacher to reflect on the lesson and comment
on it in retrospect provides insights into aspects of teaching which would be
difficult to obtain in any other way. It also enables the voice of the teacher to
be heard. (For insights into the importance of obtaining multiple perspectives
on classroom processes and interaction, see Green and Harker 1988.) When
used in association with other techniques, the results can be both reliable and
valid. (We shall examine the validity and reliability of introspective and retrospective techniques in the next chapter, and I shall present some additional
data from the listening lesson.) The technique can be particularly useful as an
initial step in the research process, acting as a stimulus for the framing of
questions for more formal investigation. As a result of the data collected in
the foregoing study, I was led to extend the research to include the following
questions:

- What is the nature of the linguistic data made available to learners?
- How are the data contextualised, presented, and exploited?
- What is the basis on which interactive decisions are made?

Observation schemes

Over the years numerous schemes have been developed for documenting
classroom interaction. Chaudron (1988), extending an analysis originated by
Long (1980), identifies twenty-four different schemes which have been developed over the last twenty-five years. In selecting an observation scheme, it is
necessary to match the scheme to the purpose of the research. The following
questions, which can assist in evaluating and selecting a scheme, have been
derived from the Long/Chaudron analysis.

1. Does the scheme employ a sign or category system? (A category system allows the observer to document a behaviour–e.g., teacher asks question– every time it occurs, while a sign system requires an observation to be made at regular intervals of time.)
2. Does the scheme require the documentation of high or low inference behaviours? (A high inference behaviour requires observers to interpret the behaviour they observe – e.g., on-task or off-task behaviour.)
3. Does the scheme allow a particular event to be assigned to more than one category or event?
4. Is the instrument intended to be used in real time or on video/audio recordings?
5. Is the scheme intended principally for research or teacher education?
6. What is the focus of the instrument? (Schemes can enable the researcher to focus on one or more of the following: verbal, paralinguistic, nonlinguistic, cognitive, affective, pedagogical content, or discourse.)

Since their first appearance on the research scene, observation schemes have become increasingly sophisticated – an inevitability, given the relative simplicity of the earlier schemes. For example, one early scheme provided eight categories of teacher language (e.g., teacher explains a grammatical point/ teacher praises/teacher criticises) and only three categories of learner language (learner asks a question/learner answers a question/learner talks to another learner). The insights generated by such simple schemes are extremely limited, and for research purposes (as opposed to teacher education purposes) the simple early schemes were replaced by increasingly sophisticated schemes.

One such sophisticated scheme is the Communicative Orientation of Language Teaching (COLT), which was developed to enable researchers to compare different language classrooms (Chaudron 1988 identifies 84 different categories in the COLT scheme). The aim of the scheme is to enable the observer to describe as precisely as possible

some of the features of communication which occur in second language classrooms. Our concept of *communicative feature* has been derived from current theories of communicative competence, from the literature on communicative language teaching, and from a review of recent research into first and second language acquisition. The observational categories are designed (a) to capture significant features of verbal interaction in L2 classrooms, and (b) to provide a means of comparing some aspects of classroom discourse with *natural* language as it is used outside the classroom. (Allen, Fröhlich, and Spada 1984: 233)

The COLT consists of two parts. Part A focuses on the description of classroom activities and consists of five major parts: the activity type, the participant organization, the content, the student modality, and the materials. Part B relates to communicative features, and isolates seven of these: the use of the target language, information gap, sustained speech, reaction to code or message, incorporation of preceding utterance, discourse initiation, and relative restriction to linguistic form. Some of the key questions relating to each of these features are set out in Table 5.2.

In Table 5.2, I have simplified (although, I hope, not oversimplified) one of the more comprehensive of the observation schemes to have been developed. It is worth noting that, while the developers of COLT have tried to devise a set of procedures which enable trained researchers to obtain reliable data (and the reliability can be enhanced by the use of more than one observer or rater), the categories and communicative features are subjective to the extent that they have been selected with reference to a particular theory of language, and also with reference to current research. This serves to underline the point that there is no such thing as 'objective' observation, that what we see will be determined, at least in part, by what we expect to see. Our vision will also be influenced by the instruments we develop, adapt, or adopt to assist us in our observations. While the use of observation schemes can provide a sharper focus for our data collection than unstructured observation, it can also serve to blind us to aspects of interaction and discourse which are not captured by the scheme, and which may be important to our understanding of the classroom or classrooms we are investigating. Later in the chapter we shall look at some research which utilized the COLT scheme.

Interaction analysis

Another method (or cluster of methods) for analysing classroom interaction involves the discursive analysis of classroom talk. There are numerous schools of thought and a range of methods and techniques for carrying out such analysis. For illustrative purposes, I have chosen an approach adapted from the work of Halliday, and Halliday and Hasan, by Lemke (1985). Lemke embraces a social perspective on language that sees schools not as 'knowledge delivery systems' but as social institutions in which people affect each other's lives. He argues that classroom education is talk: 'It is the social use of language to enact regular activity structures and to share systems of meaning among teachers and students' (p. 1). Interpreting education as the use of language in the context of social activity enables the researcher to observe, document, and interpret how teachers and students use language across all school subjects to build relationships, define roles, and so on. Two key constructs in Lemke's approach to discourse analysis are 'activity structures' and 'thematic systems'. He begins his analysis by pointing out that classroom language fulfils important functions in addition to providing information. It is also used as a tool for social action, and for creating meaningful contexts. Lemke's aim is to develop a system of analysis which captures the dynamics of social interaction at the same time as analysing the thematic content of the subject being taught. Such a system must allow for the simultaneous interpretation of the

TABLE 5.2 QUESTIONS RELATING TO THE PRINCIPAL FEATURES OF THE COLT
SCHEME

Feature	Questions
Part A: classroom activities	
1a. Activity type	What is the activity type – e.g., drill, role play, dictation?
2a. Participant organization	Is the teacher working with the whole class or not?
	Are students working in groups or individually?
	If group work, how is it organized?
3a. Content	Is the focus on classroom management, language (form, function, discourse, sociolinguistics), or other?
	Is the range of topics broad or narrow?
	Who selects the topic – teacher, students, or both?
4a. Student modality	Are students involved in listening, speaking, reading, writing, or combinations of these?
5a. Materials	What types of materials are used?
	How long is the text?
	What is the source/purpose of the materials?
	How controlled is their use?
Part B: classroom language	
1b. Use of target language	To what extent is the target language used?
2b. Information gap	To what extent is requested information predictable in advance?
3b. Sustained speech	Is discourse extended or restricted to a single sentence, clause, or word?
4b. Reaction to code or message	Does the interlocutor react to code or message?
5b. Incorporation of preceding utterance	Does the speaker incorporate the preceding utterance into the his or her contribution?
6b. Discourse initiation	Do learners have opportunities to initiate discourse?
7b. Relative restriction of linguistic form	Does the teacher expect a specific form, or is there no expectation of a particular linguistic form?

utterance in interactional and substantive terms, and thus show how each utterance contributes to the enactment of specific activity structures and the development of the thematic systems.

Lemke illustrates the ways in which interactional and thematic aspects of classroom discourse operate with reference to the following episode from a New York science classroom:

```
 1  T:  Before we get started . . . before I erase the board –
 2  Ss: Sh!
 3  T:  Uh – Look how fancy I got – [points to the board]
 4  S:  [Makes a funny noise]
 5  Ss: Sh!
 6  T:  This is a representation of the 1S orbital.
 7      S'posed to be of course – three dimensional.
 8      What two elements could be represented by such a diagram?
 9      Jennifer?
10  J:  Hydrogen and helium?
11  T:  Hydrogen and helium. Hydrogen would have *one* electron –
12      somewhere in there – and helium would have?
13  S:  *Two* electrons.
14  T:  Two [pause] This is 1S, and the white would be?
15      Mark?
16  M:  2S
17  T:  Two S, and the green would be? uh . . . Janice
18  J:  2P . . . 2P
19  J:  2P
20  T:  Two P. Yeah the green one would be 2Px and 2Py. If I have
21      one electron in the 2Px, one electron in the 2Py, two
22      electrons in the 2S, two electrons in the 1S, what element
23      is being represented in this configuration?
24      [screeching noise] Oo! that sound annoys, doesn't it?
25      Ron?
26  R:  Boron?
27  T:  That would be – that'd have uh – *seven* electrons, so you'd
28      have to have one here, one here, one here, one here, one here,
29      one here. Who said it – you?
30  S:  Carbon
31  Ss: Carbon Carbon
32  T:  Carbon. Carbon. Here. Six electrons.
33      And they can be anywhere within those – confining orbitals.
34      This is also from the notes from before. The
35      term orbital refers to the average *region* traversed by
36      an electron. Electrons occupy orbitals that may differ
37      in size, shape, or space orientation. That's – that's from
38      the other class, we might as well use it for review.
```

(pp. 3–4)

What sense does Lemke make of this classroom episode from the perspective of activity structure and thematic development? The following verbatim extracts answer this question. I have included them as good examples of how discursive analysis 'works' (we shall look in greater detail at the method in Chapter 8).

Activity Structure
In Episode 1, once it gets underway, the teacher asks a question and calls on Jennifer to answer (lines 8 and 9). Her answer is made with a questioning intonation, but is evaluated by the teacher with a firm declarative repetition of what she said (line 11). You can see that this teacher regularly confirms answers by repeating them. He may preface a question with a brief preparatory remark (as in lines 11 and 12), and he may follow the evaluation with a brief supplementary comment (as in line 20). These are regular options in this special classroom dialogue pattern. You can readily see that it would be possible to rewrite the whole dialogue as a teacher monologue with essentially the same science content being presented, but the social interaction would of course be radically different.

In lines 21–32 we find a difficult question asked. A bright student (Ron) is called on to answer it, but his answer is not acceptable to the teacher, and the thematic development is in danger of ending up in confusion. Just then another student calls out the answer the teacher wanted, *Carbon*, interrupting him. The teacher tries to ascertain who said it, perhaps with an eye to acknowledging him by name and getting a repetition as with Janice, but many students now call out this same answer, and the teacher simply proceeds to confirm it and go on. He could well have persisted in finding out who said it first, could have admonished the class by saying 'Alright don't call out, raise your hands' as he and other teachers often do in this situation, but he here sacrifices the orderliness of the interaction pattern and his own position of control, briefly, in order to get the thematic development back on track, to complete the exposition through dialogue of the science content he had begun with his question. (Lemke 1985: 18–19)

Thematic structure
If you compare the exact phrasing of the teacher's questions in line 8 and in lines 20–23, you can see that they are part of an entirely implicit development of a contrast, important to the whole lesson, between orbital diagrams that can represent several elements, and electron configurations which represent a particular element. This in turn is part of a complex system of thematic relations among the notions of *atom* (not explicitly mentioned, but always implicit), *element, orbital, electron, orbital diagram, number of electrons,* and *electronic configuration*.

These relations can only be learned by experience of their usage in relation to one another in the language of the classroom or textbook. . . . To a greater degree than we may realise, thematic systems are learned in much the same way that we learn the semantic system of our own native language: implicitly, by hearing, speaking, being corrected, but mostly by shaping our speech to conform to what we hear around us. . . . The discourse of the science classroom constantly and pervasively shows this kind of subtle implicit structure of building thematic relations to a

TABLE 5.3 A COMPARISON OF METHODS FOR CLASSROOM RESEARCH

Method	Typical questions
Formal experiment	Is Method A superior to Method B?
	Do authentic listening texts lead to greater language gains than non-authentic listening texts?
Stimulated recall	What is the basis upon which teachers decide to depart from their lesson plan in the course of a lesson?
	Why do teachers decide to correct some errors and not others?
Observation schemes	What is the range and distribution of language functions by teachers and pupils in the language classroom?
	In mixed ability classrooms, how often are low proficiency students addressed by the teacher?
Interaction analysis	How do teachers maintain power and control through classroom discourse?

degree that is probably outside the conscious recognition of teacher or students as it happens. By contrast, explicit formulation of definitions and relationships is brief and occasional. (Lemke 1985: 20–21)

I have included the description of Lemke's work both because of its intrinsic interest and to illustrate a procedure which identifies significant patterns and events without assigning classroom talk to predetermined categories, as is the case with observation schemes. The different methods discussed in this section are summarised in Table 5.3.

A review of research

When one examines the literature on classroom observation and research, one is struck by the relative paucity of research such as Lemke's where the data were actually collected within genuine classrooms. (As I have said, by 'genuine' classrooms, I mean classrooms which were specifically constituted for the purposes of teaching and learning, not to provide a venue for research.) In a recent review, I examined fifty widely cited studies from the classroom research literature (a report of this survey can be found in Nunan 1991b). The five dimensions of the analysis were as follows:

1. the environment in which the data were collected (whether they were collected in genuine classrooms or not)
2. the rationale for the research (whether the principal aim of the researcher was to provide insights which might be acted upon in pedagogy, or

whether it was to investigate processes of acquisition with only a secondary rationale relating to pedagogy)
3. the research design and method of collection
4. the type of data collected
5. the type of analysis

The survey revealed that of the fifty studies, only fifteen were actually carried out in genuine language classrooms. A further seven collected some of their data in classrooms, and some of their data out of class. The great majority collected their data outside of the classroom in laboratory, simulated, and naturalistic settings. Despite this, the researchers had no hesitation in claiming pedagogic relevance for their research. The design (whether or not a formal experiment was used) and the data collection methods employed are set out in Tables 5.4, 5.5, and 5.6. (Note that some studies utilised more than one method.)

One of the disturbing outcomes of the survey was the fact that only fifteen of the studies were classroom based. If context is important to research outcomes, then we need far more of these classroom-based, as opposed to classroom-oriented, studies. Such a view is strongly put by van Lier (1988: 47), who argues that the key task for classroom researchers is 'to identify, describe and relate, in intersubjective terms, actions and contributions of participants in the L2 classroom, in such a way that their significance for language learning can be understood'. If this is indeed the case, then extracting any one action and studying it out of context 'complicates rather than facilitates their description'.

In the development of classroom-based as opposed to classroom-oriented research, it would be good to see the emergence of studies in which a number of data collection methods are employed. This would enable the researcher to obtain a more complete picture of the phenomena under investigation. For example, an investigation of teacher beliefs and classroom interaction should desirably include not only classroom observation, but also stimulated recall, teacher interviews, and teacher diaries. I would also like to see a more active role for classroom practitioners in applied research. The development of skills in observing and documenting classroom action and interaction, particularly if these foster the adoption of a research orientation by teachers to their classrooms, provides a powerful impetus to professional self-renewal. This is exemplified in the action research programs described by Nunan (1989) and also in the introduction to classroom research for language teachers by Allwright and Bailey (1991). However, I also feel that such research, particularly if carried out in collaboration with university-based researchers, can do more than act as a tool for professional development. It also has the potential to extend the current research agenda, as well as give researchers access to a greater range of classrooms than is currently encountered within the research

TABLE 5.4 CLASSROOM-BASED
STUDIES: DESIGN AND METHOD

Design	Experiment	2
	Non-experiment	13
Method	Observation	7
	Transcript	5
	Elicitation	3
	Diary	1
	Introspection	1

TABLE 5.5 LABORATORY, SIMULATED,
AND NATURALISTIC STUDIES: DESIGN
AND METHOD

Design	Experiment	13
	Non-experiment	15
Method	Elicitation	21
	Interview	5
	Transcript	2
	Questionnaire	2
	Diary	1
	Case study	1

TABLE 5.6 MIXED STUDIES: DESIGN
AND METHOD

Design	Experiment	3
	Non-experiment	4
Method	Observation	3
	Transcript	2
	Diary	2
	Elicitation	1
	Interview	1
	Introspection	1
	Case study	1

literature. (It is no accident that so much research is carried out within university language centres!)

Ultimately, the central question that research of the type reviewed here seeks to answer is whether successful second language development can and does take place in the classroom. In his own review of the relevant research, which focused on outcomes rather than research methods, Ellis (1988) argues that it can. While his examination of the discourse processes contributing to such development is somewhat tentative, he suggests that eight aspects of discourse might be important (pp. 128–130):

1. Quantity of 'intake': The amount of the target language which learners attend to is significant – quantity alone is insufficient.
2. A need to communicate: This can be provided if the target language serves as the medium as well as the target of instruction.
3. Independent control of the propositional content: Learners have a choice over what is said, and part of this should be content known to the learner but not the teacher.
4. Adherence to the 'here and now' principle: In the early stages at least, encoding and decoding is facilitated if the things being talked about are present in the learning environment.
5. The performance of a range of speech acts. The learner should be encouraged to use a range of language functions, and perform a variety of roles with the classroom discourse (for example, initiating as well as responding to discourse).
6. An input rich in directives: Particularly in the early stages of learning, directives occur in familiar and frequently occurring contexts, they refer to the 'here and now', they are morphosyntactically simple, and, as they require a non-verbal result, they are more likely to count as successful communication than interactions requiring a verbal response.
7. An input rich in 'extending' utterances: These are teacher utterances which pick up, elaborate, or in other ways extend the learner's contribution.
8. Uninhibited 'practice': This refers to the right 'to use language without communicative intent, and also to the opportunity to repeat utterances that are meaningful to the learner'.

These principles have the virtue of having emerged from a wide range of classroom-oriented and classroom-based research. This empirical, rather than speculative, dimension is only now becoming the norm in foreign language education. The principles show that research can have something positive to say to those looking for directions and signposts to practice. This is not to say that they should be accepted uncritically by the classroom teacher. The important thing is for such research outcomes to be applied and evaluated in an informed way through action-based research on the part of practitioners.

Classroom research: sample studies

In this section, the process of carrying out classroom research is exemplified by two sample studies reported in Spada (1990). The studies are particularly relevant to this chapter because they utilise one of the most comprehensive

105

observation instruments yet devised – the COLT (Communicative Orientation of Language Teaching) scheme. As we saw earlier in the chapter, this scheme was originally devised to capture varius aspects of communicative language use in the classroom. The scheme has two parts, A and B. Part A, derived from the communicative language teaching literature, captures organisational and pedagogical aspects of the classroom. Part B, which is intended to reflect issues in first and second language acquisition research, documents aspects of teacher–student interaction. The instrument has been used in a number of instructional contexts, including ESL for children, core, immersion and extended French, and intensive ESL for adults.

Study 1: ESL study

One of the studies described in some detail by Spada was a comparative investigation of three classes of an adult ESL program which was run as a six-week intensive summer course. Each class was observed for five hours a day, once a week, over a four-week period. The investigation sought to determine (a) how different teachers interpreted theories of communicative language teaching in terms of their classroom practice, and (b) whether different classroom practices had any effect on learning outcomes. Studies such as these, which attempt to establish causal links between classroom processes and learning outcomes, are called process-product research, and are notoriously difficult to carry out.

At the beginning of the experiment, students were given a battery of tests including the Comprehensive English Language Test; the Michigan Test of English Language Proficiency; teacher-designed tests of reading, writing, and speaking; and a multiple choice sociolinguistic and discourse test.

The data yielded by the COLT observation scheme indicated that one of the classes, Class A, differed from the other two in a number of ways:

A spent considerably more time on form-based activities (with explicit focus on grammar), while classes B and C spent more time on meaning-based activities (with focus on topics other than language). Classes B and C also had many more authentic activity types than class A. Furthermore, the classes differed in the way in which certain activities were carried out, particularly listening activities. For example, in classes B and C, the instructors tended to start each activity with a set of predictive exercises. These were usually followed by the teacher reading comprehension questions to prepare the students for the questions they were expected to listen for. The next step usually involved playing a tape-recorded passage and stopping the tape when necessary for clarification and repetition requests. In class A, however, the listening activities usually proceeded by giving students a list of comprehension questions to read silently; they could ask teachers for assistance if they had difficulty understanding any of them. A tape-recorded passage was then played in its entirety while students answered comprehension questions. (Spada 1990: 301–302)

The qualitative analysis confirmed the class differences, showing, for example, that class A spent twice as much time on form-based work as class C and triple the time spent by class B. To investigate whether these differences contributed differently to the learners' L2 proficiency, pre- and posttreatment test scores were compared in an analysis of covariance. (You will recall from Chapter 2 that ANCOVA is similar to ANOVA in that it is used to compare differences between means, but that it can also compensate for any initial differences in proficiency among subjects. Such differences are a distinct possibility when intact classes rather than randomly assigned subjects are utilised in an experiment.)

Among other things, results indicated that classes B and C improved their listening significantly more than class A, despite the fact that class A spent considerably more time in listening practice than the other classes. The researcher concluded that there are measurable differences in the way in which instruction is carried out in classrooms, and that these differences are reflected in different learning outcomes. This research demonstrates the fact that qualitative observation and analysis are needed in order to interpret the quantitative results obtained from the administration of standardised tests. In other words, the finding that some students did significantly better than others on the posttreatment tests would have been uninterpretable had the research not obtained qualitative data on different classroom practices.

Study 2: Core French study

A second study reported by Spada involved eight eleventh grade core French classes. The classes were selected because they purported to represent two contrasting orientations to instruction, being either 'analytical/structural' in orientation or 'experiential/functional' in orientation. The aim of the research was to determine how these different orientations were actually realised at the level of classroom pedagogy, and whether the different orientations would lead to different learning outcomes.

All the students taking part in the investigation were given a battery of pre-experiment and post-experiment proficiency tests, including a multiple choice grammar test, a writing test, and a test of listening comprehension. In addition, each class was observed on four occasions during the school year, and the classroom interactions and behaviours were documented utilising the COLT scheme. These observation data were used to characterise classes as either Type E (experiential/functional) or Type A (analytical/structural).

Classes were categorized as Type E or Type A by taking the total percentage of time spent on each of the experiential features in Parts A and B of COLT (e.g., group work, unpredictable language use, sustained speech, focus on topics/meaning, reactions to message), adding them together for each class, and ranking the individual class totals. (Spada 1990: 304)

On this basis, two classes were categorised as experiental, with the remaining six being classed as analytical. Type A classes spent more time on teacher-controlled topics, on tasks involving minimal written work, and on form-focused activities. Also, surprisingly, Type A classes spent less time in whole-class interaction than their Type E counterparts. Analysis on Part B of the COLT scheme revealed that

students in Type E classes spent a greater amount of time producing sustained speech, reacting to message, and expanding each other's utterances than students in Type A classes. In addition, students in Type E classes were less restricted in language use than students in Type A classes. Finally, while teachers in Type A classes reacted significantly more to code than message, teachers in Type E classes did the reverse. (Spada 1990: 305)

Having established several statistically significant differences in instructional treatment between the two types of classes, the researchers then set out to determine whether these differences resulted in different learning outcomes. In attempting to derive causal links between instructional processes and learning outcomes, the researchers first compared the scores of the two groups of students using analysis of covariance and found that there was no difference on any of the measures of proficiency. They then compared just two classes, one from either end of the experiential–analytical continuum. Here, the only significant result was that the analytical students were better on the grammar test than the experiential learners. Finally, the researchers correlated posttreatment test scores with all categories of Parts A and B of the COLT scheme. This analysis resulted in rather mixed outcomes. On Part A of the COLT scheme, successful classrooms seemed to be those in which the teacher did relatively more talking than individual students, relatively more time was spent on classroom management and form-focused activities than on general discussion, the students themselves spent relatively little time speaking, and visual aids and L2 materials were used relatively often. On Part B, it was found that 'genuine questions, reaction to message and topic incorporation were positively related to improvement, whereas sustained speech by students, predictable questions, and reaction to code were negatively related. These results imply that learners benefited from both the analytical and experiential aspects of instruction' (Spada 1990: 305–306).

The studies reviewed in this section illustrate a number of important points. In the first instance, they show that collecting pre- and posttreatment test data is insufficient, that in addition, one requires process data on what actually goes on in the classrooms. The studies are also of interest because they are examples of process-product studies, which are notoriously difficult to carry out. In the first place, it is not always possible to carry out a true experiment in which subjects are randomly assigned to groups. Secondly, the treatment might not show an effect because the length of time is not sufficient to show proficiency gains. Finally, there is the problem of operationalising the constructs one is working with, particularly that of proficiency. One possible reason for the mixed results in the core French study is that the 'analytical'–'experiential' distinction is more ostensible than real. It may also be that proficiency measures selected lack construct validity [for example, it may be questioned whether the multiple choice grammar tests used by the researchers capture the notion of proficiency as the ability to carry out communicative tasks in the target language (Richards 1985)]. Another question concerns the relative contributions of form- and meaning-focused activities to the development of communicative competence – simply tabulating the amount of time devoted to different activities may be too crude as an index of analytical–experiential teaching. The insight that both analytical and experiential instruction are necessary may be only a first faltering step in the direction of developing effective instruction. To act on this insight, a teacher would want to know how much of each type of instruction is appropriate for a given group of learners, when they should be introduced, and how they relate to one another.

Conclusion

In this chapter I have set out some of the issues and methods relevant to the investigation of language learning and use in classroom contexts. Obviously, with such an enormous area, about which entire volumes can, and have, been written, it is only possible to provide some initial signposts which might assist you as you read further in the field and, it is hoped, also begin your own exploration of classroom teaching and learning processes. This last point is, I believe, an important one because:

The teacher is the researcher's link with learners, and also the learners' link with research. The teacher is contracted to help learners learn, but can do so better by knowing about previous research and by using the procedures of classroom research to understand better what is happening in his or her own classroom. In this way, the exploratory teacher will not only improve achievement but will also contribute to our general research knowledge about how language classrooms work. (Allwright and Bailey 1991: 197)

In addition to outlining methods and issues, I have tried to give some indication of the problems confronting those currently engaged in classroom research. Much of the research which purports to provide teachers with guidance on pedagogic practice is not derived from genuine language classrooms, and the research agenda needs to be extended to incorporate a greater range and number of classroom-based as opposed to classroom-oriented research. (Although, to repeat, I am not questioning the value of, or necessity for, classroom-oriented research.)

Questions and tasks

1. One of the disadvantages of observational instruments is that they act as mental 'blinkers' on the user. They also encapsulate the author's ideological beliefs about the nature of teaching and learning. What ideological assumptions about the nature of instruction are revealed by the authors of the COLT scheme? What questions or hypotheses might be investigated using schemes such as these?

2. Select three or four papers relating to some aspect of teacher talk, learner talk, or teacher–student interaction, and carry out a comparative analysis similar to that carried out by Nunan (1991b) and reported in this chapter in the section, 'A Review of Research'.

3. Study the classroom extracts and stimulated recall statements presented in the first section of this chapter. What research questions and issues do they suggest? Alternatively, carry out a similar task using the extract in task 4 below. How might these research questions and issues be followed up?

4. a. What similarities and differences are there between Ellis's list of eight conditions for successful language development and the conditions implicit in the COLT scheme?

b. Study the following classroom extract (author's data) in terms of the questions from the COLT scheme as set out in Table 5.2. (You may not be able to complete all categories.)

c. To what extent does the teaching/learning sequence reflect the following eight discourse conditions hypothesised by Ellis (1988) to be important in fostering second and foreign language development? (These principles are glossed in this chapter.)

    (1) quantity of intake
    (2) a need to communicate
    (3) independent control of the propositional content
    (4) adherence to the 'here and now' principle
    (5) the performance of a range of speech acts
    (6) an input rich in directives
    (7) an input rich in 'extending utterances'
    (8) uninhibited 'practice'

Transcript
Step 1: Teacher puts students into small groups and gives out a handout containing the following information:

> Student A: What helped me most to learn English? Let's see – reading all sorts of printed material, listening to native speakers on the radio, TV and films, finding opportunities to use English out of class.
> Student B: The things that helped me least – well, I would say memorizing

grammar rules, reading aloud one by one around the class, doing boring grammar exercises.

Student C: Language taught inside the classroom is not sufficient to make a person a competent speaker in the real world. You need to use the language outside of the classroom.

Student D: Practising through conversations and using the media, especially TV with subtitles and newspapers. You must have someone who is proficient in the language to speak with in order to learn the language sufficiently well.

Student E: I find that motivation is vital in the success of learning a foreign language. Strong interest, sheer determination and motivation to learn a second language were the most important things for me.

Student F: I would say 'teacher talk' helped me least. Looking back, I wish he had given me more opportunities to use the language in class, especially speaking it inside and outside the classroom. It would have been more fun and challenging if I was thrown into the deep end.

Student G: The thing I liked least was negative oral criticism and punishment for wrong answers. Dull teachers who are inactive/cannot be heard clearly.

Student H: What helped me most was constant drilling, and when I had my own textbook and made notes from teacher explanations.

The teacher tells the group that some additional students will be joining the class. The handout contains statements from these students. The students have to decide which of these additional students they would most like to join their group, and which they definitely would not like.

Step 2: *Small group discussion.* The students spend 25 minutes completing the task.

Step 3: *Debriefing.* The teacher leads a whole group discussion.

T: All right, this group has finished so we can all stop. What I'd like to do is get a short oral summary of the discussion you had in your group – what responses you came up with in each group. I'd like to start with the group down the back. G.

S: Our group strongly agree with A, C, and er E. And we disagree or neutral with the rest of the student. Definitely we will have/hate(?) to join our group the student H . . .

T: Which one was that? Let me see.

S: The last one.

T: You would like that person to join your group (no we don't). You don't want that person in your group (no). Mmm.

S: We would like to, to join to our group the student C – and if possible to have student A as well.

T: So you have a back up – a reserve. Why did you choose student C?

S: Because we think that is more er dynamic, that method the student is using – you know, is more . . . more aggressive, more er . . . come on, give me help (laughter).

T: All right, you've done very well. Did anybody in your group disagree, or did you all agree on the points you discussed? (yes, we agree/we agree) I suppose that's why you're sitting together, it is? (laughter)

T: Which group can I pick now? What about this group over here?

S: Can I ask you one question before I answer any question?

T: Sure.

S: Do we suppose to only choose one person as er dis . . . agree or disagree – or have more . . .

T: Well, I er the instructions were pick one (only one) pick one student

S: That's it, yes. I our group, we are most agree with the student E, and we are disagree with student F.

T: So you'd like student E to join your group and you would not like student F to join your group (exactly). Can you give . . . can you tell me the reasons that you decided?

S: Um the reason being is because the student E um mention very clearly the most important aspect – that is what is important for learning – and student F was very narrowed the subject and just point the negative point of view of learning, so . . . (mm)

T: OK Does anybody want to ask this group any questions? No? OK, this group.

S: In our group, we would like student E to join our group.

T: Student E? Golly, two votes for student E, so far. Mm

S: You want to know the reason why? (yeah) Yeah. Because we think that the student got a motivation to learn something er we can pay attention to it and then we can progress quickly. (yeah, OK) Er, we dislike student A to join our group (student A) yeah

T: Why is that?

S: Er, we feel the student, he pay attention too much on er hearing, but he did not pay attention to writing English – written English. Not much time to use er written English.

T: OK, right – Right . . . this group. Come on, don't be shy (laughter)

S: Actually we agree with student A . . .

T: Student A isn't that good, great, we've got one group at least that one group would like student A and one group would hate student A in their group.

S: And, er, student D is strongly agree (student?) D(D) strongly agree. Yes.

T: Mmm. But, but you'd like student A to join your group.

S: No, D

T: Student D? (D) D? Sorry (yeah) And you wouldn't like student A to join your group. (inaud) So which is the one you, you dislike?

S: Dislike? Student H.

S: Student H.

T: Yeah, why?

S: It's er neutral

T: (Mm) Can you give the reason why?

S: We'll have an headache, if he join to us (laughter).

T: OK – this group.

S: Um, the student which we most like to join the group is student C (Mm) And the one which we don't like to join the group is student F.

T: All right. Can you give – can you tell me the reasons?

S: Well student C – er, reason why we like him to join the group is because he's looking at the practical – at the practice of language outside the classroom. And we think – we all agree that it is very important for the student to practise the language. So, he learn the language inside the classroom, and he go outside and practise it, and that's what help him to learn English.

T: Right, and the negative one?

S: Er, the negative one – I, I think the teacher the teacher talking too much it does help the student because they're learning English. Secondly, he saying that the teacher didn't allow him to practice English in, in the classroom – well there is a limit to that because she can't give everybody all, she can't give one person all the time she have – she has to give an opportunity to the rest of the student. Secondly, er, thirdly, he said that she didn't allow him to use the language outside the classroom but she had no control over him outside the classroom – he can go and do whatever he like. So he's blaming the teacher for that.

T: I'm sure all the teachers in the room will love you. (laughter). OK. Um.

S: Er, the student we like most is E (E) Yeah We dislike B. Because as to E we think er it's (E yes) very important for learning a language its interest and determination and motivation that if you er – if you have strong strong interest and motivation then you will try to find the how to learn a language is very creative, you will find a creative way to (uhuh) learn a language.

T: OK (yes) Good. Did you all agree, or did you have to discuss it for a long time before you (we discuss) OK fine, thanks. And, last, but not least . . .

S: We, er, we disagree with student B, strongly disagree (uhuh) because er he thinks that grammar – memorizing grammar rules and doing boring grammar exercise – exercises – is er not useful, that helped him least. So, we think er the grammar, is a construction of language . . . that if you want to explain anything and you know every word in the dictionary, you don't want er what can be, er what order it must be used – in what order it must be used.

T: OK. So that's the negative – that's the student you don't want. (Yes) Which student do you want?

S: We chose er student H which who is er constant drilling and er doing exercises with teacher who explain him if he's correct or not and why – so er I think we er we have experience in this way of learning so we chose it.

Step 4: *Conclusion.* The teacher spends five minutes introducing students to the idea that different learners have different preferred learning styles and strategies, and describes how a focus on learning-how-to-learn will be an important aspect of their course.

5. a. What do you see as the key constructs underlying the investigations reported by Spada? What do you think might be the chief threats to the validity and reliability to the research? How might these be guarded against?

b. Spada argues that the qualitative and quantitative data are complementary. What evidence is there in the descriptions of the studies to support this claim?

c. What criticisms, if any, would you make of the studies and the conclusions reached by the researchers?

6. Select a classroom-based study from a recent journal such as *Language*

Learning, TESOL Quarterly, or the *Modern Language Journal.* Summarise the study by providing the following data:

a. Question/hypothesis
b. Significance/value of the study
c. Subjects
d. Procedure
e. Type of data
f. Type of analysis
g. Conclusions
h. Further research
i. Critique

Further reading

Allwright (1988) is an excellent annotated collection of important papers on classroom observation. Van Lier (1988) puts forth the case for an ethnographic approach to the analysis of language classrooms. A very different and therefore complementary perspective is provided by Chaudron (1988). Nunan (1989) provides a guide to classroom observation and action-based research for the practitioner who may not have had formal training in research methods. For a review of thirty-three methods comparison studies, see Beretta (1992). The studies in collections by Brumfit and Mitchell (1990) and Nunan (1992) illustrate what can be achieved through small-scale, action-oriented classroom research. Frölich, Spada, and Allen (1985) and Spada (1990) exemplify larger-scale classroom research.

6 Introspective methods

Here is Edward Bear coming downstairs now, bump, bump, bump on the back of his head . . . it is, as far as he knows, the only way of coming downstairs, but sometimes he feels that there really is another way, if only he could stop bumping for a moment and think about it.

(A. A. Milne, The World of Pooh)

One of the problems confronting the language researcher is that a great deal of the hard work involved in language development and use is invisible, going on in the head of the learner. During the days when behaviourist psychology dominated language research, it was considered both futile and irrelevant to investigate this invisible work, the researcher being interested only in the observable characteristics of human behaviour. These days, however, such research is generally considered inadequate, and the focus of attention is much more on the cognitive processes underlying human performance and ability. It is widely accepted that if we want to understand what people do, we need to know what they think. Researchers often go to considerable lengths to derive insights into the mental processes underlying observable behaviour, and in this chapter, we shall look at the introspective techniques which are designed to help them do this.

Introspection is the process of observing and reflecting on one's thoughts, feelings, motives, reasoning processes, and mental states with a view to determining the ways in which these processes and states determine our behaviour. The tradition of using introspective methods has come from cognitive psychology, where it has aroused considerable controversy. In fact, many psychologists assume that verbal reports have nothing at all to do with causal cognitive processes. Its use in research into language learning is more recent, although it is certain to arouse a similar amount of controversy as it becomes more widely used. Particularly contentious is the assumption made by researchers that the verbal reports obtained through the introspection carried out by their subjects accurately reflects the underlying cognitive processes giving rise to behaviour. In other words, there might be a discontinuity between what the subjects believed they were doing and what they were actually doing.

In this chapter, I shall use the term *introspection* to cover techniques in which data collection is coterminous with the mental events being investigated. I shall also use it to cover research contexts in which the data are collected retrospectively, that is, some time after the mental events themselves have taken place. The amount of time which elapses between the mental event and the reporting of that event may distort what is actually reported, and one needs to be aware of this when actually using one of these techniques. (In one sense, all the techniques reported here are retrospective in that there will always be a gap, however slight, between the event and the report.) In this chapter I shall consider the following questions:

– What do researchers mean by introspection and retrospection?
– What techniques are there for obtaining introspective and retrospective data?
– Which introspective research tools are particularly appropriate for investigating language learning?

Some early introspective methods

The earliest introspective studies involved free association tasks in which subjects were required to say the first word they thought of in response to a stimulus word. This technique was widely used by psychiatrists such as Jung (1910). Another technique, reported by Ericsson and Simon (1984, 1987), involved getting subjects to respond as quickly as possible if they did or did not understand cue sentences which were either ambiguous or difficult to interpret. They cite as an example the sentence: 'We deprecate everything that can be explained', which was used by Buhler (1951) to investigate processes of comprehension. The researcher would read out sentences such as this and the subjects were required to indicate immediately whether or not they understood.

These techniques were fraught with problems and aroused considerable controversy. Ericsson and Simon (1987) argue that techniques such as free association and sentence recall are not particularly useful for developing models of the mental processes underlying performance, because there is no way of knowing whether a subject's responses were determined before the presentation of the task. It is also possible that the response may have been determined by a procedure which is irrelevant to the task. In free association, any response is acceptable regardless of how unusual or even peculiar it might be. These early tasks assumed that subjects were reliable, and that they could be trusted to follow the procedures and instructions devised by the researcher. More recently, techniques have been developed in which the trustworthiness or otherwise of the subjects and the status of their response are irrelevant because the researcher decides the correct solution or answer in advance.

Recent studies of thinking have primarily used tasks in logic . . . mathematics . . . probability . . . and so on, where a given task has a single correct answer. Using tasks in a formalized domain has many advantages. It is easy to generate a large

116

number of different problems among which only the surface elements differ. In addition, the investigator can make a careful analysis of the task, which may suggest what kinds of theory may be reasonable before observations of people performing the task are gathered. (Ericsson and Simon 1987: 27)

Think-aloud techniques

Think-aloud techniques, as the name suggests, are those in which subjects complete a task or solve a problem and verbalise their thought processes as they do so. The researcher collects the think-aloud protocol on tape and then analyses it for the thinking strategies involved. The following is a transcript of a think-aloud protocol from a subject mentally multiplying 36 times 24 reported in Ericsson and Simon (1987: 34).

OK
36 times 24
um
4 times 6 is 24
4
carry the 2
4 times 3 is 12
14
144
0
2 times 6 is 12
2
carry the 1
2 times 3 is 6
7
720
720
144 plus 72
so it would be 4
6
864

The think-aloud technique is closer than retrospective techniques to the mental action in which subjects think back on actions performed at some prior time (for example, when they are asked to talk about why they gave certain answers in a standardised test). However, we may still question whether the verbalisation accurately reflects the mental processes which normally underlie such problem-solving tasks. It may well be that the act of spelling out our thought processes alters those processes. This worry is not peculiar to introspection. I have already pointed out that researchers, regardless of the methods they use or the traditions to which they adhere, will (if they are honest) often have to confront the possibility that their results are in some ways artifacts of the procedures they have used.

Anagram tasks

A similar technique, but this time related to letters and words rather than numbers, is the anagram task. An anagram is a word or phrase whose constituent parts have been rearranged, resulting in 'nonsense' words. Here, subjects are presented with an anagram, or nonsense word, and are required to think aloud as they unscramble it to make a meaningful word. Table 6.1 presents transcripts of three think-aloud protocols from subjects solving the anagram NPEHPA. (A protocol, as you can see from Table 6.1, is a written record of what the subjects say as they complete the task.)

What do the protocols in Table 6.1 tell us about the processes involved in mental computation, and what sort of generalisations or hypotheses, if any, would data such as these enable us to formulate? According to the researchers, two types of strategies are frequent in anagram tasks. The initial strategy is to draw on long-term memory to select likely combinations of letters – that is, combinations that occur frequently in English – and use these to generate words containing these combinations. This provides a basis for attempts at generating a list of possible solutions.

These can derive from attempts to sound out letter combinations or can be related words evoked from LTM [long-term memory]. . . . These protocols depend heavily upon recognition processes and evocation of information from LTM. A computer model could be programmed to produce qualitatively similar protocols, but it is impossible, in the absence of detailed knowledge of how subjects have information stored and indexed in LTM, to predict the sequence of events in any particular subjects' thinking-aloud protocol. In spite of the use of common processes, different subjects arrive at the anagram solution along different routes. (Ericsson and Simon 1987: 48)

While these think-aloud techniques represent an advance on earlier, rather crude techniques such as word association, they still suffer from a number of problems. For example, the question remains as to whether the verbalisation process accurately reflects the cognitive operations underlying performance, or whether these are somehow transformed by the subject's efforts to verbalise. The relevance of some of this research for language learning, coming as it does from a particular area of cognitive psychology, might also be questioned. Nevertheless, we need to acknowledge the contribution to research methodology made by cognitive psychology, a contribution which may yet provide a significant resource for language researchers.

Diary studies

Diaries, logs, and journals are important introspective tools in language research. They have been used in investigations of second language acquisi-

TABLE 6.1 THINK-ALOUD PROTOCOLS FROM SUBJECTS SOLVING THE ANAGRAM 'NPEHPA'

Protocol 1	Protocol 2	Protocol 3
N-P neph, neph	start with P	All right
Probably PH goes together	No, it doesn't	Let's see
Phan	the two P's go together	NPEHPA
Phanny	Happen	Let's try what letters go together
I get phan-ep		Do you want to tell me
no Nap-		when I miss,
Phep-an, no		okay
E is at the end		PH go together
Phag-en		but they're not very likely
People – I think of		so how about APP
Try PH after the other letters		Oh, happen
Naph, no		Got it
I thought of paper again		
E and A sound alike		
couldn't go together without		
a consonant		
try double P		
happy		
Happen		

Source: Based on data provided in Ericsson and Simon (1987: 49).

tion, teacher–learner interaction, teacher education, and other aspects of language learning and use. Diaries can be kept by learners, by teachers, or by participant observers. They can focus either on teachers and teaching, or on learners and learning (or on the interaction between teachers and learners, or between teaching and learning). In this section, we shall look at the advantages and disadvantages of using diaries as research tools in language acquisition and development.

Bailey (1990: 215) defines the diary study as 'a first-person account of a language learning or teaching experience, documented through regular, candid entries in a personal journal and then analyzed for recurring patterns or salient events'. She points out that diary studies are part of a growing body of literature on classroom research. As with the classroom observation checklists which we looked at in the preceding section, diaries can be used either for research or for teacher education. While our principal point of focus is research, it is worth noting in passing the following benefits which can accrue when using research in teacher education programs (based on Porter et al. 1990):

1. Students can articulate problems they are having with course content and therefore get help.
2. Diaries promote autonomous learning, encouraging students to take responsibility for their own learning.
3. By exchanging ideas with their teacher, students can gain confidence, make sense of difficult material, and generate original insights.
4. Keeping journals can lead to more productive class discussion.
5. Students are encouraged to make connections between course content and their own teaching.
6. Journals create teacher–student and student–student interaction beyond the classroom.
7. By matching training methodology with second language teaching methodology, they make a class more process oriented.

By extension, most of these benefits can also be applied to second language learning.

In using diaries for research, Bailey (1983, 1990) and Bailey and Ochsner (1983) recommend a five-stage procedure, beginning with an account of the diarist's personal learning history. The data collection should be as candid as possible, despite the possible embarrassment of some of the entries. This initial database is then revised for public consumption. Patterns and significant events are identified, and those factors which appear to be important in language learning are interpreted and discussed. In carrying out a procedure such as this, it is probably a good idea to avoid analysing and interpreting the data until a substantial amount of material has been collected. This can help the researcher avoid coming to premature conclusions which may be inaccurate or incorrect. In addition, it is often the case that in the early stages the entries do not make a great deal of sense, and patterns emerge only in the longer term.

It is probably not surprising that most of the diary studies in the second language acquisition literature are by applied linguists and language teachers documenting their own attempts at learning a second or foreign language. Most of these studies provide valuable insights into both social and psychological aspects of language development, and in most of them affective factors emerge as being particularly significant in language learning. Bailey (1983), for instance, kept a diary of her experiences in learning French. To her surprise, the affective factors of competitiveness and anxiety emerged as highly significant in the learning process.

The importance of affectivity also emerges in a study by Schmidt and Frota (1985). This case study documents the attempts of one of the authors, a native speaker of English, to learn Portuguese while in Brazil. The study is interesting for several reasons, not the least of which is the light it throws on the interaction of 'in class' and 'out of class' experiences on language development.

The study consisted of three phases. In the first phase, the subject, 'R', attempts to pick up a little Portuguese while interacting with native speakers. Extract 1 from his diary illustrates this particular phase. In the extract, one is immediately struck by the importance of social, interpersonal, and affective factors to R in his initial attempts to make sense of the language.

EXTRACT 1

Journal entry, Week 2

I *hate* the feeling of being unable to talk to people around me. I'm used to chatting with people all day long, and I don't like this silence. Language is the only barrier, since it is certainly easy to meet Brazilians. I've noticed that it is acceptable to ask anyone on the street for a cigarette. It . . . appears to have no relationship to age, sex or class. Last night an attractive and obviously respectable young woman, accompanied by her boyfriend, stopped me and bummed a cigarette. If I take a pack to the beach, it disappears within an hour, so that's 20 people I could have met. . . . Today P and I were at the beach, a guy came up for a cigarette, sat down and wanted to talk. He asked if I were an American and I said *sim*. He said something I didn't comprehend at all, so I didn't respond. He said, "well, obviously communication with you would be difficult" (I *did* understand that, though I can't remember any of the words now), and left. (p. 242)

Phase 2 of the study occurred when R enrolled for formal instruction in Portuguese. Once again, affective factors emerge as particularly important for R, as can be seen in Extracts 2 and 3.

EXTRACT 2

Journal entry, Week 4

P and I started class yesterday. There are 11 in the class (of various nationalities). The teacher is young and very good. She introduced herself to us (in Portuguese): I am X, my name is X, I am your teacher, I am a teacher, I am a teacher of

121

Portuguese, I'm also a teacher of English, I'm from [place], I'm single, I'm not married, I don't have children, I have a degree in applied linguistics, etc. She went around the class, asking the same kinds of questions: what's your name?, where are you from?, what kind of work do you do?, do you have any children?, etc. Most of the students could answer some of the questions, e.g., I know what my title is at the university. Everyone was rapidly picking up new things from the others' answers. For the rest of the class, we circulated, introducing ourselves to each other and talking until we exhausted the possibilities. At the end of the class, X put the paradigm for SER on the board, plus a few vocabulary items. Great! This is better than *bom dia* and then silence. . . . I'm sure I'll be asked all those questions thousands of times before I leave here. So I went out last night and talked to four people. It worked, and I'm invited to a party tomorrow night. Of course I quickly ran out of things to say and quickly stopped understanding what people said to me, but that just makes me eager to get back to class. (p. 243)

EXTRACT 3
Journal entry, Week 4
A half hour into the class, X showed up and pulled me out. There's a new section of the intensive course that's just opened and if I want I can move. I said yes . . . and went to the new class, which was already in session . . . When I sat down, a drill was in progress. SER again, which must be every teacher's lesson one. Teacher asks, student responds: *Você é americana?* ["Are you an American/"]; *Sou, sim* ["I am, yes"]. When it was my turn the question was *Você é casado?* ["Are you married?"]; so I said *não*. L corrected me: *sou, sim*. I objected: *en não sou casado*. L said [in English], "We are practicing affirmative answers." I objected again, I'm not married, and L said, "These questions have nothing to do with real life." My blood was boiling, but I shut up. The remainder of the class was choral repetition of the first conjugation verb **FALAR:** *falo, fala, falamos, falam,* over and over. I didn't like that much either, and when it was my turn to perform individually I tried to put the forms in sentences: *en falo português* ["I speak Portuguese"], *você fala inglês* ["you speak English"]. L did not appreciate that at all. What a sour start! But I think I will stick with it. There are only three students in the class, and the other two are as eager as I am . . . This class will give me almost twice as many hours a week as the other one, and L says we will cover about twice the material I would get in that course. So I guess I can remember that I am not the teacher here, try not to provoke L too much, and make the best use of the resources that I get. (pp. 243–244)

In the third and final phase of the study, R abandons the formal classes and attempts to manage his own instructional program. His focus is now on acquiring the target language through interacting with native speakers, and then reflecting on that interaction. Extracts 4, 5, and 6 illustrate the strategies he adopts, and his reactions to success and failure in out-of-class interactions.

EXTRACT 4
Journal entry, Week 11
H and I ate dinner at Caneco 70. He complained non-stop about his job. I tried to say "you don't seem comfortable" with the job: *sinto que você não está comfortável,* and his face showed complete non-comprehension. I grabbed my dictionary.

"Comfortable" is *comfortável,* but it flashed through my mind that perhaps you can only say chairs are comfortable, not people. A few minutes later H said something with *não deve.* I was taught **DEVER** as "have to" or "must," and I've been thinking that *não deve* + Verb would mean "don't have to" and *deve não* + Verb would mean "must not," but H's remark obviously meant "should not." So I learned something, but in general H is a terrible conversationalist for me. He doesn't understand things I say that everyone else understands. When I don't understand him, all he can ever do is repeat. (p. 246)

EXTRACT 5
Journal entry, Week 18
Last night I was really up, self-confident, feeling fluent . . . At one point, M said to F that she should speak more slowly for me, but I said no, please don't, I don't need it anymore.

EXTRACT 6
Journal entry, Week 20
Last night I met X, who's just come back from Argentina. Before we were introduced, I overheard M and U talking to X about me at the other end of the table. X: *ele fala protuguês?* ["Does he speak Portuguese?"]; U: *fala mal* ["He speaks poorly"]. M said I make lots of mistakes, and mentioned *marida* and *pais.* X saw me looking at them and said: *mas você entende tudo?* ["But you understand everything?"] I was annoyed and wanted to let them know I had been listening, so I replied: *entendo mal também* ["I also understand poorly"].

These extracts provide a flavour of the study as a whole. They also illustrate the ways in which diary and journal entries provide insights into processes of learning which would be difficult, if not impossible, to obtain in any other way. The fact that R is a language teacher and researcher, as well as an applied linguist, also means that he has definite ideas on what is worth recording, and also on how his observations might be interpreted. Of course, the question arises as to the extent to which the observations and conclusions made by Schmidt and Frota can be applied to second language learners who are not language teachers and researchers.

Diary studies face problems and threats similar to other introspective data collection methods. In terms of external validity, critics of the method ask how conclusions based on data from a single subject can possibly be extrapolated to other language learners. Such critics would probably accept that diaries are ground-clearing or hypothesis-raising preliminaries to real research, but that they are not of themselves valid or reliable means of doing research. Another criticism relates to the status of the data, and the interpretations derived from them. Here, the essential critical question is: To what extent do the diary entries realistically reflect what was really going on at the time the recordings were made?

Notwithstanding such criticisms, it is difficult to see how the sort of data yielded by diaries and journals could be collected in any other way. Even a cursory reading of the diary extracts provided by Schmidt and Frota reveal rich insights into some of the psychological, social, and cultural factors implicated in language development (see also Rivers' 1983 diary account of her attempts to learn a sixth language). I believe that they also have a great deal of potential for the investigation of learning strategies and learning preferences of second language students (see, for example, O'Malley and Chamot 1990; Oxford 1990; Willing 1988). Even as a ground-clearing preliminary to psychometric research, diaries, logs, and journals have a valuable place in the overall methodological repertoire of the language researcher.

Retrospection

As I indicated at the beginning of this chapter, retrospective data are collected some time after the event under investigation has taken place. Retrospection has been criticised by a number of researchers (see, for example, Nisbett and Wilson 1977) on the grounds that the gap between the event and the reporting will lead to unreliable data. It has also been claimed that if subjects know they will be required to provide a retrospective account, this will influence their performance on the task. Ericsson and Simon (1984) argue that the reliability of the data can be enhanced by ensuring that the data are collected as soon as possible after the task or event has taken place. If subjects are provided with sufficient contextual information, the reliability will also be enhanced. Steps should also be taken to ensure that subjects do not make inferences which go beyond the task, and that researcher bias is eliminated. (In interviews and stimulated recall sessions, the researcher may fall into the trap of 'leading the witness'.) Fianlly, where possible, subjects should not be informed that they will be required to retrospect until after they have completed the task.

Given the problems associated with retrospection, one may question why the technique should be used at all. Unfortunately, there are occasions when it is simply not feasible or desirable to collect data from subjects during the task performance. Consider the research on teacher decision-making which I referred to in the preceding chapter, where the focus of attention is on the decisions teachers make in the course of teaching. In this instance, it would simply not be feasible for the teachers simultaneously to teach and at the same time to report on their thoughts and decisions. Researchers have therefore been forced to use a stimulated recall technique, in which they observe and record the lesson. Immediately after the lesson, the teachers are interviewed and prompted to talk about the decisions they made during the course of the lesson. The lesson is subsequently transcribed, and the retrospections are matched against the relevant parts of the transcript. Table 6.2 illustrates the database resulting from this process (this is from my own data).

In the study referred to in Table 6.2, Ericsson and Simon's 'immediacy' condition was fulfilled by collecting the data immediately after the lesson.

TABLE 6.2 TRANSCRIPT AND RETROSPECTIVE DATA FROM A TEACHER
DECISION-MAKING PROJECT

Lesson transcript	*Retrospection*
T: What's the question you can ask for smokes? S: Are you smoke? T: Are you smoke? Do you smoke, or does she smoke? Does she smoke? What question does the interviewer ask? The interviewer? What question does the interviewer ask? What's the question in here? S: You smoke? T: You smoke? You smoke? That's not a proper question is it really? Proper question is do you smoke? So he says 'you smoke?' We know it's a question because . . . why? You smoke? . . . S: The tone. T: The tone . . . the . . . the . . . what did we call it before? You smoke? What do we call this? S: Intonation. T: Intonation. You know by his intonation – it's a question. T: Drinks. What's the question? Drinks. Do you drink? Yeah. What's the, what's the question he asks? S: Drink? T: Drink. Just one word. Drink? How do we know it's a question? Intonation.	[The students have listened to a taped interview in which the interviewer asks someone about their personal habits. While the objective of the lesson is for the students to extract key information from the interview, the teacher at this point contrasts the (native speaking) interviewer's questions with 'proper' questions.] In the post-lesson retrospection, the teacher refers to this incident as one of the spontaneous decisions she made. R: So you hadn't actually planned to teach that? T: No, I hadn't. I mean, really, that would be an excellent thing to do in a follow-up lesson – you know, focus on questions. R: In fact, what you're asking them to do in their work is focus on the full question forms, and yet in the tape they're using a . . . T: Wasn't, yeah. So, I suppose it's recognising one question form by the intonation, then being able to transfer it into the proper question 'Do you drink?' rather than 'Drink?'

Key: T = teacher, S = student, R = researcher

The technique could have been extended by providing the teacher with the transcript and getting her to reflect on it, and provide a further commentary on the action (this, of course, violates the immediacy condition, as there is an inevitable gap between the time of the recording and the provision of a transcription). It is worth noting that at one point during the retrospection the researcher almost fell into the trap of 'leading the witness' when he alluded to the contradiction inherent in the use of authentic language on the one hand, and the assertion that such language is not 'proper' on the other.

The data yielded by this retrospective way of investigating teacher decision-making gave rise to a number of important questions which were pursued in follow-up research. These included:

- How much decision-making is reflective and how much occurs as a spontaneous reaction to events occurring in the classroom?
- What theories of language learning and teaching underpin spontaneous decisions?
- What is it that teachers focus on (e.g., the instructional process, students' characteristics, student behaviour) when making decisions?
- What biographical variables (such as teaching experience and professional qualifications) correlate with different types of decisions?
- What is the nature of the linguistic data which are made available to learners, how are they made available, and to what pedagogic effect?

Another situation in which it is neither feasible nor desirable to collect data during task performance is when one is investigating learners' test-taking performance under genuine test conditions. In such a situation, it is necessary to use retrospection. The technique is illustrated by Aslanian (1985), who investigated the reading comprehension strategies of her learners in a second language context. She set out to discover, among other things, the extent to which responses on objective tests accurately reflect a learner's understanding of written texts in the target language. Her procedure was quite straightforward. The subjects read a passage in the target language, and then completed a multiple choice test. The researcher then interviewed the students, and encouraged them to think about and report to her the reasons why they had given particular responses. She concluded from her research that multiple choice tests do not always accurately reflect the language processing abilities of the test-takers. While some of her subjects gave correct answers without adequately comprehending the text, there were others who got the answers wrong, but whose introspections revealed that they had, in fact, comprehended the intentions of the writer.

Feldmann and Stemmer (1987) use a similar technique to investigate learners' test-taking performance. Their study is of interest because they use a combination of introspection and retrospection. The purpose of the study was to investigate the operations and processes used by foreign language learners when working on a foreign language test. The test they chose to investigate was the C-test, a type of gap test in which only parts of the word, rather than the whole word, are deleted. The researchers wanted to investigate the construct validity of this relatively new type of test. In other words, their aim was to find out what the test really measures.

The procedure followed by the researchers was as follows: Subjects (native speaking Germans learning French or Spanish) were tested individually. Having been introduced to the test, they were left alone in the room to complete the C-test. While completing the test they were asked to 'think aloud', and

TABLE 6.3 SAMPLE RECALL AND EVALUATION STRATEGIES IDENTIFIED BY
FELDMANN AND STEMMER (1987)

Strategy type	Example
A. *Recall*	
By structural analysis	S (looking for item *que* in 'je pense q___'): je pense again a relative pronoun starts with q ∧ ∧ ∧
Recall by adding letters/ syllables to beginning of item	S (subject is looking to item 'fastida' in 'el aire les fast ___'): el aire les fast ∧ ∧ fasto not fasta ∧ hm ∧ I really don't know.
Recall by substitution	S (subject is looking for *dirais* in 'je dir___' and uses 'something' as a filler): je di dir something . . . (continues reading).
B. *Evaluation*	
Check on meaning of item	S (translates *se mueren de calor* into mother tongue): . . . si estan querradas ∧ ∧ ∧ ∧ s-s-e mueren de calor they die with h ∧ yes se mueren (writes 'se') de calor (writes 'de') . . .
Check on form of item	S (subject is checking on endings of *retrouvent*): . . . pour elles ∧ ∧ representent has to be plural . . . or is it represent la vie quotidienne ∧ ∧ no has got to be the scenes.

their utterances were tape-recorded. The subjects and researchers then ret-rospectively reviewed the audiotape, and the subject was invited to comment on his or her utterances and behaviour, as well as answer the interviewer's questions. The researchers then analysed the responses and developed a typology of strategies used by the subjects. A strategy was defined as 'a potentially conscious plan for solving what, to the individual, presents itself as a problem in reaching a particular goal' (Feldmann and Stemmer 1987: 258). Two types of strategies were identified: recall strategies and evaluation strategies. Recall strategies were employed when the item was not retrieved automatically, whereas evaluation strategies were used to check on the appropriateness of the retrieved item. Table 6.3 sets out a sample of the strategies identified in the research.

The researchers suggest that the strategies can be ranged on a continuum from top-down processing strategies (for example, recall of past situation) to bottom-up processing strategies (for example, structural analysis), although they admit that strategies cannot be unambiguously assigned a place on the continuum. In substantive terms, there did not seem to be differences in strategy preferences according to the target language being studied. Finally, the question of the construct validity of the C-test was left unanswered.

In a fascinating investigation of classroom interaction from the learner's perspective, Slimani (1992) used retrospection to obtain data on what learners felt they had learned from particular lessons (what she calls 'uptake'). At the end of every lesson she observed, learners were given a questionnaire, or 'Uptake Recall Chart', on which they were required to recall everything they had learned in terms of the following categories:

1. Grammar
2. Words and phrases
3. Spelling
4. Pronunciation
5. Punctuation
6. Ways of using the language
7. Suggestions about using the language
8. Other

Around three hours later, learners were given the uptake recall chart they had completed at the end of the lesson as well as a second questionnaire, called an 'Uptake Identification Probe'. This required the learners to differentiate between the items they believed they had really learned in that particular lesson and those they had encountered in a previous lesson. Once uptake items had been documented, the researcher went back to the lessons (which were audio-recorded) and located the points in the lesson where the events occurred. Learners were also interviewed by the researcher.

Methodologically, this study is of interest because of the care which Slimani took, through the use of two questionnaires and an interview, to obtain reliable and valid data. She makes the point that while the procedures raised subjects' consciousness of the learning process and their role within it, the data collection procedures may also have had an effect on the learners' behaviour. However, she discounts this possibility on the grounds that the data collection took place over a relatively short period of time (six weeks).

In substantive terms, Slimani provides a vivid portrait of the contrast between the 'syllabus as reality' in contrast with the 'syllabus as plan' (see also Nunan 1988). There were, in the classroom data, 256 items which were topicalised by the teacher, and therefore made available for the learners to learn. Of these, only 112 were claimed by at least one student to have been learned. Ninety-two items (almost 34%) went completely unnoticed. Slimani concludes:

[These figures] provide us with a picture of the 'syllabus as reality' as opposed to the 'syllabus as plan'. The former represents what actually happens in the midst of interactive work done by the participants. The on-going interaction leads to the creation of a whole range of learning opportunities, some of which are the results of the teacher's plan; others arise as a by-product of the plan, but some others arise independently of any intentions, perhaps as a by-product of classroom interaction. (Slimani 1992: 209)

128

In this section, we have looked at techniques employing retrospection. I pointed out that as the length of time between the task and the retrospection increases, so also do threats to the reliability of the research. Despite this, there are certain circumstances in which retrospection, rather than introspection, is to be preferred. In investigating such things as teachers' on-line decision-making and learners' test-taking behaviour, it is simply not possible for the subjects to act and reflect/report simultaneously.

A sample study using introspection

In this section, we shall look in detail at a study utilising some of the techniques discussed in the preceding sections. The study I have chosen is Haastrup's 1987 investigation of learners' lexical inferencing procedures, published in Faerch and Kasper's book on introspection in second language research.

QUESTION/HYPOTHESIS

What knowledge sources do learners at different proficiency levels make use of, and how do they use the different sources to infer the meaning of unknown words?

SIGNIFICANCE/VALUE OF THE STUDY

An investigation of the inferencing procedures employed by second language learners when confronted by an unknown lexical item is of interest for two reasons. In the first place, it should illuminate the ways learners form hypotheses. Secondly, it should facilitate the development of a model of L2 reception.

SUBJECTS

Subjects were 124 Danish high school students who were learning English as a foreign language. Half of the subjects were judged to have high proficiency in English, and half were judged to have low proficiency. Subjects were put into pairs so that there were 31 pairs of high proficiency learners and 31 pairs of low proficiency learners.

PROCEDURE

The dyads were given a simplified passage to read. The passage contained 25 unknown test words in a comprehensible context, as the following sample text shows:

At the beginning of the nineteenth century some of the Zulu clans were ruled by a king called Chaka. He was a clever military leader with *insatiable* political ambitions. He won most of south-eastern Africa and united all the Zulu clans into one great empire, the Zulu nation. Soon afterwards, however, the downfall of the Zulu empire started by *dissention* among the blacks themselves, and ended in conflicts with the whites. (p. 198)

The dyads were asked to read the texts and to guess the meaning of the unknown words (which were italicized), verbalising all their thoughts as they did so. The discussions are transcribed and analysed.

Half of the pairs also took part in a retrospection exercise. These pairs were monitored by two researchers as they completed the think-aloud task. They were then interviewed and asked to explain certain aspects of the think-aloud task, such as why they made lengthy pauses and what led them to suggest certain meanings.

TYPE OF DATA

The study yielded two types of protocols: the dyadic interactions and the retrospective statements. A sample think-aloud protocol from the study is reproduced below:

Test word in context: In the rich world many diseases are caused by *affluence*.
Think-aloud protocol:

A. affluence – do you think it is the opposite of influence? (A + B laugh) – non-influence.
B: what does fluence mean?
A: I don't know – I know what influence means – fluence (A laughs)
B: isn't the idea that in the rich world you don't catch diseases – they are not infectious – it's more mental problems, perhaps – mental influence more than in the poor world when it's simply infection – don't you think?
A: well, yes
B: shall we say external influence – that fits with influence too
A: yes that's okay

(Haastrup 1987: 198)

TYPE OF ANALYSIS

The protocols were analysed qualitatively, and a taxonomy of cue types was established. The researcher identified three main types of cue:

interlingual: cues based on L1 (loan words in L1 or knowledge of foreign languages) other than English
intralingual: cues based on knowledge of English
contextual: cues based on the text or on the informants' knowledge of the world

Table 6.4 illustrates the ways in which the protocols were analysed.

TABLE 6.4 ANALYSIS OF THINK-ALOUD AND RETROSPECTION PROTOCOLS

Test word in context: Doctors should analyse why people become ill rather than take such a keen interest in the *curative* effect of medicine.

Excerpts from protocol		Analysis	
Thinking aloud	*Retrospection*	*Cues*	*Hypotheses*
A: this is easy I think – it must be something with the therapeutic effect	A: very easy – one knows cure and then it fits the context	intralingual, lexis + semantics	⎫
B: yes			⎪
A: of the medicine			⎬ "therapeutic"
B: yes it has to do with *kurere*[a]	B: a bit of guessing – something to do with *kurere* – if one were to use something that resembles it	contextual, the immediate context of the test word — interlingual, L1, lexis + semantics	⎭

[a] *Kurere* in Danish means "cure" (verb in the infinitive).
Source: Reprinted with permission from Haastrup (1987: 201).

CONCLUSIONS

In substantive terms, the researcher found that there were three main sources of information drawn on by the subjects. There were cues based on the first language, cues based on current knowledge of the target language, and cues based on knowledge of the world. The differences between the high proficiency and low proficiency groups were slight.

Methodologically, Haastrup found problems with both of the data collection techniques used. Overall, retrospection was less useful than thinking aloud, adding little to the data yielded by the think-aloud technique. Nevertheless, the two techniques in combination proved superior to either in isolation.

The main problems with the method of thinking aloud are (1) the varied quantity and varied informative value of the data, which makes identification of procedures difficult, and in the most unfortunate cases leaves the analyst to infer on the basis of the products only (the written result of the inferencing task) and (2) the difficulty in controlling sociopsychological variables for peer thinking aloud. For retrospection, the problems are that the data are only partly informant initiated, and that it is difficult for the researcher to strike a balance between the too-loose and too-controlled interview. To some extent these shortcomings are overcome when the two methods are combined. Such a procedure provides distinct advantages. Firstly, the two sessions provide a larger quantity of data than either in isolation. Secondly, the quality of the data are improved in two ways: (1) by using informant-initiated data as the starting point and enriching them by eliciting additional information, and (2) by using pair work that invites the verbalisation of thought, supplemented by deeper probing into the individual's thought processes. By using the methods as complements, one has the best of both worlds, although for this particular study retrospection did not add a great deal of information (Haastrup 1987: 211).

Conclusion

Introspective methods have grown in popularity in recent years, as researchers have experimented with different ways of finding out how learners go about learning and using language, and also as the questions researchers ask become more sophisticated and complex. In the next few years the popularity of such methods should continue to grow. Diaries, logs, and journals in particular have a great deal to offer research in foreign language learning. These can be kept either by teachers or learners or both, and may be used as the main data collection tool, or as a supplement to other tools.

Questions and tasks

1. Get three or four individuals to complete the NPEHPA anagram task, thinking aloud as they do so. Record, transcribe, and analyse the protocols. To what extent do the transcripts bear out the observations made by Ericsson and Simon? Are any other strategies apparent in the data?
2. List the advantages and disadvantages of the different methods discussed in the chapter. Can you suggest a question which might be investigated by one or more methods?
3. The journal extracts which follow have been taken from Schmidt and Frota (1985). Read through them and then complete the tasks which follow.

Journal entry, Week 3
The first department meeting was today. . . . It started off well, and I actually got the gist of the first topic . . . about university personnel policies and changes in the requirements for appointment and promotion to various ranks (*níveis*, my word for the day). No doubt I understood that much because it's all too familiar in my own work, and the chairperson had a clear diagram on the blackboard. However, after

that topic was closed, I did not understand another word for the remainder of the meeting, which dragged on to 9 p.m. I am totally exhausted. The only observation I can report is that turn-taking rules for meetings in Brazil are different from those in the U.S. There was a great deal of overlap among participants, and the general atmosphere was a lot rowdier than what I'm used to. (pp. 242–243)

Journal entry, Week 3
Just came back from [a sidewalk café], where I finally had something close to a conversation with someone . . . another nonnative speaker . . . a linguist, half Chinese, half Spanish, who works on comparative Romance phonology somewhere in France. . . . I was amazed that I could understand a fair bit of what he said. He spoke slowly and with difficulty and it didn't sound like Portuguese, but words only. No Portuguese sentences I am sure . . . Now I must break out of the trap I'm in. I want to be fluent in Portuguese by the time I leave here, and I want to get started. Krashen is absolutely right that native speakers are generally unable or unwilling to provide comprehensible input to beginning nonnative speakers. I wouldn't waste my time talking to someone who knew as little English as I know Portuguese. I know some people prefer to wait and get settled before tackling a language, but in my case this silent period has been maddening and against my will. I can't wait for class to start on Monday. (p. 243)

Journal entry, Week 6
L and I are still giving each other a hard time. Today in class, K's sentence in a substitution drill had a negative before the verb, followed by *nada*. I wanted to find out whether other double negatives are possible, so when it was my turn I said *en não conhecia niguém* ['I didn't know anyone']. This was not the sentence I was supposed to produce. I don't remember whether L corrected me to *alguém* or not. I only remember her annoyance that I was not performing the drill as I was supposed to, so I didn't find out what I was after. But in general, the class is OK now, even though much too structured. We start out every day with "what did you do yesterday?" and always end with "what are you going to do today after class?" In between, we have the structure of the day, each beginning with explanations and a few examples and far too many drills. I don't mind the drills as much as at first, but I will not say sentences which I don't understand, so I ask a lot of questions. This has not endeared me to L, but I think we are now getting to the point of grudging mutual respect. (p. 244)

Journal entry, Week 7
S and I made the first recording today for our project. I felt very strange at first, because this was absolutely the first time we have ever talked to each other in Portuguese . . . This is somewhat different from my difficulty in using Portuguese with native speakers of English. In that case, it's just so much easier to say it in English that it's hard to avoid switching. But with native speakers of Portuguese who are English teachers . . . I am ashamed to show my ignorance of their language when they speak mine so well. With monolinguals, it's different: we are equally ignorant of each other's language and I feel no embarrassment at all. So S and I talked in English right up to the moment she turned the tape-recorder on. Then it was fine. It was good to find that I wasn't as embarrassed as I expected to be, in fact quite comfortable. (pp. 244–245)

133

Journal entry, Week 7
Last night we [the members of the Portuguese class] and L's other class went to a
Japanese restaurant in Copacabana . . . an official exercise in communication
outside of the class . . . The event went well . . . I was proud of myself because I
managed to produce a couple of instances of *tão* + adj. and *mais do que*
constructions [comparatives], which is what we practiced in class yesterday
morning. K noticed it, and said she was impressed because she never remembers to
use in conversation what we learn in class. I think it's easier for me because I've
been making it a habit, and . . . simply because I have fewer resources [than K] to
draw on. Whatever I can get, I need. (p. 245)

Journal entry, Week 12
Portuguese 3 met for the first time this morning. From my point of view, it's a
disaster. The first sign that things were not going to be perfect was when I arrived
and found 17–18 people outside a classroom that only holds 10. K was there and
told me . . . Portuguese 4 had been cancelled and everyone is being put into one
class. . . . For the group as a whole, the average length of residence in Brazil seemed
to be about 4 years . . . I do not belong in this group. The class started off with a
discussion of the imperfeito vs. perfeito . . . Then Y said we would do a
communicative exercise. She got us into groups of three and passed out pictures.
The exercise was for each of us to make up three sentences about our picture, using
the present subjunctive. I have no idea how you make the present subjunctive or
any other subjunctive . . . What really bothered me most was that Y speaks so
rapidly that I didn't understand much of what she said at all. She apologized for it,
said that everyone tells her she speaks much faster than most native speakers, but
she can't control it. I don't know what to do about this situation. I have the option
of going back to Portuguese 2, but I might be bored there . . . I'm tempted to drop
completely . . . I'm doing pretty well outside of class, meeting people constantly,
speaking Portuguese 2–3 hours every day and I think learning something from
almost every interaction . . . I have until Monday to change my mind, because
that's when I have to pay my tuition. (p. 246)

From your reading of the extracts, what would you say are the social and
interactional variables which may foster or inhibit language acquisition? Summarise your thoughts by completing the following table.

	In the classroom	*In naturalistic environments*
Facilitates		
Inhibits		

a. Formulate a research question or hypothesis relating to the effect of social
and interactional variables on second language acquisition.
b. Do you find the data from the journal entries convincing, or are they too
anecdotal to be of any real value?
c. Study the following statement from one of the researchers.

Research in second language acquisition (SLA) has to date typically concentrated on the acquisition of systems central to linguistic analysis, especially morphology and syntax. Indeed, SLA has virtually been defined (implicitly, in most cases) as the acquisition of linguistic forms, structures and rules. Only recently has there been widespread recognition among SLA researchers that it is important to study the acquisition of other components of language ability as well, especially those interactional and social aspects of language ability that are frequently referred to under the rubric of 'communicative competence'. (Schmidt 1983: 137)

Based on the journal extracts, how do you think the authors would define *communicative competence?* What are the different components making up the construct?

4. Find a study in the literature which utilises one or more of the techniques discussed in this chapter. Summarise and critique the study by supplying the following information:

a. Question/hypothesis
b. Significance/value of the study
c. Subjects
d. Procedure
e. Type of data
f. Type of analysis
g. Conclusions
h. Further research
i. Critique

5. With reference to your own professional context, design a study utilising one of the introspective methods outlined in the chapter.

Further reading

Without doubt, the most important collection of papers on introspection in language research is Faerch and Kasper's *Introspection in Second Language Research*. It contains a mixture of position papers on the use of introspection in both cognitive psychology and applied linguistics, as well as research reports. A particularly useful paper in the collection is Grotjahn's, which locates introspection within a conceptual research framework.

For a practical introduction to techniques for collecting data through diaries, see Bailey (1990).

7 Elicitation techniques

Before I came here I was knowing all the English language tense(s) . . . present tense
. . . past tense . . . present perfect tense . . . perfect tense . . . future tense . . . future
in the past . . . everything . . . I was knowing . . . I am knowing now . . . I just
asked, er, one day the boss, I said to him "How you knowing this tense?" for
example 'go' . . . How can you use this word? . . . past tense? present tense? the
other tense? He just looked me like that . . . he told me "I don't know Genghis."
This is Australian people. I am Turkish people. I am knowing, he doesn't know.
Can you explain this?

(Genghis, cited in Johnston 1987)

Studies utilising elicitation are extremely common in the applied linguistics
literature. In fact, in a recent survey I found that it was the most frequently
employed data collection method, being used in half of the studies analysed
(Nunan 1991b). Elicitation techniques have been a feature of second language
acquisition research since the original morpheme order studies of the 1970s,
which collected their data through the use of the Bilingual Syntax Measure
(this device is explained in the next section). Elicitation techniques vary enormously in scope, aim, and purpose. They include studies which obtain their
data by means of a stimulus, such as a picture, diagram, or standardised test,
as well as those based on questionnaire, survey, and interview data.

In this chapter, we shall only be able to take a selective look at some of the
more commonly used instruments. If you are interested in exploring any of
the techniques reviewed here in greater detail, you will find numerous references in the body of the chapter. This chapter addresses the following
questions:

- What is elicitation and how has it been used?
- How is elicitation used to obtain production data from learners?
- What are the strengths and weaknesses of surveys, questionnaires, and
  interviews, and how can they be used in applied linguistic research?
- How can we quantify qualitative data from surveys, questionnaires, and
  interviews?

Production tasks

In investigating language learning and use, one can attempt to obtain naturalistic samples from learners as they interact in the target language. The

problem with such a procedure is that it can be extremely time-consuming and difficult. In addition, it may not result in the outcomes one desires. The learners may simply not use the language items which the researchers are interested in. Focused investigations (that is, investigations in which the researchers have an idea of the linguistic features they are looking for) attempt to overcome these problems by employing elicitation to obtain samples of learner language for linguistic analysis. For example, second language acquisition studies of the type carried out by Dulay and Burt (1973, 1974) and Bailey, Madden, and Krashen (1974) were designed to provide the researchers with evidence on the appearance of certain grammatical morphemes. The aim of the research was to determine the order in which these particular morphemes appeared, and the effect of such variables as instruction and first language background on the order of acquisition.

The elicitation device used by these researchers was known as the Bilingual Syntax Measure. This consisted of a series of cartoonlike drawings. Subjects were shown the drawings and asked a series of questions which were designed to elicit the target language items under investigation. More recently, a similar technique has been used to obtain elicitation data from immigrants. The Interview Test of English as a Second Language (ITESL) is designed to obtain information from immigrants in Australia for diagnosis, placement, and remediation (Griffin 1986). The test consists of twenty items designed to elicit twenty target grammatical items. Each item contains a stimulus picture, cue questions, instructions for the test administrator, and a set of scoring criteria. The following sample illustrates the test items.

Item 6: Test probe for personal pronouns

Stimulus pictures: Picture 1: Illustration of man working in garden
Picture 2: Illustration of woman working in garden
Picture 3: Illustration of man and woman working in garden

Instructions to tester:

DO	SAY
Point to picture of man working and say: (emphasise "he's")	*Look at him.* *He's working.*
Point to picture of woman working and say:	*And her?*
Point to picture of man and woman working: Indicate both people and say:	*And them?*

Scoring criteria:
0   neither she nor they is used as required
1   one of she or they is used
2   both she or they are used as required

All responses may include hesitation, uneven fluency, and self-correction. Pronunciation can be poor but the required pronoun must be clearly understood. The pronoun may occur with or without the verb 'to be'. That is *she's, she is,* and

TABLE 7.1 HYPOTHESISED ORDER OF
ACQUISITION ACCORDING TO THE
INTERVIEW TEST OF ENGLISH FOR
MIGRANTS

Grammatical item	Rank
nouns	1
verbs	2
adjectives	3
verb *be*	4
possessive pronouns	5
personal pronouns	6
adverbs of time	7
requests	8
simple present	9
futures	10
wh- questions	11
present continuous	12
directions	13
possessive adjectives	14
comparatives	15
offers	16
simple future	17
simple past	18
infinitives/gerunds	19
1st conditional	20

she are all considered acceptable. Similarly *they're*, *they are*, and *they* are all
considered acceptable.

(adapted from Griffin 1986)

The authors of this test claim that in the course of developing it, they discovered a developmental order of grammatical acquisition. The test was administered to a large sample of subjects whose scores were analysed according to
a relatively new statistical model, the partial credit model. The order identified by the study is set out in Table 7.1. This order is at variance with that
established by other studies and is, I believe, an artifact of the elicitation
instrument, a point I shall address in greater detail shortly.

Research such as this based on elicitation techniques differs from naturalistic observation in a number of important respects, most particularly in that
the researcher determines in advance what is to be investigated. Researchers
need to be aware of two possible threats to the validity of such investigations.
The first is that by determining in advance what is going to be considered
relevant, other potentially important phenomena might be overlooked. The
other danger, and one which needs to be considered when evaluating research

utilising such devices, is the extent to which the results obtained are an artifact of the elicitation devices employed (see, e.g., Nunan 1987 for a discussion on the dangers of deriving implications for second language acquisition from standardised test data). One needs to be particularly cautious in making claims about acquisition orders based on elicited data, as Ellis (1985) has pointed out. In the case of the ITESL data, which are at variance with other SLA studies, it seems clear that the so-called order of acquisition is the creation of the elicitation device and the statistical procedures used to analyse the data.

There is evidence that the so-called developmental order of acquisition uncovered by the ITESL is an artifact of the test itself. Consider the following response of a subject to Item 6.

Tester: Look at him, he's working. He's working.
Subject: Yeah, working in the . . . er . . . park or . . . or . . . government park.
Tester: And her?
Subject: And same change flower or put fresh one. (Hmm) Or watering, I think so.
Tester: Yeah. And them?
Subject: And them working together.

(Author's data)

According to the scoring criteria, this subject gets a score of 0 and is deemed not to have acquired 'personal pronouns'. However, in response to a question later in the test, she does use personal pronouns appropriately. Similarly, in the above response, there is evidence that the subject is capable of using the present continuous tense. However, when it comes to the probe designed to test for evidence of the present continuous, she fails to use the required form, as is evidenced by her response:

Subject's response:
Tester: What are these people doing? What are they doing?
Subject: Have music, coffee, radio. Listen music and have toast and cup of tea. Er, have a sleep. Girlfriends . . . er . . . is the girl drink coffee. And, er, excuse me this is here? Telephone? Oh, worry, looks like worry. Some fight together.

(Author's data)

Scoring criteria:
0   no continuous form used or understandable
1   a number of continuous forms are used but production of the list contains painful hesitation and self-correction; little or no fluency in production of list
2   a clear list of verbs in the continuous form

The dangers of making claims about acquisition based on a single production task is underlined by Eisenstein, Bailey, and Madden (1982), who carried out a study into the acquisition of verb tenses. They used two different tasks to elicit data from their subjects. The first of these was a production task similar to the Bilingual Syntax Measure, and the second was an imitation task – the researcher read aloud sentences containing the target items, and the subjects were required to imitate these. Eisenstein et al. concluded that the second task provided more accurate information on the subjects' current state of morphosyntactic development. The major problem, as they saw it, with the production task, was in interpreting the data that resulted from the task.

It is evident that serious questions must be raised about data from production tasks. When a particular structure does not appear, several alternatives are possible: The structure may simply not be present in the grammar of the learner, or the learner may have some knowledge of the structure but lack the confidence to use it and may be exhibiting an avoidance strategy. A third possibility is that the learner knows the structure but has not used it as a matter of chance. When a structure is used correctly in a form that has high frequency in the language, it could be part of an unanalyzed chunk which does not reflect the learner's creative use of grammar. (p. 388)

Perhaps the best way of guarding against threats to the reliability and validity of studies employing production tasks is to do as Eisenstein et al. did and obtain one's data from more than one source. While this increases the practical problems of carrying out the research, it greatly enhances the internal validity of the study and enables the researchers to be more confident in the claims they make.

Surveys

Surveys are widely used for collecting data in most areas of social inquiry, from politics to sociology, from education to linguistics. Surveys of community attitudes, opinions, and practices on many subjects, from current voting intentions to eating habits, appear in the popular press with monotonous regularity. According to Cohen and Manion (1985), surveys are the most commonly used descriptive method in educational research, and may vary in scope from large-scale governmental investigations through to small-scale studies carried out by a single researcher. The purpose of a survey is generally to obtain a snapshot of conditions, attitudes, and/or events at a single point in time.

Survey research is distinguished from experimental studies in a number of important respects. The most significant difference concerns the role of the researcher. As we saw in Chapter 2, the experimental researcher manipulates the environment in order to examine the interaction among variables. In survey research, on the other hand,

the researcher doesn't "do" anything to the objects or subjects of research, except observe them or ask them to provide data. The research consists of collecting data

Step 1: Define objectives → What do we want to find out?

Step 2: Identify target population → Who do we want to know about?

Step 3: Literature review → What have others said/discovered about the issue?

Step 4: Determine sample → How many subjects should we survey, and how will we identify these?

Step 5: Identify survey instruments → How will the data be collected: questionnaire/interview?

Step 6: Design survey procedures → How will the data collection actually be carried out?

Step 7: Identify analytical procedures → How will the data be assembled and analysed?

Step 8: Determine reporting procedure → How will results be written up and presented?

Figure 7.1   Steps in carrying out a survey

on things or people as they are, without trying to alter anything. A survey researcher might want to know about teachers' honest attitudes toward their school principals, unaltered by the act of asking. The more intrusive a survey, the lower the chances that it will accurately reflect real conditions. (Jaeger 1988: 307)

In carrying out a survey, one works through a series of steps similar to those for other types of research. These are set out in Figure 7.1.

One of the most important questions a survey researcher must confront is: What is the population covered by the survey? Political surveys, particularly those preceding an election, generally purport to cover the entire population of eligible voters. Of course it would not be practicable to obtain data from the entire population (in fact, this is exactly what the election itself purports to do), and a major task for the researcher is to select a representative sample from the population as a whole. Perhaps the most comprehensive type of survey is the national census, which aims to obtain data on every individual in the nation. In more modest investigations it may in fact be possible to survey the entire population. For example, a researcher who has been commissioned to evaluate the introduction of a computer-assisted language program in a single school district may be able to survey all of the language teachers who have used the new program.

In those instances in which it is not feasible to collect data from the entire population, the researcher must resort to sampling. The concern here is to ensure that the sample is representative of the population as a whole. Numerous sampling strategies are open to the survey researcher, as Table 7.2 shows. (These strategies have been adapted from Cohen and Manion 1985.) The first four strategies yield probability samples. Using these procedures, we can

TABLE 7.2 STRATEGIES FOR SURVEY SAMPLING

Strategy	Procedure
1. Simple random	Select subjects at random from a list of the population.
2. Systematic	Select subjects in a systematic rather than random fashion (e.g., select every twentieth person).
3. Stratified	Subdivide population into subgroups (e.g., male/female) and randomly sample from subgroups.
4. Cluster	Restrict one's selection to a particular subgroup from within the population (e.g., randomly selecting schools from within a particular school district rather than the entire state or country).
5. Convenience	Choose nearest individuals and continue the process until the requisite number has been obtained.
6. Purposive	Subjects are handpicked by the researcher on the basis of his/her own estimate of their typicality.

Source: Adapted from Cohen and Manion (1985).

determine the probability of selection of each respondent. Procedures 5 and 6, on the other hand, will result in non-probability samples, in which the probability of selection is unknown. Small-scale studies may decide to use non-probability samples because they are easier to establish and, in consequence, cheaper. They may also be perfectly satisfactory for a preliminary or pilot study whose aim is to trial survey instruments and procedures, not to obtain data which can be generalised from sample to population.

The question of how big a sample should be is taken up by Fowler (1988). He dismisses the common misconception that the adequacy of a sample depends on the fraction of the population included in that sample, arguing that 'a sample of 150 people will describe a population of 15,000 or 15 million with virtually the same degree of accuracy, assuming all other aspects of the sample design and sampling procedures were the same' (Fowler 1988: 41). A key consideration in determining sample size concerns the subgroups within a population that may need to be separately identified – for example, whether to separate men from women, or whether to separate the responses from members of different ethnic groups.

Survey data are collected through questionnaires or interviews, or a combination of questionnaire and interview. The construction of questionnaires and interview schedules that yield valid and reliable data is much more complex than might at first be thought. In the next section, we shall look in some detail at questionnaire construction and at the analysis of questionnaire data. Then we shall turn our attention to interviews.

Questionnaires

I have found that among graduate students, the questionnaire is a relatively popular means of collecting data. It enables the researcher to collect data in field settings, and the data themselves are more amenable to quantification than discursive data such as free-form fieldnotes, participant observers' journals, the transcripts of oral language. However, as I indicated at the conclusion of the preceding section, the construction of valid and reliable questionnaires is a highly specialised business. In this section I shall set out some of the pitfalls to be aware of in questionnaire construction.

Types of questions

Questionnaire items can be relatively closed or open ended. A closed item is one in which the range of possible responses is determined by the researcher, for example: 'Foreign languages should be compulsory in high school. Agree/ neutral/disagree'. An open item is one in which the subject can decide what to say and how to say it, for example: 'What do you think about the proposal that foreign languages should be compulsory in high school?' Questionnaires can consist entirely of closed questions, entirely of open questions, or a mixture of closed and open questions. While responses to closed questions are easier to collate and analyse, one often obtains more useful information from open questions. It is also likely that responses to open questions will more accurately reflect what the respondent wants to say.

Youngman (1986), cited in Bell (1987), has subcategorised closed questions. His categories, along with examples, are set out in Table 7.3.

Question wording

When constructing a questionnaire, one needs to pay careful attention to the wording of the questions. As we have already seen, a danger with any type of elicitation device is that the responses one gets will be artifacts of the elicitation devices themselves. It is particularly important that the researchers not reveal their own attitudes through leading questions such as the following: 'Do you think that the concept of learner-centredness is utopian and unrealistic?' Questions should not be complex and confusing, nor should they ask more than one thing at a time. The following example from Cohen and Manion (1985: 105–107) is likely to be confusing to respondents:

Would you prefer a short, non-award course (3, 4 or 5 sessions) with part-day release (e.g. Wednesday afternoons) and one evening per week attendance with financial reimbursement for travel or a longer, non-award course (6, 7, or 8 sessions)

TABLE 7.3   CLOSED QUESTION TYPES IN SURVEY QUESTIONNAIRES

Question type	*Example*
List	Indicate your qualifications by circling any of the following: diploma, B.A., M.A., Ph.D.
Category	Indicate your salary range by circling one of the following: less than 20,000 20,000–40,000 40,000–60,000 more than 60,000
Ranking	Rank the following from 1 to 4 in order of preference. 'I like to learn best by studying': – with the whole class – in small groups – in pairs – independently
Scale	Circle one of the following to indicate your attitude to the following statement: 'I like to learn through interacting with native speakers'. strongly agree, agree, neutral, disagree, strongly disagree
Quantity/ frequency	Circle one of the following: How often did you practise English outside class last week? 0, 1, 2, 3, 4, 5, 6, 7, 8, 9, 10, more than 10
Grid	How many NESB students are there in the following classes?

	0–5	5–10	10–15	15+
Year 1				
Year 2				
Year 3				
Year 4				

Source: After Youngman (1986), cited in Bell (1987).

with full-day release, or the whole course designed on part-time release without evening attendance?

(For a discussion of this issue see Briggs 1986; Brislin, Lonner, and Thorndike 1973.)

In language education, another danger to avoid is culturally biased questions. Numerous authors, including Briggs (1986), Brindley (1990), and Brislin et al. (1973) have pointed out that there is considerable cross-cultural variation concerning the type of information which can be sought by a stranger. Major differences may exist between the culture of the interviewer and that of the respondent, and these differences may affect the responses given (for examples of problems caused by the interviewer's behaviour and language, see 'Questions and Tasks' at the end of this chapter, task 3). Factors such as the following should be taken into consideration:

- the willingness of respondents to make critical statements
- the willingness of respondents to discuss certain personal topics, such as age, salary, or opinions on political and social issues
- the shared values which can be assumed, for example, the concept of freedom of the press
- the shared attitudes which can be assumed, for example, the commonly held belief among many educators in Western countries that classroom learning should be a source of enjoyment for the learner.

Interpreting responses

I have found questionnaires to be an attractive means of collecting data by graduate students. Unfortunately, the construction of a reliable questionnaire which will tell you what you want to know is difficult and extremely time-consuming. When constructing questionnaire items, it is important, first of all, to be very clear about the objectives of the study, and each item should be directly referenced against one or more of the research objectives. You should also determine in advance how the data to be gathered will be analysed. A trap for the inexperienced researcher is to collect the data and then realise that the question was asked in a way which cannot be analysed to answer the question. Because of these and other pitfalls, it is imperative to pilot any questionnaire which is developed. (In fact, I would argue strongly that all research should have a piloting phase.)

Having constructed, piloted, and administered a questionnaire, one is faced with the tasks of collating and interpreting the responses. As I have already indicated, one of the great advantages of closed questions is that they yield responses which can readily be quantified and analysed, particularly if one has access to computer statistics packages. Free-form responses from open questions, although they may result in more useful/insightful data, are much more difficult to quantify, although there are ways of quantifying this qualitative data.

As an example of the problems of reducing free-form data to manageable proportions, consider the following selected extracts from a study I was involved in which, among other things, investigated teacher beliefs about the nature of language and learning. The question was: 'State three beliefs you have about language development that determine the way you teach'. There were 372 responses. The following samples indicate the type and range of responses.

'Children learn by using the language'.
'All children benefit from immersion of the written print'.

145

'Language is developed through all curriculum areas'.

'Children should be allowed to learn any new concepts in their native language if possible'.

'Children learn best when there is a positive encouraging environment'.

The immediate task was to synthesise fifteen pages of statements in such a way as to reveal possible patterns, yet without distorting or misrepresenting the data. Of course, as soon as one places free-form statements into one category or another one runs the risk of distorting the data. The procedure I adopted was to conduct a key word analysis, generating categories from the statements made by respondents. This resulted in categories such as 'Immersion' and 'Learning by doing/experiential'. Examples of categories and the statements which generated them are as follows:

IMMERSION

'Children need to be immersed in all types of writing/reading literature'.

'All children benefit from immersion of the written print'.

LEARNING BY DOING/EXPERIENTIAL

'Children's language develops through experiences so in order for the children to gain the most out of any given lesson many experiences should be given'.

'Children learn by using the language'.

LANGUAGE ACROSS THE CURRICULUM

'It occurs across the curriculum and therefore should not be seen as a separate subject area'.

'Language is developed through all curriculum areas'.

GRAMMAR, STRUCTURE, CORRECTNESS

'A child needs to be aware of basic grammatical structures'.

'I believe grammar, spelling and reading are the basis for language development'.

ORAL/WRITTEN LANGUAGE RELATIONSHIPS

'Spoken language should be mastered (ESL) before written'.

'There is a strong relationship between oral language development and expression and the ability to express oneself in writing'.

CREATION OF RICH, POSITIVE ENVIRONMENT

'Children need to be an active part of a rich language environment'.

'Children learn best when there is a positive encouraging environment'.

TABLE 7.4 TEACHERS' BELIEFS ABOUT THE NATURE OF LANGUAGE
AND LEARNING

Category	Number
Reference to language/learning	
Modelling	43
Immersion	28
Learning by doing/experiential	25
Language across the curriculum	22
Grammar, structures, correctness	20
Oral/written language relationships	14
Importance of literature	13
Process approach	9
Valuing/importance of L1	8
Direct instruction	8
Input	5
L1/L2 similarity/contrast	3
Integration of four skills	2
Imitation	2
Subtotal	202
Reference to environment/climate	
Creation of rich, positive environment	50
Wide variety, many opportunities, frequent practice	21
Meaningful experiences/context	16
Social, collaborative, interactive learning	15
Subtotal	102
Reference to the learner	
Individual differences	22
Relevance, purposeful	13
Individual differences, readiness, stages of development	11
Confidence, motivation, experimentation, risk-taking	9
Home, parental influence	8
Active involvement, child centred	5
Subtotal	68
Total	372

Categories were then grouped together according to whether they referred to
language/learning, the learner, or the climate/environment of learning. This
enabled the fifteen pages of data to be represented in a table, which is reproduced as Table 7.4.

Quantifying qualitative data

The example in the preceding section shows one way in which qualitative
data can be condensed and quantified. In fact, it is possible to carry out sta-

tistical analyses on data such as these. For example, the researchers might want to know whether more experienced teachers, or teachers with higher degrees, gave types of responses which were different from less experienced or less qualified teachers. They could investigate this by sorting out responses according to the biographical variables of interest (in the following example I have used 'experience'), and drawing up 2 × 2 contingency tables such as:

	Experienced teachers (5+ years' experience)	Inexperienced teachers (1–5 years' experience)	Total
Reference to language/learning	126	76	202
Reference to environment/climate	35	67	102
Reference to the learner	19	49	68
Total	180	192	372

Using the procedure for calculating chi-square set out in Chapter 2, the researchers can determine whether these different responses are significant. The final, and most difficult, task is to interpret the results. If, in the foregoing example, it should transpire that the relatively more experienced teachers made significantly more references to principles of language and learning, one might be led to hypothesise that as teachers increase their mastery of technical aspects of instruction and knowledge of language, their teaching practices become less dependent on local environmental and affective factors. Such an observation would have implications for teacher education.

An alternative way of quantifying qualitative data is presented by Lincoln and Guba (1985). (See also the description of a 'grounded' approach to qualitative data analysis provided by Strauss 1988.) The first step is to place each individual entry onto library index cards.

1. Given the pile of cards that has resulted from the unitizing process, and that will be more or less haphazardly arranged, select the first card from the pile, read it, and note its contents. This first card represents the first entry in the yet-to-be-named category. Place it to one side.
2. Select the second card, read it, and note its contents. Make a determination on tacit or intuitive grounds whether this second card is a "look-alike" or "feel-alike" with Card 1, that is, whether its contents are "essentially" similar. If so, place the second card with the first and proceed to the third card; if not, the second card represents the first entry in the second yet-to-be-named category.
3. Continue on with successive cards. For each card decide whether it is a "look/feel-alike" of cards that have already been placed in some provisional category or whether it represents a new category. Proceed accordingly.
4. After some cards have been processed the analyst may feel that a new card neither fits any of the provisionally established categories nor seems to form a new category. Other cards may now also be recognised as possibly irrelevant to

the developing set. These cards should be placed into a miscellaneous pile; they should *not* be discarded at this point, but should be retained for later review.

(Lincoln and Guba 1985: 347–348)

At the beginning of the process, new categories emerge rapidly, but the rate of emergence declines as more and more cards are processed. Once all the cards have been assigned, the analyst must devise categories and labels for each of the groups. The internal reliability of the procedure will rest on the extent to which an independent analyst agrees on the categories and the assignment of individual cards to the different categories.

Interviews

The oral interview has been widely used as a research tool in applied linguistics. In addition to its use in survey research, it has been used by second language acquisition researchers seeking data on stages and processes of acquisition (Johnston 1985), and also by language testers, who use the oral interview as a means of assessing proficiency (Ingram 1984). The 'sociolinguistic interview' has also been used to investigate linguistic variation, conversational analysis (see the preceding chapter), pragmatics, and cross-cultural communication.

Interviews can be characterised in terms of their degree of formality, and most can be placed on a continuum ranging from unstructured through semi-structured to structured. An unstructured interview is guided by the responses of the interviewee rather than the agenda of the researcher. The researcher exercises little or no control, and the direction of the interview is relatively unpredictable. In a semi-structured interview, the interviewer has a general idea of where he or she wants the interview to go, and what should come out of it, but does not enter the interview with a list of predetermined questions. Topics and issues rather than questions determine the course of the interview. In the most formal type, the structured interview, the agenda is totally predetermined by the researcher, who works through a list of set questions in a predetermined order. The type of interview one chooses will be determined by the nature of the research and the degree of control the interviewer wishes to exert. Because of its flexibility, the semi-structured interview has found favour with many researchers, particularly those working within an interpretive research tradition. For Dowsett, the semi-structured interview

is quite extraordinary – the interactions are incredibly rich and the data indicate that you can produce extraordinary evidence about life that you don't get in structured interviews or questionnaire methodology – no matter how open ended and qualitative you think your questionnaires are attempting to be. It's not the only qualitative research technique that will produce rich information about social relationships but it does give you access to social relationships in a quite profound way. (Dowsett 1986: 53)

The advantages of the semi-structured interview are, in the first instance, that it gives the interviewee a degree of power and control over the course of the interview. Secondly, it gives the interviewer a great deal of flexibility. Finally, and most profoundly, this form of interview gives one privileged access to other people's lives. Dowsett illustrates this third point with a number of moving anecdotes.

I've had a number of interviews with people that have changed my life . . . : interviewing a mother of a girl from one of the schools in the Making the Difference study [the study Dowsett was currently researching], who announced, about 15 minutes into the interview, that she was dying of cancer and wasn't expected to live more than four or five months. She was perfectly healthy looking at the time. The husband knew but the kids didn't. The family relations, the whole education experience of the girl, the way she functioned in her life at that moment, was going to be changing quite dramatically in the next four months. As I watched that woman talk to me about how they were planning to negotiate the future and where it was going and what plans they had for the two girls in the family, I couldn't be anything but moved. (1986: 55)

On several occasions in this and other chapters, I have mentioned the bias inherent in most research methods. In the case of the oral interview, one source of bias is the asymmetrical relationship between the participants. In other words, the participants do not have the same rights, and even in an unstructured relationship, the interviewer has much more power than the interviewee. The inequitable relationship between the interviewer and interviewee will affect the content of the interview as well as the language which is used. In terms of content, biographical factors such as gender and ethnicity can affect the validity and reliability of the research. Briggs (1986) cites an interview he conducted with an elderly Spanish-speaking couple in New Mexico. The interview failed because the interviewees regarded the sessions not as interviews, but as 'pedagogical encounters between two elders and a young person with little knowledge of the community' (Briggs 1986: 103). It is therefore important for researchers using interviews to incorporate into their interpretation of the data the effect of biographical variables, belief systems, and so on.

In linguistic terms, the asymmetry will be reflected in the actual language used (van Lier 1989). This is something which will need to be taken into consideration by second language acquisition researchers who wish to draw conclusions about such things as acquisition orders based on the data. Several researchers (see, for example, Johnston 1985) have pointed out that interviewees rarely ask questions, a major problem when one considers that questions are important signposts to a learner's stage of morphosyntactic development. Various strategies have been tried for overcoming this problem, from role plays to the technique of passing the interviewee a note suggesting that they ask the interviewer questions. While such strategies may call into question the validity of the research, it is difficult to see how those data might be obtained in any other way.

Van Lier (1989) provides a number of alarming examples of interactions between interviewers and second language subjects in which the interviewees are treated in a highly questionable manner. In the following extract, for example, the interviewer concludes that the subject (a young child) has no target language skills.

I: What's your father's name?
S: [no response]
I: What does your father do?
   Where does he work? Where does your father work?
   Come on girl, talk! talk! Don't be afraid. Where does your father work?
S: [no response]
I: What does your mother do? Where is your mother? What does your mother do?
S: [no response]
I: What do you do at home? Do you help your mother? What do you do?
S: [no response]
I: ((into the microphone)) Doesn't talk.

(van Lier 1989: 503–504)

There are numerous practical suggestions in the literature for planning and conducting interviews, ranging from the sensible to the self-evident. The following procedures are recommended by Cohen and Manion (1985), Bell (1987), and Spradley (1979).

1. PREPARING THE INTERVIEW SCHEDULE

Once the research objectives have been established, the researcher has to translate these into interview questions. Cohen and Manion (1985: 305) recommend that the variables under investigation be written down by name in order to facilitate this process. At this stage, the question format and response mode need to be considered. These will, of course, vary according to the nature of the variables under investigation, the type of subjects, the resources available to the researcher, and so on. However, regardless of the issues, the researcher will still need to decide on the type of questions to be used (open-ended versus closed, direct or indirect, etc.) and in what form the responses are to be collected and analysed.

2. PILOTING

Because of the potential problems in the use of the interview that we have already identified, it is very important that interview questions are piloted with a small sample of subjects before being used. This gives the researcher the opportunity to find out if the questions are yielding the kind of data required and to eliminate any questions which may be ambiguous or confusing to the interviewee. (I would go further and say that it is important for all

151

elicitation instruments to be thoroughly piloted before being used for research.)

3. SELECTION OF SUBJECTS

Bell (1987) points out that efforts should be made to secure a representative sample, even in a small-scale study. This will involve selecting appropriate proportions of subgroups of the population, using whatever variables you have determined to be important. In the selection process, it may be necessary to negotiate access to subjects or data collection sites with individuals or institutions.

4. ELEMENTS OF THE INTERVIEW

The structure of the interview itself will depend on the extent to which the sequence of questions is fixed. However, it is possible to delineate a number of key elements which may be present. These are as follows (see Cohen and Manion 1985: 306 ff and Spradley 1979: 59–60):

Briefing and explanation. Before the interview begins, the researcher explains the nature of the research and the purpose of the interview to the interviewee and answers any questions that he or she may have. This includes telling the interviewee how the data are to be used. If the data are to be recorded and, in particular, if the data are to be made available to other people, the interviewee's permission must be sought.

Questioning. In the less structured ethnographic interview a range of question types may be used. In order to encourage the respondent to recount his or her experiences, opinions, and so on, the researcher may also use a variety of other strategies. These are outlined by Spradley (1979: 67).

Walker (1985) makes a number of practical suggestions about the actual conduct of the interview. He considers first of all the physical positioning of the interviewer and interviewee, suggesting that sitting side-by-side can often result in a more productive interview than sitting face-to-face (sitting side-by-side can convey the message that the interaction is meant to be cooperative rather than confrontational). The researcher must also decide how the interview is going to be recorded. While tape-recording is the obvious choice for someone collecting linguistic data, it is not the only option. The other option is for the interviewer to take notes and to use these to reconstruct the interview at a later date. Walker points out that tape-recording and note-taking are not simply alternative data collection techniques, but represent quite different ways of going about doing research. Some of the relative strengths and weaknesses of the two recording devices are set out in Table 7.5.

Applied linguistics researchers are generally interested in the language used by their subjects, even when they are investigating intercultural and attitu-

TABLE 7.5   STRENGTHS AND WEAKNESSES OF TAPE-RECORDING AND NOTE-TAKING

Instrument	*Strengths*	*Weaknesses*
Tape-recording	Preserves actual language Naturalistic Objective record Interviewer's contributions recorded Data can be reanalysed after the event	Possibility of data overload Time-consuming to transcribe Context not recorded Presence of machine offputting Core issues masked by irrelevancies
Note-taking	Central issues/facts recorded Context can be recorded Economical Off-record statements not recorded	Recorder bias Actual linguistic data not recorded Encoding may interfere with interview Status of data may be questioned

dinal phenomena rather than linguistic development. For this reason, they are more likely than other types of social science researchers to want to use tape recorders. The most sensible procedure would probably be to tape-record interviews, but supplement these with written notes. I have found in classroom research that taking copious notes in addition to recording the lessons under investigation greatly enhances the subsequent tasks of transcribing and interpreting the taped lessons. The same should also hold for interviews.

A sample study

In this section, we shall look in detail at a research project which used an elicitation device for obtaining its data. The study, by Cohen and Olshtain (1981), investigated the feasibility of using rating scales to assess sociocultural competence.

AREA FOR INVESTIGATION

The sociocultural competence of second language speakers.

RESEARCH QUESTIONS

Can a rating scale be developed for asessing sociocultural competence? Do non-native speakers misuse or omit semantic formulas in an apology in a way that natives would not? Can we also rate utterances as to their stylistic appropriateness in the given context?

RATIONALE

At the time this study was carried out, language researchers were beginning to broaden the focus of their attention from the development of grammatical competence to other areas of target language development, such as discourse and pragmatic competence. The focus of this study was the development of sociocultural competence, defined as 'the ability to use the appropriate socio-cultural rules of speaking (also referred to as "sociolinguistic" rules), i.e., the ability to react in a culturally acceptable way in that context and to choose stylistically appropriate forms for the context' (p. 113).

In order to investigate this aspect of language use, however, it is necessary to operationalise the construct through an instrument which enables it to be measured. It was this concern for a measure of sociocultural competence which motivated the study in the first place. Because there are so many speech acts constituting sociolinguistic competence, the researchers restricted themselves to just one of these – that of apology. They chose this particular speech act because they believed it to be 'emotionally charged', and therefore more likely to elicit a natural response than a more emotionally neutral speech act.

SUBJECTS

Subjects were 44 college students in Israel. Thirty-two of these were native speakers of Hebrew who were enrolled in an EFL program, and who were judged to be at an intermediate-high level of proficiency in English. The other 12 subjects were native speakers of English. The subjects were divided into three groups. The native speakers acted as informants for native speakers' apologies, 12 of the Hebrew speakers served as informants for apologies in comparable situations in Hebrew, and the remaining 20 Hebrew speakers served as subjects apologising in English.

RESEARCH METHOD

The researchers used a role play based on an elicitation instrument which was administered to all subjects. The instrument consisted of the following instructions, followed by eight role cards (the 12 Hebrew informants had cards which had been translated into Hebrew).

Instructions
You will be asked to read eight brief situations calling for an apology. In each case, the person whom you owe the apology will speak first. I will role play this person. Respond as much as possible as you would in an actual situation. Your response will be tape-recorded. Indicate when you've finished reading.

Sample situations
You're at a meeting and you say something that one of the participants interprets as a personal insult to him.

He: "I feel that your last remark was directed at me and I take offense."
You:

You completely forget a crucial meeting at the office with your boss. An hour later you call him to apologize. The problem is that this is the second time you've forgotten such a meeting. Your boss gets on the phone and asks you:
Boss: "What happened to you?"
You:

(Cohen and Olshtain 1981: 132)

TYPE OF DATA

Administration of the instrument resulted in protocols in both English and Hebrew.

TYPE OF ANALYSIS

In assessing non-native deviation from native patterns, the researchers used the following list of semantic formulas developed by Fraser (1979). While the examples given are in English, the formulas must, presumably, be relevant to Hebrew as well.

1. An expression of apology
    a. An expression of regret (e.g., 'I'm sorry')
    b. An offer of apology (e.g., 'I apologise')
    c. A request for forgiveness (e.g., 'Excuse me' or 'Forgive me')
    d. An expression of an excuse (not an overt apology but an excuse which serves as an apology)
2. An acknowledgment of responsibility
3. An offer of repair
4. A promise of forbearance (i.e., that won't happen again)

In analysing the data, the researchers were careful to differentiate between deviations from native speaking norms resulting from negative transfer from the native language and those resulting from lack of proficiency in the target language.

RESULTS

1. In certain situations, both the second language subjects and the Hebrew informants used semantic formulas considerably less often than native English speakers. For example, Hebrew speakers were less likely to express an apology than native English speakers in 'insulting someone in a meeting' and 'forgetting to take their son shopping'. This would indicate that the deviations are a result of negative transfer from the target language.

2. In some situations the deviation seemed to be a matter of lack of proficiency rather than negative transfer.

3. In some situations non-native English speakers responded more like native English speakers than like Hebrew speakers.

4. On the question of whether a rating scale could be developed for assessing sociocultural competence, the researchers felt that they had produced at best a crude measure of such competence.

CRITIQUE

This is a carefully thought out and well conducted investigation of an area of language development which has been generally neglected. As such, it represents an important addition to the applied linguistics literature. However, it is always possible to identify problems and shortcomings.

As with any study employing elicitation instruments, there is always the concern that the results have been determined, at least in part, by the instrument itself. In the case of the study we have looked at here, would the subjects have responded in these ways if the situations were genuine rather than elicited? (Problems associated with the use of elicited data are acknowledged and discussed in detail by the researchers.) The validity of role-play data has been extremely contentious among those scholars concerned with this kind of pragmatic research. However, the question remains as to how one would collect relevant data on this aspect of pragmatic interaction if the role play were not used.

In addition, the researchers' judgments were based on an examination of the percentage of responses assigned to each category. No tests were applied to determine whether or not the differences were statistically significant.

Conclusion

In this chapter, we have looked at a range of research instruments which have been drawn together under the rubric of 'elicitation': stimulus pictures and role plays, as well as surveys, questionnaires, and interviews. The breadth of the chapter reflects the fact that elicitation is probably the single most frequently used method in language research.

In terms of intervention and control, elicitation resides somewhere between the formal experiment and naturalistic observation. While most researchers are aware of threats to the validity of their research posed by the use of elicitation devices, in many instances, these devices are the only practical means whereby relevant data can be collected.

Questions and tasks

1. What are the possible advantages and disadvantages of the different data collection procedures set out in the chapter? What are the situations in which one might select one strategy rather than another? In terms of external validity, which method do you think would be most likely/least likely to give results which accurately reflect the population from which the sample is drawn?

2. You have been commissioned by your institution to conduct a survey of people who enrol in your courses. The institution is interested in finding out why people do the courses and if there is a typical student profile. Part of the survey will therefore involve an investigation of their attitudes and motivation. Identify some research questions or hypotheses that you might start with.

3. Study the following extracts from van Lier (1989). What 'procedural problems' can you identify? How do you think the interviewer's behaviour or language might have influenced the data collected?

a. (From an oral proficiency interview)
   Interviewer: Where is your mother? What does your mother do?
      Subject: She's dead.
   Interviewer: Ah – she's dead. Very good.

(van Lier 1989: 499)

b. (From an interview aimed at eliciting data on the subject's syntactic development)

Interviewer	*Subject*
1. In Colombia do the lobsters have claws?	2. Claws?
3. Claws. Do they have . . . the lobsters, do they have have claws (form my hands into claws)?	4. Octopus?
5. No. The lobsters. Do the lobsters have hands?	6. Huh?
7. I don't know how to say it. I know . . . I am a lobster. This is my . . . I am a lobster. This is my claw (hands formed like claws).	8. Hm. Hm.
9. Do lobsters in Colombia have claws? Like this, you know? They pinch people.	10. Lobster?
11. On Sunday do you catch many lobsters?	12. Eh, huh?
13. Yeah, do you get many?	14. Eh. Dictionary?
15. Oh, do you want to go get your dictionary?	16. No. No necessary.
17. How many, how many do you get? How many do you catch?	18. Catch?

157

Interviewer	*Subject*
19. On Sunday. Yeah. How many do you catch on Sunday?	20. Thirty or forty.
21. Thirty or forty?	22. Depend.
23. What do you do with them?	24. Huh?
25. The lobsters. What do you do with the lobsters?	26. You do?
27. Yes, where do they go?	28. In morning.

(Butterworth, cited in Hatch, Wagner Gough, and Peck 1985: 55)

c. (From a second language acquisition research project interview)

Observer	*Adolescent*
1. Do you know what a question is?	2. Question mark.
3. Yeah. What do we mean when we say questions?	4. Question?
5. What do we mean by question marks? What do we mean? What does question mark mean?	6. This a (points)
7. Yeah. But why do we put that mark there?	8. This.
9. Why do we put that mark there? See, we don't have it there. We just have a period there.	
10. Do you wrestle?	11. No.
12. No?	13. I like look.
14. You like to watch.	15. No me wrestle.
16. You don't like to do it yourself. You'd rather watch. Let's say "watch."	17. Hm?
18. Say "watch." Same thing. Look – watch, look – watch.	19. Watch
20. Watch. You like to watch. . . .	
21. What are you gonna do tonight?	22. Tonight? I don't know.
23. You don't know yet? Do you work at home, do the dishes or sweep the floor?	24. Water (garbled).
25. You water?	26. Flowers.
27. Flowers.	28. Mud.
29. Oh, you wash the mud down and all that. What else do you do at home?	30. Home?

(Hatch et al. 1985: 54)

Further reading

Briggs (1986) provides a wealth of practical information on what to do (and what not to do) when interviewing subjects.

For a general introduction to surveys, questionnaires, and interviews in education, a useful text is Cohen and Manion (1985).

8 Interaction analysis

'When I use a word', Humpty Dumpty said, in rather a scornful tone, 'it means just what I choose it to mean – neither more nor less'.
(Lewis Carroll, *Through the Looking Glass*)

In this chapter, we shall look at the analysis of interactions occurring in naturalistic environments, that is, in non-experimental, non-elicited environments. In doing so, we shall test Humpty Dumpty's assertion that speakers are free to make words mean whatever they want them to mean. I shall devote the first section of this chapter to studies of first language interaction, focusing in particular on some of the work which has been carried out in child–adult interaction. This work is of interest to second and foreign language researchers because it is frequently claimed that second language pedagogy should be guided by the conditions under which first languages are acquired. We shall also look at the procedures developed by interaction analysts for studying adult interaction in social and transactional encounters. The chapter addresses the following questions:

- What is interaction analysis?
- How can data from children acquiring their first language be analysed?
- What does the research literature have to say about the relationship between first and second language acquisition?
- What methods exist for the analysis of transactional and interpersonal interactions between adults?

Comparing discourse analysis, interaction analysis, and conversation analysis

Before proceeding with the main business of the chapter, I should like to address the distinction between discourse analysis, interaction analysis, and conversation analysis. In looking at the literature, it quickly becomes apparent that the distinction is by no means clear-cut, and in many instances, the distinction is one of emphasis rather than distinct categories. I have found it useful to distinguish between the different analytical methods in terms of four different factors: firstly, the means whereby the data have been collected; secondly, the mode of language which is admitted into the analysis; thirdly,

159

whether the researcher brings to the analysis a predetermined set of analytical categories; and finally, whether the focus of attention is essentially linguistic or non-linguistic.

In looking at the means whereby the data were collected, the salient question is whether the data were collected through some form of elicitation or whether the researcher has tried to obtain naturalistic samples for analysis. In general, in all forms of analysis, the preference is for naturally occurring language. However, while conversation analysts rigidly eschew the use of elicited or invented samples of language, both of these practices are acceptable to some discourse analysts. When considering studies based on natural samples of language, we need to keep Labov's observer's paradox in mind, and ask whether it is ever possible to obtain natural samples of language. In other words, is it ever possible, through observation, to collect the sort of language speakers use when they are not being observed? Interaction analysts do not use invented samples of language, and, like conversation analysts, generally favour the collection of naturally occurring, non-elicited language.

The second factor is the mode of language which is admitted into the analysis. Discourse analysis is carried out on both written and spoken language (although individual analysts generally favour one form rather than another). Conversation and interaction analysis, on the other hand, are both concerned exclusively with spoken language.

The third question concerns whether or not the analyst brings to the analytical task a predetermined set of categories. Once again, discourse analysis is distinguished from conversation and interaction analysis in the use of predetermined analytical categories. Conversation and interaction analysts favour a discursive, interpretive type of analysis.

The final distinction I should like to draw here concerns the substantive focus of analysis. Discourse analysis has developed within linguistics, and it is therefore hardly surprising that the analysis is generally carried out in linguistic terms. In the same way as sentence grammarians are concerned with what makes a well-formed sentence or utterance, the discourse analyst investigates what it is that makes for well-formed discourse. Discourse analysts have studied textual factors such as the use of reference and conjunction, which contribute to cohesive discourse, as well as the ways in which speech acts such as 'inviting', 'apologising' and 'denying' are performed and interpreted within coherent discourse (see, for example, Brown and Yule 1983). Conversation analysis, on the other hand, has emerged from a school of sociology known as ethnomethodology, and the rules and procedures employed are sociological rather than linguistic in character. Substantively, this form of analysis investigates such things as the management of turn-taking, repair strategies, the resolution of ambiguity, speaker selection, and topical relevance. It also investigates the way certain speech acts, such as question–answer and offer–decline, combine as adjacency pairs; in this regard, conversation analysis overlaps with discourse analysis. The essential difference is

TABLE 8.1 DISTINGUISHING CHARACTERISTICS OF DISCOURSE, CONVERSATION, AND INTERACTION ANALYSIS

	Discourse analysis	Conversation analysis	Interaction analysis
Method of generating data	Invented Elicited Naturalistic	Naturalistic	Elicited Naturalistic
Mode	Spoken Written	Spoken	Spoken
Type of analysis	Categorical	Interpretive	Interpretive
Units of analysis	Linguistic	Non-linguistic	Both linguistic and non-linguistic

that the discourse analyst is concerned with the rhetorical routines realised in speech, while the conversation analyst is interested in the social routines (for an extended discussion with examples, see Aston 1986). Interaction analysts are concerned with both the linguistic and non-linguistic aspects of spoken language, and attempt to articulate links between the linguistically focused rhetorical routines and social aspects of interaction.

The various features and characteristics which I have discussed are set out in summary form in Table 8.1, and this should make clear points of similarity and divergence between the three approaches.

Which of these is the preferred type of analysis? In his book on pragmatics, Levinson (1983) synthesises the debate in the following manner.

DA [discourse analysis] theorists can accuse CA [conversation analysts] of being inexplicit, or worse, plain muddled, about the theories and conceptual categories they are actually employing in analysis . . . CA practitioners can retort that DA theorists are so busy with premature formalization that they pay scant attention to the nature of the data. The main strength of the DA approach is that it promises to integrate linguistic findings about intrasentential organization with discourse structure; while the strength of the CA position is that the procedures employed have already proved themselves capable of yielding by far the most substantial insights that have yet been gained into the organization of conversation. (Levinson 1983: 287)

From the foregoing discussion, you can see that interaction analysis shares characteristics both with discourse and conversation analysis. It is narrower than discourse analysis in terms of mode and method of generating data, but somewhat broader when it comes to analysis. While it shares the same broad, interpretive approach to the analysis of data as conversation analysis, it is broader in terms of the range of features subjected to analysis. I have chosen the term *interaction analysis* as the title for this chapter because of its breadth of focus. This will allow me, in parts of the chapter, to stray into the domains of discourse and conversation analysis. For an alternative approach, which subsumes interaction and conversation analysis under discourse analysis, see Hatch (1992).

Child–adult interaction

As intimated at the beginning of this chapter, it is useful for foreign language educators to be aware of research issues and methods in the field of first language acquisition, because numerous methodologists and materials developers claim a privileged place for their approach on the basis of a supposed relationship to the conditions which account for first language acquisition. Asher (1977), for example, claims that his methodology (Total Physical Response) is underpinned by important characteristics of first language acquisition. These include the comprehension-first principle (that infants have a silent period in which they comprehend but do not speak), the here-and-now principle (that parents or primary caregivers only talk to the infant about things that are present in the immediate environment), and the physical response principle (which is based on the conviction that much early language is in the form of imperatives to the child to carry out actions, such as 'pick up the ball', 'give the blocks to Nana'). By familiarizing ourselves with some of the literature on first language acquisition, we shall be better placed to evaluate the claims made by these methodologists and materials developers. The research is also interesting because of the methods employed for data collection and analysis.

Other claims (and I emphasise the fact that these are *claims,* not truths) in the literature which have been taken up by second language specialists include the following:

1. Contrary to popular belief, the child does not first learn structures which are then deployed in conversational interaction. Rather the child learns how to 'do' discourse, by interacting verbally with primary caregivers, and it is out of this discoursal interaction that syntactic structures develop.
2. Children learning their first language plan conversations and gamelike interactions. Adult interlocutors facilitate this process by providing conversational 'scaffolds' for the child. The adult does a great deal of interpretive work to ensure that the interaction does not break down. Typically, the child is allowed to take the lead, with the adult following and supporting.
3. In child–adult interactions, the focus is on the meanings being conveyed, not the forms in which the meanings are couched. Virtually all parental corrections relate to violations of meaning, not form.

(For detailed discussion on these and other points, see Asher 1977; Hatch 1978; Krashen 1981, 1982; van Lier 1988; Wells 1981.)

Not surprisingly, a great deal of research is devoted to recording and ana- lysing the developmental patterns and stages through which children pass in acquiring the phonological, morphosyntactic, semantic, and pragmatic sub- systems of the target language. Much of this research takes the form of detailed case studies. Fletcher (1985), for example, provides a book length study of the language development of one child, Sophie, from the age of 2 years and 4 months through to 3 years and 11 months.

In this section, I shall restrict my focus to investigations of children's inter- actional abilities. This work is interesting because it is now widely believed that children learn interactional skills first and then begin to master other aspects of the language, such as the phonology and the grammar of the lan- guage. (This is the reverse of many second language methods.) The following two extracts from Wells (1981) illustrate this point. They are between a child, Mark, and his mother. As you read the extracts, consider the following questions:

What differences are there between the two extracts?
Is there any evidence that Mark's language has developed between the first and second conversations? (In Extract 1, Mark is 23 months of age, and in Extract 2 he is 28 months old.)
What is the precise nature of Mark's contributions to the interactions?
What has Mark learned about 'doing' conversations?
What does his mother do to make the conversation work?

Extract 1
Mark is looking in a mirror and sees reflections of himself and his mother.

1	Mark:	Mummy (v)
2		Mummy
3	Mother:	What?
4	Mark:	There – there Mark
5	Mother:	Is that Mark?
6	Mark:	Mummy
7	Mother:	Mm
8	Mark:	Mummy
9	Mother:	Yes that's Mummy
10	Mark:	*
11		Mummy
12		Mummy (v)
13	Mother:	Mm
14	Mark:	There Mummy
15		Mummy (v)
16		There. Mark there.
17	Mother:	Look at Helen
18		She's going to sleep (long pause)

Mark can see birds in the garden
19	Mark:	[ ] (= look at that)
20		Birds Mummy (v)
21	Mother:	Mm
22	Mark:	Jubs (birds)
23	Mother:	What are they doing?
24	Mark:	Jubs bread
25	Mother:	Oh look
26		They're eating the berries aren't they?
27	Mark:	Yeh
28	Mother:	That's their food
29		They have berries for dinner
30	Mark:	Oh

(Wells 1981: 102)

Extract 2

Mark has seen a man working in his garden
1	Mark:	Where man gone?
2		Where man gone?
3	Mother:	I don't know
4		I expect he's gone inside because it's snowing
5	Mark:	Where man gone?
6	Mother:	In the house
7	Mark:	Uh?
8	Mother:	Into his house
9	Mark:	No
10		No
11		Gone to shop Mummy

The local shop is close to Mark's house
12	Mother:	Gone where?
13	Mark:	Gone shop
14	Mother:	To the shop?
15	Mark:	Yeh
16	Mother:	What's he going to buy?
17	Mark:	Er – biscuits
18	Mother:	Biscuits mm
19	Mark:	Uh?
20		Mm
21	Mother:	What else?
22	Mark:	Er – meat
23	Mother:	Mm
24	Mark:	Meat
25		Er – sweeties
26		Buy a big bag
27	Mother:	Buy sweets?
28	Mark:	Yeh
29		M – er – man – buy the man buy sweets
30	Mother:	Will he?

31	Mark:	Yeh
32		Daddy buy sweets
33		Daddy buy sweets
34	Mother:	Why?
35	Mark:	Oh er – [ ] shop
36	Mark:	Mark do buy some – sweets – sweeties
37		Mark buy some – um –
38		Mark buy some – um –
39		I did

(Wells 1981: 107)

In commenting on Extract 1, Wells argues that despite Mark's obvious lack of linguistic resources, in interactional terms, the conversation is remarkably similar to ordinary conversation. Mark is able to take turns appropriately, and is also capable of maintaining a particular conversational topic over several turns. In functional terms, Mark's language is pragmatic rather than propositional. For example, in lines 1, 12, and 19 he attempts to initiate an interaction; he draws attention to what is currently of interest in lines 4, 6, 14, and 20, and in lines 27 and 30 he acknowledges his mother's contributions. The mother, on the other hand, does a lot of interpretive work to ensure that the conversation flows smoothly. She uses simple utterances and restricts the semantic content to immediate topics. Pragmatically, she lets Mark take the initiative. For example, in lines 5, 9, 18, 23, 25–26, and 28–29 she uses cohesion to maintain the coherence of the interaction. 'Mark is being given the opportunity to learn both the referential links between words and structures and the objects and events to which they refer, and also the intralinguistic meaning relations that hold between these words which all belong to the same semantic field' (Wells 1981: 104).

In Extract 2, there are numerous indications that Mark's language has progressed. In lines 1, 11, 26, and 36 we see an increase in the length and complexity of his utterances. There is evidence of his ability to respond appropriately to information-seeking questions in lines 17 and 22. He also refers to persons and events which are not present in the here and now. The extract also shows the mother continuing to provide a scaffold for the interaction. She follows Mark's lead despite his rejection of her suggestion that the man has gone inside because of the weather. She checks her understanding through clarification requests and confirmation checks in lines 12 and 14, and then assists Mark in building a fictional account involving a sweets shop. In fact the interaction owes as much to the structure provided by the mother as to Mark's contributions:

The meaning is 'negotiated' and the resulting story is a collaborative achievement. Firstly, there is the need for the adult to interpret the child's contribution in the light of the immediate context and the focus of joint attention; secondly, to maximise uptake, the adult's own contributions need to be closely related to the child's preceding communication and current interest; thirdly, whilst being modified in timing, form and content to the child's receptive capacities, these adult contributions must also provide the means whereby the child can enlarge his linguistic resources and, through them, his understanding of the content of the communication (Wells 1981: 108)

This textual commentary is typical of the analysis engaged in by those who favour an interpretive approach to their data. As we saw in Chapter 3, the 'intensive immersion' in recorded data (Edelsky 1981) is typical of ethnography. The key characteristic of this approach is the suspension of preformed judgments and beliefs. It has been suggested that the researcher should approach the data in the same way as an ethnographer might investigate an unknown culture – not by specifying in advance what will count as significant, but by assuming that anything that occurs in the data might potentially be of significance (van Lier 1988). In this 'intensive immersion in the data', Wells shares common ground with the conversation analyst. However, by admitting into his analysis an investigation of the development of different speech acts, he also draws on techniques and strategies from discourse analysis. Wells's research is summarised in Table 8.2.

Another important issue concerns the context and environment of the research. Most forms of interaction analysis take into account the context in which the data were collected. In child language studies, contextual factors include not only where the interaction takes place and what is happening at the time, but also the relationship between the interlocutors. This is exemplified in Extracts 3 and 4, which are from my own data. Both extracts involve a child, Rebecca, interacting in two different contexts, with different interlocutors. In Extract 3 she is interacting with her older sister and older cousins. In Extract 4, on the other hand, she is interacting with her mother.

As you read these extracts, consider the different communicative roles played by Rebecca and the different 'messages' she gets about interaction in the two different encounters. Both interactions were recorded on successive days when Rebecca was 27 months of age (almost the same age as Mark).

Extract 3
[This interaction takes place in Rebecca's bedroom. The older children, Jenny, Zoe, and Jodie, are playing 'mums and dads' and want to exclude Rebecca.]
R: A, a play, a ready . . . a mum a dad.
Je: Darling, you're only a darling, now stay here, stay here.
Z: I want a drink.
Je: Now darling, it's time to go to ni nis. Lie down. (forces Rebecca down in her cot.) Go ni nis. You can stay up darling tonight. (inaud) . . . go ni nis. (puts up side of cot)
R: Ah, ah, darling. How, a shutting you.
Je: There darling. No. Do you wanna get out? (Yeah).
  Do you wanna play with your sister? (secured side of cot)
R: Ah ni nis, ah ni nis. Ni nis.

TABLE 8.2 SUMMARY OF FIRST LANGUAGE ACQUISITION STUDY BY WELLS (1981)

Question	How is it that the human infant is able to acquire its first language rapidly and successfully?
Rationale	Although we know a considerable amount about the organisation of formal systems of language in isolation from the contexts in which they are used, we are still largely ignorant about the principles that underlie the orderliness of conversation. We are also ignorant about how the human infant is able to acquire language.
Subjects	A male infant, Mark, followed from the ages of 23 to 28 months, and his mother.
Procedure	Natural samples of language are collected from Mark and his mother as they interact at home.
Types of data	Transcripts of interactions.
Type of analysis	Interpretive.
Results	1. Children learn key aspects of interaction, such as turn-taking, gaining the floor, and negotiating meaning very early.
	2. The mother does a lot of work to ensure that the interactions 'work'.
	3. Pragmatic language functions are acquired before propositional ones.
	4. Children learn to do discourse through interaction, and out of this interaction, syntactic structures develop.

Je: OK, ni ni.
R: Ah (protests).
Je: [Turns out the light]
R: No! No! No!
Je: Now it's ni nis time. (No.) Ni ni. (No.) I'm going to go and get Zoe and Jodie and Jared and we'll come back. [leaves room]
   [Silence]
R: Get. Zoe. Jenny.
   [Silence]
R: (Sighs)
   [Silence]
R: I'm a go [?] Muuummy! Muuummy!
Jo: Hello.
R: A getting out. Jenny a cot a me in.
Je: See, I got her in the cot. Now, that's . . . she can just walk around in the cot for her sleep and we'll pretend she's gone to sleep.

                             (Author's data)

Extract 4
[In this extract, Rebecca and her mother are talking as Rebecca has her after-sleep snack.]
R: Mm. Wash it.
M: Washed it – yeah, I washed the tomato.
R: A bump.
M: Pardon! Don't bang it – no. It'll squash.
       You bite it. (Mm)
R: Ah
M: Oh, you've still got a mouthful. Well chew it up and swallow it. Chew, chew, chew. Chew it on your molars. That's right. How are your molars, good? Oh, yeah, big aren't they. Well now, you going to have a bite of your tomato?
R: A bobble (bottle)
M: Drink. OK.

(Author's data)

Rebecca's role is very different in these two interactions, as is her language. In the interactional roughhouse in Extract 3, she is on the periphery, marginalized by her status as the youngest interlocutor. She has to work hard to become part of the interaction and have her communicative bids heeded. In Extract 4, on the other hand, she is allowed to take the lead. The mother supports her and interprets her utterances, as the mother did in the Wells transcript, so that the interaction proceeds smoothly. The child learns quite different things about what language can do in both interactions. I would argue, not that one context is more appropriate than the other for language development, but that the child needs a variety of communicative encounters to develop a complete functional repertoire. In terms of research, a complete picture of Rebecca's linguistic repertoire will emerge only if data for analysis are collected in a range of contexts.

Adult–adult interaction: interpersonal encounters

In this section we shall look at the work of conversation analysts. The major aim of this work has been to describe and ultimately to account for the ways in which conversations are carried out in socially organised interactions. The basic research question addressed by conversation analysts is: How is it that conversational participants are able to produce intelligible utterances, and how are they able to interpret the utterances of others (Garfinkel, 1967)?

As we saw earlier, conversation analysts insist that their analyses be based on naturally occurring instances of everyday interaction. They specifically reject the use of data obtained through formal experiments, interviews, and other forms of elicitation, and the use of precoded observational schedules of the type we examined in Chapter 5. The rejection of these methods, which are widely utilised in other areas of social and behavioural science, identify this approach as a separate research discipline. In addition, they reject the use of examples which have been invented by the researcher – a practice favoured by certain schools of linguistics and applied linguistics. In a key collection of papers on conversation analysis, Atkinson and Heritage (1984) point out that virtually none of the data in their volume could conceivably be the product of recollection or intuition in generating data by comparison with the richness and diversity of empirically occurring interaction, 'nor would such invented "data" prove persuasive as *evidence* relevant to the analysis of interaction. Data of this sort can always be viewed as the implausible products of selective processes involving recollection, attention or imagination' (p. 3). They are just as critical of the use of formal experiments, arguing that the success of an experiment will depend on the extent to which the researcher has been able to limit, control, and manipulate the behaviour in question. It is the researcher who decides before the event which behaviours are relevant and which are irrelevant. Yet the question remains as to where the variables came from in the first place.

Without previous exposure to a range of naturally occurring interactional data, the experimenter is unlikely to anticipate the range, scope, and variety of behavioural variation that might be responsive to experimental manipulation, nor will he or she be in a position to extrapolate from experimental findings to real situations of conduct. By the same token, while certain of the experimenter's data may or may not be artifacts of the more general experimental situation in which the data were produced, such influences (if any) can be determined only by systematic comparison with a large corpus of naturally occurring data. (Atkinson and Heritage 1984: 3)

A characteristic feature of this type of research is the elaborately detailed, interpretive analysis of relatively small chunks of language. For example, Schegloff (1984) devotes twenty-five pages to a discussion and analysis of the use of the utterance 'for whom' in a sixteen-line interaction taken from a radio 'call-in' show. His focus, in this analysis, is on the ambiguity inherent in interaction, and the ways in which such ambiguity is resolved. He demonstrates that the linguistic form of an utterance does not necessarily coincide with the functional intention of that utterance. In the case of 'for whom', Schegloff shows that while this looks to be a question, it in fact does not function as a question within the interaction. You might like to consider your own interpretation of 'for whom' in the extract, part of which follows.

B: He says, governments, an' you know he keeps – he talks about governments,
   they sh- the thing that they sh'd do is what's right or wrong.
A: For whom.
B: Well he says – he –
A: [By what standard]
B: That's what – that's exactly what I mean.

(Schegloff 1984: 28)

A similar type of analysis is carried out by Davidson (1984), who investigates what happens in a conversation when an invitation, offer, request, or proposal is rejected. Her database, which is somewhat more extensive than Schegloff's, includes rejection sequences such as the following:

A: I was gonna say if you wanted to you could meet me at UBC and I could show you some of the other things on the computer, maybe even show you how to program Basic or something.
B: Well, I don't know if I'd want to get all that involved.
A: It's really interesting.

(adapted from Davidson 1984: 108)

Among other things, Davidson claims to have found that, following a rejection, speakers typically reformulate their offer, and that the subsequent version provides the interlocutor with an alternative which provides a face-saving way for the interlocutor to reject the offer.

In these studies, there is no attempt to provide 'representative samples' of the phenomena under investigation. The number of instances of the behaviour can range from a single instance which is analysed in great detail, to a dozen or more. A sample from the contents of the Atkinson and Heritage collection reveals the sorts of things conversation analysts are interested in investigating.

Orientations
• On some questions and ambiguities in conversation
Preference organization
• Agreeing and disagreeing with assessments: some features of preferred/
   dispreferred turn shapes
• Subsequent versions of invitations, offers, requests, and proposals dealing with
   potential or actual rejection
• Speakers' reportings on invitation sequences
• Pursuing a response
Topic organization
• Generating topic: the use of topic initial elicitors
The integration of talk with nonvocal activities
• Notes on story structure and the organization of participation
• Talk and recipiency: sequential organization in speech and body movements
Aspects of response
• On the organization of laughter and talk about troubles
• Public speaking and audience responses: some techniques for inviting applause

(adapted from Atkinson and Heritage 1984: v–vi)

Adult–adult interaction: transactional encounters

In the preceding section, we looked at the analysis of conversations which, essentially, have a social function. Similar methods for recording and analysing data are used by researchers who are interested in investigating transactional interactions. These are interactions whose primary purpose is the exchange of goods and services (Merritt 1976). Of particular interest are encounters involving the exchange of professional services. The contexts for this research include courts of law, hospitals, doctors' and dentists' consulting rooms, and so on. Shuy (1973), for example, investigated the interactional patterns between medical practitioners and patients. He found that while the potential success of medical treatment depended almost entirely on obtaining accurate information from patients, physicians in training received little or no training in techniques for carrying out diagnostic interviews.

In a more recent investigation, Candlin, Coleman, and Burton (1983) studied interactions between dentists and patients. The focus of their investigation was those points in the consultation in which the patients described their complaint. Building on previous research into doctor–patient communication within a cross-cultural context, they posed the question: How do patients communicate complaints and how do dentists respond? From this, they hypothesised that 'dentists and patients bring to consultations different discoursal sets' (p. 59) – that is, awareness by coparticipants of what is expected/allowable behaviour in an encounter. A patient's perceived lack of opportunity to talk is related, not to the amount of actual talk, but to their opportunity to engage in relevant talk, that is, talk related to symptoms.

The database for the investigation was 66 dentist–patient consultations carried out in a range of settings. The data yielded by the investigation are illustrated in the following extract.

Extract 5
[The patient, female, is already well acquainted with the dentist. She has begun talking as she enters the consultation room.]

P	(must have something) that was left in and I kept thinking it would come

P	out come out because I didn't want a repetition
D	right come and sit down
DSA	( )

P	I didn't want a repetition of all that bleeding and rushing to the
D	now
P	hospital and restitching and so I just thought well I'll keep persevering

P		oh a real old do
D	oh you had some er	infection and some secondary hemorrhage on it
DSA		(excuse me)

P		yes I'm a I'm a real bleeder when the teeth come out always have
D	didn't	you

P	been and the health hasn't been too good and I kept having
D	no that's right

171

{ P   ( )   well it's still there and it er it { ( )
{ D   and what's your trouble now   { there's

{ P   { yes I think it's an old tooth or something
{ D   something brewing there is { there
   P   that didn't come up didn't come out and I thought while there's no trouble in the mouth and I've (got) I keep getting ulcers in the mouth and I thought while it's quiet and er my chest's better than it's been for a

{ P   while I'll   { ( ) I'll drive in to see you
{ D   { is it yeah   right let's have a look now

{ P   mm
{ D   it's still o-on the same side there
                       [6 seconds]

{ P   [chuckles]
{ D   that's a piece of a tooth it's not a whole tooth by any

{ P   { I kept hoping it would come { out
{ D   means it's a piece of { a tooth   { that's come along ah

{ P   [chuckles] { (four years)
{ D   I don't know when they had that out { it's er no it's not

{ P   ( )   I
{ D   one I took out for you   I've taken nothing as far back as that
   P   think it was was it four years this October coming
                    [2 seconds]

   P   ah it's about that time since all I had all that trouble about four years

{ P   since this October
{ D   yes ( ) yes but that was nearer the front that was

{ P   yes yes this has been I've never been to
{ D   after you'd had teeth out down here

{ P   anyone since ( ) I've tried to hope it would work itself out
{ D   yes well

{ P   no   {   ( )
{ D   that's not one I took out for you it's er it's { one that's been taken

{ P   is it really   [chuckles]   { ( )
{ D   out years ago   yes   and em { a little piece has come through

                      (Candlin et al. 1983: 68–69)

What is going on in this interaction, and how can we make sense of it? The discursive analysis provided by the researchers is illustrated in the following extract from the research report. The analysis is similar to that used by those engaged in analysing casual conversation. However, a major difference between this work, in which transactional interactions are analysed, and that which looks at the analysis of casual conversation is that the latter carries out detailed analysis on small quantities of data, whereas transactional analysts generally work with extensive transcripts.

In this consultation the patient does not wait to be invited to present her report; even before entering the consulting room, she has begun to make her report. The patient is typical in that her report is made indirectly, although she is a little unusual (but not unique) in reporting on two different aspects of her complaint. Thus the patient reports first that "must have something that was left in." That is to say, she reports not on the pain or discomfort which she is suffering but instead on what she assumes to be the cause of the discomfort, the fact that something was "left in." Second, the patient reports on her fears concerning complications experienced during previous dental treatment which led her to delay seeking treatment again. The precise nature of the complaint for which the patient has been delaying seeking treatment is left unspecified. The patient's report is also, clearly, highly elaborated. The dentist follows this introduction by presenting the patient with an invitation to report on her complaint ("and what's your trouble now") which is almost immediately repeated ("there's something brewing there is there"). In this way, the dentist ensures that the consultation proceeds according to the standard procedure despite its rather unconventional introduction.

The patient responds to her dentist's invitation by returning to the first of the two aspects of her complaint in "I think it's an old tooth or something that didn't come up didn't come out." Again, therefore, she reports on the cause of the discomfort which she is suffering – the sudden appearance of a nonerupted tooth – rather than on that discomfort itself.

The particular interest of this consultation lies in the dentist's response to his patient's report. The patient has told him that "it's an old tooth," but in an extraordinarily peremptory manner, which the transcript cannot reveal adequately, the dentist declares, "that's a piece of tooth . . . it's not a whole tooth by any means it's a piece of a tooth." This then is the third technique available for dentists when responding to patient's reports: in addition to ignoring reports or minimizing their significance, the dentist can openly declare them to be incorrect. (Candlin et al. 1983: 69–70)

You can see that this type of analysis consists of an extensive interpretive gloss on the interaction. The analysis faces similar threats to reliability and validity as other forms of ethnography. Because of the rich database, it is generally not feasible to include enough primary data in an article or paper to enable an independent researcher to conduct a reanalysis. The studies can also face the charge of subjectivity. In the foregoing commentary, for example, there are several assertions which we must take on trust – for example, that the beginning of the consultation is unconventional, and that the dentist treats the patient in an 'extraordinarily peremptory manner'. Generalisability is also an issue here. The researchers assert that there are three techniques available for dentists to respond to a patient's complaint. Elsewhere in their study, they claim that the process by which patients report complaints involves a three-stage procedure, that dentists give patients only one opportunity to present their report, that patients report their complaints indirectly, and that dentists either ignore the report, disagree with it, or agree with it but minimise its significance. As critical readers, we need to ask ourselves how many instances of this behaviour would be required in order for us to be convinced that a general principle of interaction had been identified. We would also need to know the extent to which contextual and environmental factors influence outcomes. For example, do these principles hold in private clinics where the patient pays as well as in public clinics where the state pays? Is similar behaviour observed when the patient and dentist are from different cultural and/or linguistic backgrounds? Are similar results obtained when the interaction occurs in the course of emergency treatment as well as during routine dental visits? Finally, we need to ask whether the conclusions drawn by the researchers warrant the studies in the first place.

Thus far, we have focused principally on interactions between native speakers (although the studies all have major implications for second and foreign language interactions). In the next section, I shall analyse a major investigation of interaction in a cross-cultural context.

Interaction analysis in a cross-cultural context

In this section, I shall examine a study that was carried out in order to investigate communication tasks in professional workplaces between workers from different cultural and linguistic backgrounds (Willing 1990). As with all the other studies reported in this chapter, the overall aim of the research was to identify the patterns and regularities underlying interpersonal interactions in particular contexts. The study was carried out with a group of immigrants to Australia, who had professional qualifications and who were undertaking an intensive language course designed to prepare them to seek employment in their chosen profession.

The point of departure of the study was the essentially practical one of providing guidelines for the development of curricula and materials for helping immigrants working in professional workplaces. In order to carry out these pedagogical tasks, however, it was necessary to obtain descriptions of workplace communication tasks, and to identify potential sources of intercultural communication difficulties.

The objectives of the study were as follows:

a) To develop a guiding taxonomy of professional workplace communication tasks in terms of encounter type, function, register, channel, and complexity.
b) To develop conceptual frameworks which can be used to provide language teaching practitioners with an understanding of:
   i) a range of communication tasks which commonly recur in professional workplace functioning;
   ii) the sub-skills which make them up;

TABLE 8.3 RESEARCH PROCEDURE FOR INVESTIGATING COMMUNICATION IN
THE PROFESSIONAL WORKPLACE

Step	Procedure
1	Literature review
2	Initial information collection from selected workplaces
3	Formation of steering committee
4	Systematic and extensive data collection from authentic workplace interactions
5	Data analysis with reference to conceptual models developed during Steps 1 and 2
6	Formulation of conclusion and recommendation; compilation of report

  iii) potential sources of intercultural communication breakdown;
  iv) the ways in which various types of encounter between native speaker and
non-native speaker (and NNS/NNS) may be made use of for purposes of
learning. This will involve an examination of how communication trouble is
signalled and dealt with by means of routines such as comprehension and
confirmation checks, clarification requests, and repairs; as well as other
conscious strategies of communication and learning;
  v) the factors which determine the difficulty and learnability of specific task
types encountered in the professional workplace.
c) To present the above information in a research report.
d) To recommend applications of that information in teaching/learning and
professional development materials.

(Willing 1990: 2–3)

The decision to investigate native speaker and non-native speaker communication in professional workplaces was prompted by a change in government immigration policy, which has brought increasing numbers of immigrants with professional qualifications into the country. Many of these
professionals fail to find employment in the profession for which they are
trained. This represents a waste of resources for the country and is demoral-
ising for the immigrants themselves. In order to design programs which
would equip non-native speakers to enter the workforce at an appropriate
level, it was felt that empirical data were needed on the communication
demands made on these speakers in their respective workplaces. In essence,
the overall task of the research team was to characterise the culture of professional workplaces. The procedure followed by the research team is set out
in Table 8.3.

The database for the study came from a group of students taking an English
for Professional Employment course. Part of this course involved spending
time on work placement. The course participants, with permission from the
organisations, tape-recorded some of their interactions while on work place-

ment. They did this by activating a lapel microphone attached to a small cassette recorder which was carried in the participant's pocket or handbag. The data yielded by this procedure were analysed in the same discursive, interpretive manner as the other studies we have looked at in this chapter. This is illustrated in the following sample transcript and commentary.

Extract 6

[Teodoro and his Australian colleague (who is, in the hierarchy of the company, Teodoro's deputy and assistant) are engaged in a morning meeting in their shared office, in which Teodoro is systematically running through various jobs and other matters which have to be dealt with. He is, in fact, following an informal agenda which he has on paper in front of him (the assistant does not have a copy of this). The following extract constitutes one of the agenda items.]

```
 1   T:  Now uh, how do you call the that
 2       special paper that fit in the sliding door?
 3   C:  In the sliding door?
 4   T:  Sno us
 5   C:  Oh ceraphic glass
 6   T:  Ceraphic gla   the have another name. That's not
 7       XYZ
 8   C:  No this one isn't, no.
 9   T:  No. Uh these ones to put to install there before
10       the third of April, meaning the XYZ product
11   C:  which Mort Adams is taking ————
12   T:  Mort Adams is working on it
13   C:  OK
14   T:  Mort, Mort Adams told me that he is not sure about
15       it if he have the material or not yet. He will let
16       me know tomorrow, which is Wednesday
17   C:  That's right
18   T:  And he is planning to install the new XYZ material
19       on Thursday.
20   C:  OK
21   T:  But he asked me to clean those one. He told me
22       that's very simple only to peel off.
23   C:  Yeah?
24   T:  Just, just scratch one corner
25   C:  Peel it off
26   T:  And then peel off all it
27   C:  OK
28   T:  back, and get it a special kind of cleaner.
```

[Extract continues to line 100]

(Willing 1990: 13)

ANALYSIS

In this segment, the beginning of the new agenda item is marked by Teodoro's use of the marker *now* (line 1). He signals the satisfactory completion of the problem-solving episode at line 88 ("thank you, I put away"). . . . A key factor in this interaction is of course the status differential between the two participants. Teodoro is clearly in charge. This is evident throughout, and is shown from the beginning by the fact that he controls the agenda, he provides the transition, topicalises (lines 1–6), and lays the problem situation before his assistant. Teodoro *defines* the problem situation in lines 9–10 ('these ones to put to install there before the third of April'), and describes it in lines 11–28. (Willing 1990: 15)

Having provided data samples, along with an analysis, the task for the researchers is to interpret the data – that is, to make sense of it within the context of the workplace culture they are seeking to characterise. Of course, a large scale study such as this will generate numerous outcomes, and it is impossible to detail these here. However, I would like to present one of the findings to illustrate the way in which the data were interpreted.

The researchers found that an important construct which helped them make sense of the data was that of the 'meeting'. Most of the interactions which occurred, whether they took place in formal settings such as board rooms, or informally in corridors, shared characteristics commonly associated with meetings. In particular, they were:

- oriented to a shared, external goal
- fitted within an explicitly or implicitly agreed upon time frame
- had an explicitly or implicitly agreed upon agenda
- characterised by relatively orderly turn-taking.

This research has yielded a great deal of valuable data which can be utilised in the development of curricula as well as teaching materials and classroom activities. For example, it has provided us with insights into the generic structure and discourse characteristics of 'meetings', which have emerged as key interactional events within the culture of the professional workplace. For second language learners, pedagogical procedures based on these insights should enable them to enter into, and interact within, the culture of their chosen professional workplace.

Conclusion

In this chapter, we have seen that the interpretive analysis of naturally occurring interactions is an important element in research on first and second language acquisition and use. It is particularly significant for those researchers who believe that the context in which interactions occur is an important variable which needs to be taken into consideration. Such researchers are likely to eschew the use of formal experiments, elicitation devices, and other forms of intervention in favour of an approach which allows them to investigate language use in natural settings.

As we have seen, in contrast with the experimental method, there are no highly formalised procedures for collecting and analysing data in this type of research. This flexibility can be both an advantage and a disadvantage – an advantage in that the researcher can see what is actually there without the intervening filter of a methodological procedure, a potential disadvantage in that the lack of explicit guidelines may cause the researcher to lose his or her way.

While most of the methodological developments in interaction analysis have taken place in investigations of first language use, these techniques and procedures are beginning to be used by second language researchers. The study reported in the preceding section is an excellent example of theoretical models and research procedures developed in first language research being adopted and adapted for use in second language research.

Questions and tasks

1. The following extract is a continuation of the interaction between Rebecca and her mother. Read the interaction and then complete the questions/tasks which follow.

R: [cough] A Lawrie a bobble, a same a me.
M: Yes, Lawrie has a cup the same as yours, doesn't he. That's why we have your name on the bottom. What's that say?
R: P-A-me
M: P-A-me. Ha! (Yeah) That says B-E-C-C-A Becca.
   You're a funny duck. Now, you going to have a bite of your tomato? (Yeah) Cause we really have to get going, and we're not taking big tomato in the car. No. All over your seat. A big mess.
R: Got.
M: Got what?
R: Num Num.
M: Piece – piece of num num. Piece of bacon.
R: Yeah.
M: Haa – found a piece did you? (Yawns)
R: Go sleep.
M: Go to bed. Yes, I do feel a bit sleepy.
R: (snores).
M: Why'd you wake up in the night?
R: A mummy.
M: Yes, I know that's what you said – 'Mummy'. But why did you want me?
R: Hub, bub, bub, bly.
M: Pardon?
R: Hub, bub, bub, bly.
M: Hub, bub, bub, bly? (Yeah.) Oh you're making up
R: Bubble ble . . .
M: Bubble a Bill. (Yeah.) You're making up nonsense. No mozzies [mosquitoes], were there – when you were in bed last night? No mozzies.

R: A duff.

M: Stuff, yeah I put stuff on you. Cream.

R: Cream on a mozzie.

M: Cream on you.

R: Get me. Oh! Oh!

M: Mozzies won't get you.

R: Sore

M: Mozzies smell that cream and what do they say?

R: Bzzz! Yuk!

M: Yuk, they say, and they fly away.

R: Yeah. Poo, poo, a, a got uuk yuk. Hate bees.

M: You hate bees, do you? (Yeah). I, I don't like bees, cause they sting.

R: A ding, (sting) a Jenny, a mozzie a sting a hard a Mummy cuddle.

M: Yes, I cuddled Jenny, yes. Do you remember when the bee stung you on your foot (yes) up at Grandma's (yes). Hurt, didn't it.

R: Mummy came a ail on a feet.

M: Mummy came and what, Darling?

R: A ail a feet.

M: What did I put on your foot?

R: A ail.

M: Ail? Oil (yeah). Not oil, it was, it was sting cream. Make the sting better.

R: A tissue.

M: With a tissue, that's right. And go pat, pat, pat on the bee sting with the cream. (Yeah) Yeah.

R: Oh, mato.

M: Eat it up, cause we grew that in our garden. That's delicious.

R: Delouse.

M: Delicious, yes, very tasty. Can you say 'very tasty'!

R: Very tasty!

M: Hee Ha. I love tomatoes, specially tomatoes that we grew in our garden.

R: Me a a me a me a sec a Lawrie a dancing.

M: You and me and Lawrie dancing?

R: Me, a you a, a, Jenny, Lawrie a dancing.

M: Dancing?

R: Yeah. No No (No) No Ahh.

M: Jumping (No) Dancing?

R: Ah, ah guck.

M: You're stuck. Well don't have a fit, because I didn't understand you. All right, you try and say it again, Darling. You, and me and Jenny and Lawrie

R: Dancing. Dancing.

M: Dancing (No) Dancing (No) Dancing (No). Where do we do it? (No) Oh! (Ahh) Oh, try again. Say it again. Say it again (Ahh!) Don't have a fit – you'll get stuck. You mustn't slide down like that. I'm sorry I didn't understand your word.

(Author's data)

a. Are the comments made by Wells about the interactions between Mark

179

and his mother pertinent to the interaction between Rebecca and her mother?

b. What do you think Rebecca might have learned as a result of this interactive experience?

c. Study the transcripts from Rebecca's point of view. What does she already know about 'doing' conversation?

2. To what extent are the following comments supported or not supported by the child–adult transcripts in this chapter?

When children learn their first language, they do not first learn sounds, then words, then sentences, and then finally apply this linguistic knowledge in their interaction with the social world around them. They begin by interacting with the meaningful people in their environment and they converse, play games and engage in rituals long before they are able to utter their first recognizable words. Their caretakers typically spend enormous amounts of time in setting up and developing these interactions, and language develops along the way. (van Lier 1988: 229)

It can be observed that children learning their first language often plan conversations and game-like interaction long before they are skilful users of complex syntax. Parents and caretakers help them in this planning by providing prototypical structures and gradually handing over slots and roles. (van Lier 1988: 215–216)

In interactions with children learning their first language, the focus is on the message being conveyed, and the vast majority of corrections by caretakers refer to violations of meaning rather than form. (Snow and Ferguson 1977)

[First] language acquisition is a subconscious process; language acquirers are not usually aware of the fact that they are acquiring language, but are only aware of the fact that they are using the language for communication. (Krashen 1982: 10)

3. What possible questions, issues, or hypotheses suggest themselves to you as a result of your initial contact with these data?

4. The following exchange between Rebecca and her mother took place ten months after the 'tomatoes' tape. What evidence is there that Rebecca's language has developed in that time? Refer also to Table 8.4. (You can focus on morphosyntactic, functional, pragmatic, interactional, etc., features.)

[R has just had her morning sleep. R and M are putting on one of R's tapes.]

M: That's the right way. Can you put them away?
R: Think I need a bit help.
M: You need a bit of help [yes] oh right. Where is it?
    No, it doesn't go in that way. No. No.
R: Where?
M: Upsi . . . up the other way. That's it. In that way.
R: Know what one.
M: Know what one
[Cassette with children's songs and stories begins and continues through segment.]

TABLE 8.4 REBECCA; SAMPLE UTTERANCES AT 27 MONTHS AND 37 MONTHS

27 months	37 months
1. Mm. Wash it.	1. Think I need a bit help.
2. A bump.	2. Where?
3. Ah.	3. Know what one.
4. A bobble	4. I don't want it outside.
5. A Lawrie a bobble, a same a me.	5. You hear that slurpy noise?
6. P-A-me	6. I am. I love ice block.
7. Got.	7. O . . . on a bench.
8. Num Num.	8. Yeah.
9. Yeah.	9. Baby crying [referring to tape]
10. Go sleep.	10. Baby crying.
11. (snores).	11. Why crying?
12. A mummy.	12. Wants Mummy.
13. Hub, bub, bub, bly.	13. Cause I want a drink.
14. Hub, bub, bub, bly.	14. Not really
15. Bubble ble . . .	15. Cause I want a book.
16. A duff.	16. Cause I want a . . . I want a ice block.
17. Cream on a mozzie.	17. Why?
18. Get me. Oh! Oh!	18. I can't rember.
19. Sore	19. Mmm. Hope you can't do that.
20. Bzzz! Yuk!	20. I don't know.
21. Yeah. Poo, poo, a, a got uuk yuk. Hate bees.	21. A chicken's man coming?
22. A ding, a Jenny, a mozzie a sting a hard a Mummy cuddle.	22. Mmm, I think I have some spaghetti from last night?

M: Oh, where did you get that from? I said for you to eat that outside.
R: I don't want it outside.
M: I don't want it inside.
R: You hear that slurpy noise?
M: Yeah, I can hear that slurpy noise. Who's doing it?
R: I am. I love ice block.
M: Where did you put the bubble gum?
R: O . . . on a bench.
M: On the bench in the kitchen?
R: Yeah.
M: Have you eaten any of it? [No] None?
R: Baby crying [referring to the tape]
M: Pardon?

R: Baby crying.
M: Yeah.
R: Why crying?

M: Why? Oh . . . hungry? Tired? What do you think then?

R: Wants Mummy.

M: Wants Mummy. Is that why you cry? Why do you cry?

R: Cause I want a drink.

M: [laughs] Oh – you don't cry cause you want a drink do you? No.

R: Not really.

M: Not really. Why do you cry then?

R: Cause I want a book.

M: Want a book. . . . Not really.

R: Cause I want a . . . I want a ice block.

M: Cause you . . . no, no. not really. Why did you have a fit yesterday?

R: Why?

M: I don't know why. I'm asking you. Why did you?

R: I can't rember.

M: Can't remember, no. Well, I can remember. You didn't want to come home. Remember that? Remember that?

R: Mmm. [Jumps along with the tape] Hope you can't do that.

M: I can't do that, no, it's too difficult. My poor old bones. Now, what are you going to have for lunch?

R: I don't know.

M: Don't know. Sandwich?

R: A chicken's man coming?

M: No, chicken man's not coming today. But, you going to tell what you have, what you'd like for lunch?
Mummy'll make you a nice meat sandwich.

R: Mmm, I think I have some spaghetti from last night?

M: No, we didn't have spaghetti last night.

R: (inaud)

M: No, we didn't have spaghetti last night. We had macaroni with the meat.

(Author's data)

5. Using the sample data from Rebecca as a point of departure, develop a research outline to investigate some aspect of child first/second language development.

a. Issue/question/hypothesis
b. Rationale
c. Subject(s)
d. Procedure
e. Type of data
f. Type of analysis
g. Measures to guard against threats to reliability and validity

6. Summarise the Communication Tasks in the Workplace Project by completing the following:

a. Question(s)/hypotheses
b. Rationale

c. Procedure
d. Data
e. Analysis
f. Outcomes
g. Implications
h. Critique

Further reading

Although it has been around for a number of years now, Wells (1981) is an excellent and extremely readable introduction to child language development, which focuses in particular on the development of interactional skills and highlights the importance of interaction to other aspects of child language development. It also contains useful procedural information for those interested in collecting and analysing data on child first or second language development. A standard text on language acquisition is Fletcher and Garman (1986). Two more recent introductions to child language, which introduce the reader to a wide range of research, are Reich (1988) and Foster (1990). Finally, Bennett-Kastor (1988) provides a detailed introduction to techniques for collecting and analysing children's language.

For studies of conversation analysis see the edited collection by Atkinson and Heritage (1984). The editors also provide an overview of the methodological principles and procedures involved in this type of analysis in their introduction to the volume. Another relevant collection on conversation analysis is Roger and Bull (1989).

Three excellent introductions to discourse analysis which have been written with the classroom teacher in mind are Cook (1989), McCarthy (1991), and Hatch (1992).

9 Program evaluation

'Either this wallpaper goes or I go'.

(words attributed to Oscar Wilde on his deathbed)

Making judgments and evaluations is an integral part of everyday life (even toward the end of life if we are to believe the quote above). We are constantly evaluating all aspects of our life and work, to such an extent that we rarely notice that we are doing so. This familiarity can often mask important aspects of evaluation when viewed from a formal perspective.

This chapter is somewhat different in character from the preceding chapters, most of which have focused on research methodology. In this chapter, we shall look at program evaluation. I have included the chapter for several reasons. In the first place, I believe that evaluations, incorporating as they do questions, data, and interpretation, are a form of research. Secondly, small-scale program evaluations can provide an excellent research training ground for graduate students.

In the first section, I shall define evaluation and attempt to draw a distinction between evaluation and assessment. Different types of evaluation are reviewed, and the relationship between evaluation and assessment is discussed. The chapter also provides a practical guide to the different steps in the design of an evaluation.

Defining evaluation

In the curriculum literature, there sometimes appears to be a confusion between program evaluation and student assessment. In fact, some writers use the terms *assessment* and *evaluation* interchangeably. Gronlund (1981) writes:

Evaluation may be defined as a *systematic process of determining the extent to which instructional objectives are achieved by pupils*. There are two important aspects of this definition. First, note that evaluation implies a *systematic process,* which omits casual, uncontrolled observation of pupils. Second, evaluation assumes that *instructional objectives* have been previously identified. Without previously determined objectives, it is difficult to judge clearly the nature and extent of pupil learning. (pp. 5–6)

Gronlund, in circumscribing evaluation in terms of learning outcomes, presents an extremely narrow input-output view of evaluation and, by extension, education. In fact, he is using the term *evaluation* roughly in the sense in which I would use *assessment*. I would like to suggest that, while they are obviously related, they mean rather different things – that evaluation is somewhat broader in concept than assessment.

To me there is a clear distinction between the two concepts. *Assessment* refers to the processes and procedures whereby we determine what learners are able to do in the target language. We may or may not assume that such abilities have been brought about by a program of study. Evaluation, on the other hand, refers to a wider range of processes which may or may not include assessment data.

The data resulting from evaluation assist us in deciding whether a course needs to be modified or altered in any way so that objectives may be achieved more effectively. If certain learners are not achieving the goals and objectives set for a course, it is necessary to determine why this is so. We would also wish, as a result of evaluating a course, to have some idea about what measures might be taken to remedy any shortcomings. Evaluation, then, is not simply a process of obtaining information, it is also a decision-making process. (Nunan 1988: 118)

Two important characteristics of evaluation emerge from this discussion. In the first place, it involves not only assembling information but interpreting that information – making value judgments. In fact the word *value* is contained within *evaluation*. Secondly, it involves action. We collect information about language programs not as a form of philosophical reflection, but in order to do something differently next time. Brown (1989) points out that in curriculum terms there is a degree of similarity between evaluation and needs analysis, which also involves the collection of information for decision-making purposes, and that the distinction between the program evaluation and needs analysis 'may be more one of focus than of the actual activities involved' (Brown 1989: 223).

The relationship between assessment and evaluation

While acknowledging a distinction between assessment and evaluation, Hudson (1989) argues that the measurement of student performance is the key to program evaluation. For Hudson, the essential question to be asked by a program evaluator is 'whether an examinee has mastered the content he or she has been taught, or has reached a level of competence defined as mastery' (p. 259). In his paper, Hudson focuses on what we might call product-oriented evaluation. In other words, he is concerned above all else with the outcomes of the learning process rather than with the process itself.

185

The researcher who uses assessment data as the key element in an evaluation has to give careful consideration to three factors. These are (1) the nature of the evidence to be used, (2) the relationship between the evaluation and the program goals, and (3) the appropriate measurement instruments to be used. The first factor takes us back to an issue which I raised in Chapter 1, that of construct validity, and the importance of operationalising the constructs underlying one's research. The product-oriented evaluator, no less than other researchers, has to be able to define whatever it is that he or she is trying to measure – for our purposes, language proficiency. However, such a definition needs to be consistent with the goals and objectives of the program. It would be unfair of the evaluator to operationalise language proficiency solely in grammatical terms and appply this to the evaluation of a program designed to develop interactional skills.

The other crucial consideration for an evaluator concerned with learning outcomes relates to the measuring instruments to be used. Here the evaluator must consider whether the instrument is actually measuring what it purports to measure. In Chapter 2, we looked at an investigation by Chaudron and Richards in which listening comprehension was measured through a written cloze test. It has been argued that such an instrument is an inappropriate means of measuring general language proficiency (see, for example, Alderson 1983). In the final analysis, however, the researcher needs to use some sort of instrument or assessment procedure for arbitrating between different programs, and it is a reasonable bet that someone will criticise one's procedures, no matter how carefully they have been constructed.

The relationship between these three issues – defining constructs, relating outcomes to goals, and the appropriateness of the measuring instruments – is summed up by Hudson in the following manner:

> The reason much of the discussion centers around the nature of language
> proficiency is that this directly relates to whether specific language tasks or
> program objectives can be specified for instruction and measured validly. This in
> turn relates to the degree to which a test can be used to determine mastery.
> (Hudson 1989: 261)

In selecting assessment procedures and instruments, the evaluator needs to be fair to the program being evaluated. This issue of 'fairness' can be a major problem when the evaluator is attempting to compare the relative merits of two different programs, as Beretta (1986b) shows. In his article, Beretta addresses the question of how we can get information for comparative purposes about the effects of different language teaching programs. The central problem here is to find a means of measuring student outcomes which is fair to both of the programs being evaluated and does not discriminate against one of the programs. He provides the following example of studies which fail the test of being program-fair:

Asher (1972) and Asher, Kusudo, and de la Torre (1974) investigated the effect of the Total Physical Response (TPR) method compared with a "regular" program. In the 1972 report, one of the stories used in classroom training in the TPR group is presented as an example; it is entitled "Mr Schmidt goes to the office." Later in the report, we are informed that one of the criterion measures used to compare experimental (TPR) and control (regular) groups is a listening test involving a "story entitled 'Mr. Schmidt goes to the office'" (p. 136). In view of this, it is hardly astonishing that the experimental students dramatically outperformed controls (p = .0005). (Beretta 1986b: 432)

There are strategies which the evaluator can adopt to guard against the threat of biasing the evaluation. These include the use of standardised tests, the use of specific tests for each program, the adoption of program-specific plus program-neutral measures, the identification of common and unique objectives, and the appeal to consensus (Beretta 1986b: 434). The most common strategy is to use standardised tests. Because the test items have not been derived from either of the programs under investigation, it is assumed that they will not provide an unfair advantage to one program at the expense of the other. There is evidence, however, that such tests may in fact not be impartial (Valette 1970). The second strategy is to devise specific tests for each program and administer each test to both groups. The problem here is that one can only claim superiority for one of the programs if the subjects are superior not only on their own test, but also on the one specifically designed for the other group. A compromise between these two positions would be to devise a test which contained program-specific plus program-neutral measures. This third strategy was the procedure adopted by Beretta and Davies (1985) in their evaluation of the Bangalore Communicational Teaching Project in India. The fourth strategy suggested by Beretta is to identify the objectives of both programs and from these to generate test items that are common to each program and unique to each. In criticising this approach, Beretta cites some of the objections to the use of behavioural objectives in curriculum development, and points out that the strategy will not be usable if one of the programs is not based on behavioural objectives. The final strategy is to appeal to consensus. Here, the evaluators seek a loose consensus on the construct of language proficiency from both parties, and develop testing instruments based on this.

Beretta's detailed examination of the options available to the product-oriented evaluator, and the shortcomings of each, highlights the dilemma of identifying appropriate assessment instruments when one is concerned with evaluating the relative merits of two different language teaching programs. While admitting to a certain pessimism, he suggests that recent research experience has provided us with some basic rules of thumb.

We know that program evaluation is only as good as the criterion measures used; that standardized tests are inappropriate tools for comparing programs; and that, at the very least, the claims of each specific program must be taken into account in test construction if competing interests are to be represented fairly. Whether we complement these rough-and-ready principles with increasingly elaborate appeals to the arbitration of "neutrality" or "objectives" or some other tribunal remains to be seen. In the meantime, the question of program-fair evaluation invites our further inspection. (Beretta 1986b: 441)

Bachman (1989) claims that the role of measurement in program evaluation has become increasingly unclear in recent years. This is due partly to the increasing attention paid to curriculum processes at the expense of products, partly to the increasing status of qualitative as opposed to quantitative data, and partly to the shortcomings of norm-referenced tests (that is, tests in which an individual's scores are compared with those of other individuals). For Bachman, the solution lies in the adoption of criterion-referenced tests, that is, tests for assessing what learners are able to do, and in which students are assessed, not against other students, but according to their mastery of pre-specified objectives.

While information about what learners can do at the end of a program that they could not do at the beginning is important for product evaluation, it is by no means the end of the story as far as the evaluator is concerned. In terms of internal validity (that is, being able to state confidently that it was the program which made the difference), one needs a control or comparison group. Without such a group, it is impossible to state whether or not the differences observed in the learners were brought about by the program or by factors external to the program. (It could even be argued that the learners may have made even more progress if they had been left alone to pick up the language naturally on the street!)

Unfortunately, it is not always possible for the evaluator to create a situation in which subjects are randomly assigned to experimental and control groups. In fact, it is not always possible for the evaluator to obtain data on what the learners could do before taking part in a program. I have been involved in several evaluations in which the funding authorities commission the evaluation at the conclusion of the program. In such instances, it has been necessary to engage in the comparatively messy and unreliable task of reconstructing information about what the learners were able to do before the program began from students' notebooks, interviews, and other sources. In these instances it was also difficult, although not impossible, to obtain control data for comparative purposes. This underlines the importance of appointing an independent evaluator at the beginning of an innovative program, not at the end. While this exhortation appears consistently in the literature (particularly in the reports of post-hoc evaluations), it is just as consistently ignored.

Program administrators and teachers tend to think in terms of evaluations only when their sources of funding are under threat. In a similar vein, Hargreaves (1989) points out that evaluation is the least well articulated and supported dimension of curriculum projects, that it is less often underrated than simply overlooked. Among the many reasons for this state of affairs is 'the lack of immediacy and urgency in what evaluation is concerned with; it is usually the second volume of the course book or the programme for the next in-service course which are needed by tomorrow, rather than the perhaps inconclusive assessment of the effectiveness of the first volume of the course book or the previous in-service course' (Hargreaves 1989: 35).

Ideally, product-oriented evaluators need more than pre- and post-program assessment data from control and experiment groups (Long 1984). Assessment data will tell us what learners can or cannot do (and, if we are lucky, what the learners can or cannot do as a result of taking part in the program). However, it will not always tell us why objectives have been achieved and why other objectives have not been achieved. In order to make such judgments, the evaluator needs access to information about what went on inside the classrooms themselves. Long (1980) argues this point in an article in which he refers to the classroom as a 'black box'. Particularly when attempting to evaluate and compare two different programs, it is impossible to say what made the difference (if indeed there was a difference) without access to data about what went on within the classroom. One might also want information on a range of other factors and issues which might affect learning, such as institutional facilities, the prevailing intellectual and emotional climate, relationships between administrative and teaching staff, and so on.

The importance of process data in program evaluation

In addition to information on what learners can or cannot do in the target language, it is important to obtain data about learning and teaching processes themselves. Systematic observation is one important means of collecting such data. Non-observable problems such as failure to activate language out of class can be collected through learner diaries and self-reports. Other techniques, which are described and illustrated in some detail in Nunan (1989), include interviews and questionnaires, protocol analysis, transcript analysis, stimulated recall, and seating chart observation records. Ideally, a number of such techniques and instruments should be utilised in order to obtain multiple perspectives on the program under investigation.

The desirability of obtaining data on program outcomes and teaching processes is illustrated in a study reported in Spada (1990). We looked in some detail at this study in Chapter 5 and saw that a qualitative analysis showed that, while one class spent considerably more time on listening than two other classes, the students' listening comprehension did not improve at a commensurate rate. By collecting qualitative classroom data, the researchers were able to relate the measurable differences in the listening comprehension of students to the activities and procedures which the teachers themselves employed. If the researchers had only collected pre- and post-intervention test scores, the measurable differences would have been uninterpretable.

This research demonstrated that there are in fact measurable differences in the way in which instruction is delivered in language programs that have similar ideological underpinnings, and that these differences can be related to learning outcomes. On a methodological level, it indicates that we need qualitative data based on classroom observation if we are to interpret, for the evaluative purposes of making decisions about program alternatives, the quantitative data yielded by assessment instruments of various sorts. If we do not have such qualitative data, then it is difficult, if not impossible, to say what it was about the instruction and interaction in the classroom which made a difference. In the case of no difference being observed, qualitative data also enable the evaluator to say why this should be so.

Points of focus for program evaluation

Thus far, I have argued that evaluation is concerned with determining what learners have learned from a program, and also with making judgments about why instruction has or has not been successful. I have outlined some of the problems in obtaining assessment data, and have argued that in order to interpret such data, one also needs information from a range of other sources inside and outside the classroom. While learning outcomes are of paramount importance, they are not the exclusive, or even the primary, focus of all evaluations. Having determined that Program A is more effective than Program B, one then needs to decide which of the elements within the curriculum is responsible for the outcomes. Any elements can form the focus of an evaluation, particularly limited or focused evaluations, which are concerned with part of the total program picture. The types of evaluative questions one might pose in relation to different curriculum areas are set out in Table 9.1, which has been adapted from Nunan (1988).

The scope of program evaluation, and the range of issues which can provide a point of focus for evaluators, is well illustrated in the studies collected in Alderson and Beretta (1992). For example, Mitchell investigates one particular approach to bilingual education within an elementary school setting. Palmer evaluates a university course for teaching German based on Krashen's (1981, 1982) input hypothesis of language acquisition. Coleman focuses on the shifting goals within an English as a foreign language project in Indonesia. Ross investigates the use of five different methods in the teaching of English as a foreign language in Japan. These and the other studies in the collection show just how broadly evaluators might be required to cast their net.

Within the literature on program evaluation, it is traditional to distinguish between formative and summative evaluation. Formative evaluation takes

TABLE 9.1 SOME KEY QUESTIONS IN PROGRAM EVALUATION

Curriculum area	*Sample questions*
The Planning Process	
Needs analysis	Are the needs analysis procedures effective?
	Do they provide useful information for course planning?
	Do they provide useful data on subjective and objective needs?
	Can the data be translated into content?
Content	Are goals and objectives derived from needs analysis?
	If not, from where are they derived?
	Are the goals and objectives appropriate for the specified groups of learners?
	Do the learners think the content is appropriate?
	Is the content appropriately graded?
	Does the content take speech processing constraints into account?
Implementation	
Methodology	Are the materials, methods, and activities consonant with the prespecified objectives?
	Do the learners think the materials, methods, and activities are appropriate?
Resources	Are resources adequate/appropriate?
Teacher	Are the teacher's classroom management skills adequate?
Learners	Are the learning strategies of the students efficient?
	Do learners attend class regularly?
	Do learners pay attention/apply themselves in class?
	Do learners practise their skills outside the classroom?
	Do learners appear to be enjoying the course?
	Is the timing of the class and the type of learning arrangement suitable for the students?
	Do learners have personal problems which interfere with their learning?
Assessment and evaluation	Are the assessment procedures appropriate to the prespecified objectives?
	Are there opportunities for self-assessment by learners? If so, what?
	Are there opportunities for learners to evaluate aspects of the course such as learning materials, methodology, learning arrangement?
	Are there opportunities for self-evaluation by the teacher?

place during the course of program delivery, and it therefore provides a mechanism for improving the program during the course of its delivery. Summative evaluation, on the other hand, takes place at the end of the program, and is therefore not capable of improving that particular program. Summative evaluations are carried out to provide information for the modification or curtailment of succeeding programs. Both types of evaluation may attempt to provide a comprehensive portrait of the program under study or may choose to adopt a more limited focus. Akst and Hecht (1980: 264–265) identify five key curriculum areas that may form the focus of evaluation. These are as follows:

1. Appropriateness of objective: one may take the position that program objectives are not open to question, since they are presumably the premises on which the rest of the program is based. Occasionally, however, an evaluator may take exception of objectives that appear to be misguided or unrealistic (for example, the objective in a writing program of having foreign students attain the same proficiency level as native speakers).
2. Appropriateness of content to program objectives.
3. Appropriateness of placement procedure: whatever the bases of the placement procedure – high school record, interviews, a battery of tests, or self-selection – the procedure itself should be subject to careful scrutiny. Issues meriting investigation include content and cutoff scores of a test, and reliability of interview ratings, essay scores, and high school grades. Both judgment and empirical research play a role in addressing these concerns.
4. Effectiveness of instruction: the question here is whether students are in fact learning the content and, if so, whether their learning is the result of instruction or extraneous factors.
5. Efficiency of instruction: can the same learning be provided at a smaller investment of time or money? Alternatively, can more learning be obtained for the same investment?

In addition to formative and summative evaluation, Perkins and Angelis (1985) describe norm-referenced, criterion-referenced, and growth-referenced evaluation (although they are using the term *evaluation* in the sense in which I have used *assessment*, that is, measuring student outcomes). Norm-referenced assessment refers to the practice of comparing one individual's test scores with those of other individuals. In criterion-referenced assessment, an individual's performance is compared with some prespecified standard. Growth-referenced assessment was developed by those who are critical of what is seen as the arbitrariness of prespecified standards in criterion-referenced assessment. In growth-referenced assessment, performance data are collected over time, and judgments are made according to whether performance goes up or down. In other words, students are judged not against other students nor against external criteria, but against themselves. Perkins and Angelis point out that while there are comparatively few growth-referenced studies in ESL, 'Given the disarray and disagreement about standard setting in criterion-referenced measurement, it would seem that growth-referenced evaluation is a more viable vehicle for ESL/EFL program evaluation, since growth is the construct around which all instructional programs are anchored' (1985: 86). Whatever the merits of growth-referenced assessment, and these remain to be demonstrated, the evaluator is still confronted with the task of demonstrating that any growth which occurs is a result of the program and not some external factor or factors.

An evaluation model which was influential in the 1970s and 1980s was Stufflebeam's (1971) CIPP model. Stufflebeam identified four types of evaluation – context evaluation, input evaluation, process evaluation, and product evaluation. *Context evaluation* is designed to improve a program by evaluating and critiquing its strengths and weaknesses. *Input evaluation* identifies the resources appropriate for achieving program goals. With *process evaluation,* the focus is on the evaluator providing ongoing feedback during and at the conclusion of a program, so that evaluation data may be fed back into, and thereby assist in the improvement of, the program. Finally, *product evaluation* measures the attainments of the programs. These different types of evaluation are summarised in Table 9.2.

Evaluation and research

A question of central importance to this book is: To what extent can program evaluation be considered a form of research? It could be argued that only evaluations designed in such a way as to provide outcomes that are externally and internally valid and reliable (such as comparative evaluations of different programs) can be considered research. A person holding such a view would probably argue that most evaluations making judgments about a single program are not research because they lack external validity. They do not purport to provide data beyond the research site where the data were collected.

I take a broader view, and have argued throughout this book that any investigation which contains questions, data, and interpretations of the data qualifies as research. I would therefore accept that evaluations, even those of a single program, are, in fact, research. While evaluators who are investigating a single program can usually ignore issues relating to external validity, they still have a responsibility to guard against threats to the internal and external reliability, and also the internal validity of their investigations. Internal validity can be particularly problematic for research conducted in a field setting. According to Airasian, there are eight major threats to the internal validity of field research. These are set out in Table 9.3. (See also the discussion on validity in Chapter 3.)

TABLE 9.2 THE CIPP MODEL FOR PROGRAM EVALUATION

Context evaluation	Input evaluation	Process evaluation	Product evaluation
Objective			
To define the institutional context, to identify the target population and assess their needs, to identify opportunities for addressing the needs, to diagnose problems and to judge if proposed objectives are sufficiently responsive to assessed needs.	To identify and assess system capabilities, alternative program strategies, procedural designs for implementing the strategies, budgets and schedules.	To identify and predict, in process, defects in the procedural design or its implementation; to provide information for preprogrammed decisions, and to record and judge procedural events and activities.	To collect descriptions and judgments of outcomes, and to relate them to objectives and context, input, and process information to interpret their worth and merit.
Method			
By using such methods as system analysis, survey, document review, hearings, interviews, diagnostic tests and the Delphi[a] technique.	By inventorying and analysing available human and material resources, solution strategies and procedural designs for	By monitoring the activity's potential procedural barriers and remaining alert to unanticipated ones, by obtaining specific information for programmed	By defining operationally and measuring outcome criteria, by collecting judgments of outcomes from stakeholders, and by

performing both qualitative and quantitative analyses.

relevance, feasibility, and economy. And by using such methods as literature search, visits to exemplary programs, advocate teams, and pilot trials.

decisions, by describing the actual process and by continually interacting with and observing the activities of project staff.

For deciding to continue, terminate, modify, or refocus a change activity. And to present a clear record of effects (intended and unintended, positive and negative).

Relation to decision making in the change process

For deciding on the setting to be served, the goals associated with meeting needs or using opportunities, and the objectives associated with solving problems, i.e., for planning needed changes. And to provide a basis for judging outcomes.

For selecting sources of support, solution strategies, and procedural designs, i.e., for structuring change activities. And to provide a basis for judging implementation.

For implementing and refining the program design and procedure, i.e., for effecting process control. And to provide a log of the actual process for later use in interpreting outcomes.

---

[a]The Delphi technique is a procedure in which a set of questions or tasks is sent out to experts in the field. The collective responses are then collated and analysed.

Source: Stufflebeam (1971).

TABLE 9.3 THREATS TO THE INTERNAL VALIDITY OF FIELD RESEARCH

Threat	Comment
History	Events external to the program, policy, or practice under investigation which occur between pre- and posttesting
Maturation	Natural biological, psychological, or sociological development of subjects occurring between pre- and posttesting
Instability	Unreliability of measures, which causes fluctuation in scores independent of the program, policy, or practice under investigation
Testing	The effect of taking a test at one point in time upon taking the test at a subsequent point in time
Instrumentation	The effect of changes in the measuring instrument between pre- and posttests so that observed effects are a result of the instrument change and not the program, policy, or practice
Selection	Biases resulting from differences between types of individuals recruited for comparison groups
Mortality	Differential loss of subjects from comparison groups
Statistical regression	The effect of selecting individuals on the basis of their extremely high or extremely low scores on a measuring instrument. Scores at the extreme ends of a distribution are unreliable, and retesting tends to result in either extremely high scorers scoring relatively lower, and hence 'regression' downward in test scores, or extremely low scorers scoring relatively higher, and hence 'regressing' upward in test scores. Unreliability of test scores at extreme ends of the distribution, in and of itself, results in changes in scores upon retesting.

Source: After Airasian (1974: 162–163).

Elements in the design of an evaluation study

In this section, I shall look at some of the practical issues and problems which need to be dealt with when designing an evaluation. The discussion will be organised around the following key questions:

- What is the purpose of the evaluation?
- Who is the audience for the evaluation?
- What principles of procedure should guide the evaluation?
- What tools, techniques, and instruments are appropriate?
- Who should carry out the evaluation?
- When should it be carried out?
- What is the time frame and budget for the evaluation?
- How should the evaluation be reported?

PURPOSE

As with other types of research, it is extremely important to clarify from the beginning the aims and objectives of the evaluation. This is not always easy to achieve and can involve considerable negotiation, particularly when there are numerous interest groups involved. Teachers, administrators, parents, funding authorities, and learners will often have quite different perceptions of the purpose of an evaluation. If these are not dealt with satisfactorily and put in writing before the evaluation begins, then other steps in the evaluation process, such as designing data collection instruments, will be almost impossible to carry out. There is also the danger that, at the end of the evaluation, the outcomes themselves will be unacceptable to one or more of the interest groups.

If the purpose of the evaluation is to provide information for the ongoing improvement of the program, it will be formative in nature. On the other hand, if the purpose is to provide information for accountability, then it is more likely to be summative. Whether it is to be formative, summative, or both, the evaluation needs to be planned for from the beginning of the project.

AUDIENCE

Audience is an important preliminary consideration, and one which is not always given adequate attention. As indicated earlier, different audiences will often perceive different purposes. Funding authorities will want to know whether their money is being spent wisely, and may look to a summative evaluation which measures what learners have or have not achieved as a result of taking part in the program. Teachers, on the other hand, may want a rich, interpretive account of the program which is formative in nature, non-judgmental, and reflective of multiple perspectives and interpretations.

An additional danger, and one which Hudson points out, is that the audience may change during the course of the evaluation, or even at its conclusion: '. . . evaluations will always have audiences, and the original audience seldom remains the sole audience. Peer evaluations made for a teacher trainer have a way of coming to the attention of the program director. An evaluation for the program director has an uncanny way of being quoted later by some funding agency' (Hudson 1989: 259). The fact that an evaluation report may fall into the hands of those for whom it was not initially intended places an additional burden on the researcher.

Hargreaves (1989) also suggests that the evaluator needs to consider whether the target audience is a specialist one, versed in the subject domain, or whether it consists of generalists who will not necessarily be familiar with the key concepts associated with the field or area being evaluated.

197

PRINCIPLES OF PROCEDURE

A major practical impediment to the successful completion of an evaluation may be a disagreement on the part of those closely involved in the evaluation on the scope, nature, purpose, and respective rights of those involved. Each of the key players in an evaluation, be they teachers, learners, administrators, bureaucrats, or the evaluators themselves, will bring their own perspectives, sets of beliefs, and realities to the evaluation. Unless clearly articulated principles of procedure are laid out at the beginning of the evaluation, it is quite possible that these differences of perception may jeopardise the evaluation. One way of preempting this is for the parties involved to negotiate a set of principles of procedure which can be agreed to at the outset of the project, and subsequently drawn upon in cases of disagreement. The following comprehensive set of principles were drawn up to guide the evaluation of a major curricular innovation. They provide a clear statement on the relative rights and responsibilities of the participants in relation to evaluation data as well as outcomes and recommendations.

1. No participant in the project will have privileged access to the data of the evaluation.
2. No participant will have a unilateral right to, or power of veto over, the content of the report.
3. The evaluators will attempt to represent the range of viewpoints encountered in the evaluation.
4. Explicit and implicit recommendations made by the evaluators will not be regarded as prescriptive. As far as possible, recommendations will reflect the views of the participants, not the evaluators.
5. The evaluators will assume that they can approach any individuals involved in the project to collect data. Those approached should feel free to discuss any matter they see fit, and all such discussions will be treated as confidential by the evaluator.
6. The release of specific information likely to identify informants will be subject to negotiations with these informants.
7. The criteria of fairness, relevance and accuracy form the basis for negotiation between the evaluator and participants in the study. Where accounts of the work of participants can be shown to be unfair, irrelevant or inaccurate, the report will be amended. Once draft reports have been negotiated with the participants on the basis of these criteria, they will be regarded as having the endorsement of those involved in the negotiations with regard to fairness, relevance and accuracy.
8. There will be no secret reporting. Reports will be made available first to those whose work they represent.
9. Interviews and meetings will not be considered 'off the record', but those involved will be free, both before and after, to restrict aspects of parts of such exchanges, or to correct or improve their statements.
10. The evaluators are responsible for the confidentiality of the data collected by them.

TABLE 9.4 EVALUATOR'S ROLE, CATEGORIES, AND PROCEDURES

Evaluator's role	Categories	Procedures
Outsider looking in	Existing information	– Records analysis – Systems analysis – Literature review[a] – Letter writing
	Tests	– Proficiency – Placement – Diagnostic – Achievement
	Observations	– Case studies – Diary studies – Behavioral observation – Interactional analyses – Inventories
Facilitator drawing out information	Interviews	– Individual – Group
	Meeting	– Delphi technique[b] – Advisory – Interest group – Review
	Questionnaires	– Biodata surveys – Opinion surveys – Self-ratings – Judgmental ratings – Q sort

[a] A written summary and critique of research relating to a question or issue.
[b] A procedure in which a set of questions or tasks is sent out to experts in the field. The collective responses are then collated and analysed.
Source: Reprinted with permission from Brown (1989: 233).

(L. Bartlett, 1988, 'Proposal for the evaluation of the National Curriculum Project', Adult Migrant Education Program, Australia, unpublished manuscript.)

TECHNIQUES AND INSTRUMENTS

Most of the discussion in earlier sections of this chapter has concerned the place of assessment data in evaluation, although it was made clear that assessment data alone are inadequate for the purposes of program evaluation. In fact, any of the data collection methods dealt with in this book can be used by the evaluator, as can be seen in Table 9.4, which is taken from a practical synthesis of existing possibilities in program evaluation by Brown (1989). It can be seen from the table that the evaluator can either be an outsider or someone who plays the role of a facilitator within the program being evaluated. The table also illustrates the wide range of instruments and techniques which the evaluator can draw on for collecting data.

DATA ANALYSIS

A basic question flowing from the choice of techniques and instruments concerns the types of analyses to be used and whether these are to be statistical, interpretive, or both. Evaluations have the potential to yield huge quantities of data, and decisions need to be made on how the qualitative data resulting from semi-structured interviews and questionnaires are to be reduced to manageable proportions.

TIME FRAME AND BUDGET

Establishing a realistic time frame and budget are important for the successful completion of the project. In those cases where one is competing for outside funding, the success of one's bid will often rest on the time line and budget, and whether these fit in with the time line and budget of the funding body.

In carrying out an evaluation for an external body or agency, there are generally nine essential steps:

1. Become familiar with the project, program, or innovation.
2. Submit an expression of interest.
3. Prepare an evaluation proposal.
   a. identify the objectives
   b. determine the data collection methods
   c. determine the data analysis methods
   d. identify the subjects
   e. formulate a budget
   f. establish a time line
4. Refine the evaluation proposal – consultation and negotiation with the clients.
5. Develop, pilot, and refine the data collection instruments.
6. Identify and negotiate the data collection sites.
7. Analyse the data.
8. Prepare and circulate a draft report.
9. Revise the report and submit a final version.

REPORTING

The reporting process can take much longer than anticipated, particularly if there is disagreement by funding authorities on points of fact, outcomes, or recommendations. It is important for those who commissioned the evaluation to be given a draft of the evaluation report with the opportunity to comment

TABLE 9.5 CENTRAL QUESTIONS IN PROGRAM EVALUATION DESIGN

Element	Questions
Purpose	What is the purpose of the evaluation?
	Is it basically formative or summative in nature?
Audience	What is the audience for the evaluation?
	Are the interests of the different stakeholders compatible or incompatible?
	Does the audience consist of specialists or generalists?
Principles of procedure	What principles of procedure should guide the evaluation?
	How should these be negotiated between those involved in and affected by the evaluation?
Techniques and instruments	What techniques and instruments are to be used?
	Are these appropriate to the aims of the evaluation?
	Do they imply an insider or outsider role for the evaluator?
Data analysis	Will the data analysis be statistical or interpretive?
	Is the data analysis within the scope of the evaluation?
Time frame and budget	Is the budget adequate given the evaluation brief?
	Does the time frame incorporate all the essential steps needed for the evaluation?
	Is the time frame consistent with the budget?
Reporting	How is the evaluation to be reported?
	Does the evaluation plan allow for drafts of the report to be negotiated with those funding the evaluation?

on it before it is released. If the funding authorities are not happy with the report, then there is a danger that the final report may not see the light of day. This negotiation process can greatly extend the evaluation time line.

The points and issues raised in this section are summarised in Table 9.5.

Doing evaluation: a case study

In this section, I shall provide an illustrative summary of an evaluation which was carried out recently within a school district in Australia. The general purpose of the evaluation was to provide information to the educational authorities who had funded an innovative in-service package designed to improve the writing skills of students in a cluster of 'disadvantaged' inner city elementary schools.

TITLE

An evaluation of the Disadvantaged Schools Project Writing Package.

OBJECTIVES OF THE INNOVATION

The objectives of the innovative package were as follows:

1. That students demonstrate improvements in their ability to respond effectively to the writing demands of the curriculum. Specifically, they will be able to perform effectively in written class assignments, make effective notes, do independent research, complete written homework assignments, and participate fully in classroom discussions about writing.
2. That students understand the criteria by which their writing is being assessed and act to meet these criteria in their writing.
3. That the positive impact of the teaching/learning cycle, known as the 'curriculum genre', on students' verbal and reading abilities is demonstrated.
4. That teachers participating in the genre writing package be able to identify examples of the following genres: recount, report, procedure, explanation, exposition, discussion, and narrative.
5. That teachers will be aware of the significant language features of the genres listed in Objective 4.
6. That teachers will be able to apply their knowledge of genre theory to identify the schematic structures and significant language features of genres other than those identified in Objective 4.

PURPOSES OF THE EVALUATION

There were three principal purposes of the evaluation relating to the impact of the innovation on both teachers and learners, and the elements within the package which had and had not proved to be effective. The purposes were summarised as follows:

1. To assess the impact of the writing package on students' writing.
2. To evaluate the impact of the package on teachers'
   a. capability to assess the effectiveness of students' writing
   b. pedagogy
   c. knowledge of the social functions of language.
3. To identify which elements of the package have been most beneficial and which require amendment.

DATA COLLECTION METHODS

Four principal data collection methods were used in the evaluation. These were:

1. A detailed questionnaire completed by teachers involved in the project
2. Focussed interviews with teachers and other key personnel
3. Observation and analysis of lessons

4. Analysis of students' writing samples from schools taking part in the innovation and also from schools not involved in the innovation.

TIME LINE

In the initial brief it was envisaged that the project would take seven months
to complete. The project plan and budget were based on this time line, a summary of which follows. (Note that the project took several months more than
this.)

May	Appoint principal researcher
	Devise questionnaire and distribute to schools
June	Interview consultants and authors of in-service package on goals, nature, and implementation of package
	Conduct literature review (see glossary)
	Identify non-package schools to act as control
	Collect samples of students' writing from package and non-package schools
July	Collate responses to questionnaire and select school for further evaluation
	Conduct structured interviews with teachers, students, and parents
	Record sample lessons and collect written texts relating to these lessons
August	Complete interviews, recordings of sample lessons, and collection of texts
	Begin data analysis and evaluation of students' writing
September	Complete data analysis and evaluation of students' writing
	Begin drafting report
October	Submit draft report
November	Revise report
	Submit final draft

TYPE OF DATA AND ANALYSIS

The evaluation resulted in three types of data – interview protocols, questionnaires, and samples of students' writing. The major analytical tasks confronting the evaluators were the comparative analysis of the 1,500 pieces of
writing, and the collation and analysis of the questionnaire data.

ANALYSING STUDENTS' WRITING

Assessing the quality of written language is a complex matter, and the criteria
by which one carries out such a task will depend on one's beliefs about the
nature and purpose of language. For example, if one believes that the creative
use of language is important, then one will evaluate positively writing which

TABLE 9.6 SCHEMATIC STRUCTURE OF SUCCESSFUL TEXT

Structure	Clauses	Text: 'The Skull and the Skeleton'
	1	One day there was a poor orphan girl
Orientation	2	She had to work with her stepmother
	3	Her hands were going to skin and bones
	4	So she decided to run away
	5	She saw a castle
	6	So she knocked on the door tap tap tap
	7	A skull with no body opened the door
	8	and he said "yes"
Complication	9	The girl told the skull [what had happened to her][a]
	10	She stepped into his castle
	11	She saw a body without a skull
	12	She knew that it belonged to the skull
	13	And the skull told the girl [what had happened][a]
	14	The they [sic] had dinner
	15	She stayed two night [sic]
Resolution	16	and she kissed the skull
	17	They got married
	18	They lived happily after

[a] The words in brackets were actually written by the student.

exhibits characteristics such as figurative and metaphorical images, the use of fantasy, and so on. In the present instance, the evaluators selected criteria which were consistent with the linguistic model underlying the writing package. In this model, the essence of successful writing lies essentially in the overall structure of a text, its development and cohesion, and whether or not it is written in language appropriate for its intended purpose and audience. The criteria not only had to reflect this view of 'good writing', but it had to be practically applicable within the limitations of time imposed by this evaluation (Walshe et al. 1990: 18).

Following the model, three criteria were selected for analysing the data:

1. Is the schematic structure appropriate for the genre of the text? (In the model, it is argued that texts written for different purposes will exhibit different patterns of overall organisation and text structure.)
2. Does the writer explicitly identify the topic, and was the topic developed appropriately? (If the writer fails to develop the text topic or switches from one topic to another, then the text is confusing and difficult to follow.)
3. Does the writer use reference appropriately? (Appropriate use of reference is an indicator of text cohesion and an indicator that the writer has a sense of the 'decontextualised' nature of writing in comparison to speaking.)

TABLE 9.7 SCHEMATIC STRUCTURE OF UNSUCCESSFUL TEXT

Structure	Clauses	Text: 'Aboriginal Skeletons and Skulls'
Thesis (statement)	1	All around the world the museums do need some skeletons and skulls
Argument 1 (statement)	2	Well the Aboriginals gave them some of their grandparents to put in the museum's
Argument 2 (recount)	3	Well Loir Richards is an Aboriginal
	4	and she said that some people say that Aboriginals have not got any feelings
Conclusion	5	The skeletons and skulls should go back
	6	where they come from and remain
Argument 3	7	You would not like it
	8	if they took your grandparents skeletons and skulls

The sample texts set out in Tables 9.6 and 9.7 illustrate the way in which these criteria were applied to an analysis of the texts. The successful text is a narrative, the schematic structure of which is as follows:

- orientation (the context for the story is provided and the major participants are introduced)
- complication (the problem or point of the story is presented)
- resolution (the problem is resolved)
- evaluation (the writer comments on the narrative)

Commentary on text:

[This text] like many other narratives collected for this analysis contains no evaluation and reveals that this young writer, like many others, lacks full control of the narrative genre. However, for the purpose of this evaluation of young children's writing the essential stages of the narrative have been taken to be orientation, complication and resolution, and hence is assessed as satisfying criterion 1. The topic of [the text] is developed in the sense that the adventures of the 'poor orphan girl' are related to the meeting of the 'skull' and subsequent finding of its disengaged body. While the logical sequence of some events in the narrative such as the skull telling 'what had happened' and 'having dinner' are not especially clear, there is enough information about the skull and skeleton for the reader to follow both the sequencing of events and the connection between complication and resolution. Hence the text is considered successful in terms of criterion 2. Reference is used appropriately in the text. The major participants are explicitly introduced: 'a poor orphan girl', 'a skull with no body' and thereafter referred to appropriately; 'she', 'the girl', 'he', 'the skull'. Thus it is clear at all times who or what is being referred to in the text. (Walshe et al. 1990: 20)

The unsuccessful text was produced after the writer had viewed an educational program on Aboriginal remains. The writer's task was to argue the question of whether or not these remains should be preserved in museums or whether they ought to be returned to Aboriginal people for burial. The text is an exposition and has the following schematic structure:

- thesis (the argument is introduced)
- arguments (the thesis is supported)
- reiteration of thesis

Commentary on text:

. . . the structure of Text 2 can be summarised as follows: a general statement, which could be generously interpreted as a thesis, followed by a second statement, rather than an argument. Next is a short recount rather than a second argument. . . . [This is] followed by the writer's conclusion regarding this topic and then there is a follow up argument. It is the conclusion that gives the clearest indication that the writer intended the text to be an Exposition. Other stages in the text are not those of a successful Exposition. . . . Development of topic in Text 2 is unsatisfactory. While the text is loosely cohesive around the topic of museums and skulls and skeletons, there are problems in that none of the arguments follow logically from one to another. . . . There are also minor problems with referencing. The opening statement refers to 'the museums'. Such reference is unclear as the reader is not informed which museums are being referred to. . . . Thus Text 2 is assessed as unsatisfactory on all three criteria. (Walshe et al. 1990: 21)

ANALYSING QUESTIONNAIRE DATA

The questionnaire contained thirty questions, twelve of which were closed, and eighteen of which were open ended. The open-ended questions yielded a great deal of qualitative data, and the researchers were confronted with the problem of quantifying these in a way which enabled patterns to emerge. They did this by constructing a series of analytical categories from the statements themselves. For example, the questionnaire probe which instructed teachers to 'state three beliefs you have about language development that determine the way you teach' resulted in several hundred statements. On analysis, it appeared that these related to one of three broad concepts – language/learning, the environment/climate, or the learner. These major categories were further subdivided, and the statements were assigned to the appropriate category. (The results of this analysis can be found in Chapter 7, where we looked at ways of quantifying qualitative data.)

One of the problems confronting the evaluators concerned the interpretation by teachers of the model underlying the package. They attempted to gain insights into teachers' belief systems indirectly, by posing questions such as the following:

Question 14
Assume the following scenario.
Your school participated in the Writing Package in 1990. It will enter a second

TABLE 9.8 TEACHERS' ADVICE TO COLLEAGUES ON PACKAGE: ANALYTICAL
CATEGORIES

Category of teacher advice	N
Reference to genre/model/factual writing	61
Reference to handbook/package/video/support material	44
Reference to consultants	21
No comment	19
Reference to practical nature of package/definite procedures	18
Too early to comment	16
Reference to positive reaction of children	15
Reference to purposeful nature of writing	12
Reference to complexity/difficulty of model/package/need to persevere	11
Reference to shortcomings of process writing/previous approaches	9
Reference to spoken/written language relationship/contrast	6
Reference to specific practices, e.g., joint construction	7
Empowering nature of package	7
Language across the curriculum	7
Reference to beneficial effect on writing	3
Total	256

stage of participation in 1991. A new teacher previously not involved will start at
your school in 1991. Write some brief notes to him/her in which you describe the
content of the package and in which you describe your reaction to the content.

Once again, this strategy resulted in a great deal of qualitative data which
had to be quantified in some way. In this particular case, the discursive notes
made by the teachers were scanned for key terms which were used to create
analytical categories. Statements were then assigned to the relevant categories. The result of this analysis is set out in Table 9.8.

OUTCOMES

The evaluators came to the following conclusions:

1. The innovation had an overall positive response from participating teachers, with teachers giving an overwhelmingly positive response to the writing package.
2. The innovation had a beneficial impact on students' writing. A compari-
   tive analysis of texts from package and non-package schools indicated
   that, in terms of the evaluation criteria identified by the researchers, students in package schools produced a greater range of factual texts, and
   produced them more successfully.
3. Teachers' classroom practices changed as a result of participation in the

innovation. Although teachers incorporated ideas from the package into their teaching, they adapted these significantly to suit their needs.

4. The objectives of the innovation were largely met.
5. The model of in-service upon which the innovation is based has a number of distinctive features which contributed to its effectiveness. These include the balance of theory and practice, the demonstration lessons, and the cyclical nature of the input.

CRITIQUE

The major structural shortcoming of the study stemmed from the fact that the evaluation was not commissioned until the innovation had concluded. This made it impossible to collect pre- and post-innovation writing samples and teacher comments from package and non-package schools. Despite the fact that the literature on evaluation is replete with exhortations to program innovators to build an evaluation component into their projects, this seems to be relatively infrequent. The lack of pre-intervention writing texts calls into question the internal validity of this study.

Despite the care with which the analytical categories were constructed for the analysis of the free-form comments from teachers, there is always the possibility that the categories and constructs are artifacts, and either misrepresent or distort in some way the original data. The researchers attempted to minimise this threat by the involvement in the analysis of all four members of the evaluation team.

There is a question as to the external validity of the study, since we do not know the extent to which the results can be applied beyond the groups investigated. The evaluation was focused on elementary students in a number of urban schools which had been designated as 'disadvantaged' by government fiat. To what extent the innovation would be appropriate for pupils in schools not designated as 'disadvantaged' or to other levels in the system, such as secondary students, must remain doubtful.

Notwithstanding the shortcomings in the design and execution of this evaluation, it represents a carefully conducted piece of research. The researchers piloted their procedures and instruments, including the questionnaire, and they collected data from multiple sources. Most important of all, they were guided throughout the evaluation by the theoretical model on which the innovation was based.

Conclusion

Program evaluation is an enormous subject, and many volumes have been written about the conceptual and practical aspects of doing evaluation. In this chapter, I have tried to give some indication of the scope of program evaluation from the perspective of research. I have justified the inclusion of this chapter in a book such as this on the grounds that program evaluations count as research, since they contain questions, data, and interpretive analysis. While such a claim may be said by some to stretch the definition of research to the breaking point, I believe that it is justified.

The chapter reviews recent writing on evaluation in language education. I have dealt with the scope of evaluation from the perspective of the language curriculum developer, and highlighted some of the practical problems associated with the collection, collation, and analysis of evaluation data. In the process, I have shown how any element within the curriculum may be evaluated. Processes of program evaluation are illustrated with an extended example from a recent study into an innovative program in a second language context.

Program evaluations are particularly suitable as training vehicles for graduate students. They present a ready-made area for investigation, the scope of the evaluation can be tailored to the time and resources available to the student, and there are numerous models and procedures available in the published literature for collecting and analysing data.

Questions and tasks

1. An increasingly popular means of assessing achievement is the proficiency rating scale. The following is the generic description of foreign language speaking proficiency at high intermediate level. It is taken from the American Council on the Teaching of Foreign Languages Provisional Proficiency Guidelines.

Able to satisfy most survival needs and limited social demands.
Shows some spontaneity in language production but fluency is very uneven.
Can initiate and sustain a general conversation but has little understanding of the
   social conventions of conversation.
Developing flexibility in a range of circumstances beyond immediate survival needs.
Limited vocabulary range necessitates much hesitation and circumlocution.
The commoner tense forms occur but are infrequent in formation and selection.
Can use most question forms.
While some word order is established, errors still occur in more complex patterns.
Cannot sustain coherent structures in longer utterances or unfamiliar situations.
Ability to describe and give precise information is limited.
Aware of basic cohesive features such as pronouns and verb inflections, but many
   are unreliable, especially if less immediate in reference.
Extended discourse is largely a series of short, discrete utterances.
Articulation is comprehensible to native speakers used to dealing with foreigners,
   and can combine most phonemes with reasonable comprehensibility, but still has
   difficulty in producing certain sounds in certain positions, or in certain
   combinations, and speech will usually be labored.

209

Still has to repeat utterances frequently to be understood by the general public. Able to produce some narration in either past or future.

(cited in Freed 1984: 228–229)

a. How might such a scale be used as part of an evaluation?
b. What do you see as the problems of using such a scale?
c. What additional/alternative data would you collect?

2. Prepare an evaluation brief for a curriculum innovation with which you are familiar. Include the following information:

- Brief description of innovation
- Evaluation questions
- Type of data
- Type of analysis
- Time line and budget
- Anticipated problems
- Possible solutions to problems

Further reading

As I have already indicated, there is a great deal of material available within the educational literature on program evaluation. For the language teacher, the best place to begin is with the papers on evaluation published in Johnson's (1989) collection on second language curriculum development, and then to read the studies in the collection edited by Alderson and Beretta (1992). Practical guidelines for the evaluation of language education are provided in Alderson (1992). The papers by Beretta (1986a, b) are also important contributions to the field. For an excellent case study of an educational innovation, see the evaluation of the Bangalore Project by Beretta and Davies (1985).

10 Doing research

Wise folk may or may not form expectations about what the future holds in store
but the foolish can be relied upon to predict with complete confidence that certain
things will come about in the future or that others will not.

(Medawar 1984)

In this final chapter, I shall outline some of the practical procedures to be followed in planning, carrying out, and evaluating a research project. While the
size and complexity of projects will vary, from relatively modest, action-oriented studies carried out by classroom teachers and others involved in professional practice through to major investigations by university based
researchers, all research, I believe, can benefit from the considerations contained in this chapter. The following questions are dealt with:

- How do I go about developing a research question?
- What is a literature review, and how do I carry out one?
- What should a research report contain?
- What are some of the practical problems associated with carrying out
  research, and how might these be dealt with?

Developing a research question

A minimum requirement for an activity to be considered research is that it
contain three components:

1. a question
2. data
3. analysis and interpretation.

The first component, and the key to the others, is the formulation of a question. It is this initial step which often causes researchers, particularly those
who are new to the research process, the most trouble. It is worth spending
as much time as is necessary to get the question right, and in this section, we
shall look at some of the considerations which will facilitate this process.

Before formulating a question, one needs to determine the general topic
area one is interested in. The general area itself can emerge from one's own
particular interests, from one's experience in the field, from reading widely,
or from a combination of these. Table 10.1 sets out some of the areas which

TABLE 10.1 RESEARCH AREAS AND TOPICS IDENTIFIED BY A GROUP OF
POSTGRADUATE STUDENTS AT MACQUARIE UNIVERSITY

Area	*Topic*
Pedagogy	– Teaching Korean in secondary schools: motivation and learning experiences
	– Differences in the discourse of Japanese as a second language learners in the playground and the classroom
	– The relationship between spoken and written language
	– Teaching writing for academic purposes
	– The written discourse of specialised subjects in the university context
	– Using the genre approach to teach academic writing
	– Teacher feedback in the adult ESL classroom
	– SLA in tutored environments
	– The role of cultural background in reading comprehension
Teacher education	– Team teaching: ESL and the mainstream
	– A program for community school teachers in Papua New Guinea
	– Professional development and program management
	– Supervisory feedback in the TESOL practicum
Sociocultural concerns	– Language use in social context in Japan
	– Language and culture in Western Kenya
	– Bilingual medical consultations
	– Language choice and cultural identity
	– Standard versus dialect preferences by Thai speakers in Northeastern Thailand
Learning strategies	– Learner independence and the self-access centre
	– Second language strategy preferences of secondary learners
Testing and assessment	– Testing speaking proficiency
	– The predictive validity of the IELTS[a] test
	– Assessing the language proficiency of school-age children
Language disability	– Developing bilingual/bicultural awareness in primary-age deaf students
	– The abuse of children with language disability
	– Phonological and grammatical performance of students with mild to moderate sensorineural hearing loss
	– Social interaction of hearing impaired and hearing children

[a]IELTS is the International English Language Testing Service.

a group of my postgraduate students identified. It shows the wide range of interests that can emerge from a single group of students, all of whom are doing the same course.

Hatch and Lazaraton (1991) make the excellent practical suggestion that graduate students and others who are interested in doing research should keep a research journal. Such a journal can be an invaluable resource when it comes to defining what interests you and in identifying a research area. They suggest:

Each time you think of a question for which there seems to be no ready answer, write the question down. Someone may write or talk about something that is fascinating, and you wonder if the same results would obtain with your students, or with bilingual children, or with a different genre of text. Write this in your journal. Perhaps you take notes as you read articles, observe classes, or listen to lectures. Place a star or other symbol at places where you have questions. These ideas will then be easy to find and transfer to the journal. Of course, not all of these ideas will evolve into research topics. Like a writer's notebook, these bits and pieces of research ideas will reformulate themselves almost like magic. Ways to redefine, elaborate or reorganize the questions will occur as you reread the entries. (Hatch and Lazaraton 1991: 11–12)

Having identified a general area, and a topic within that area, one begins the task of formulating a question. Not all questions are researchable. For example, the question 'Should values clarification be taught in primary school?' cannot be settled empirically. Of course we could conduct a survey of interested community members to find out what they think, but this would not provide us with an answer to the question – it would answer a rather different one, namely, 'What are community attitudes towards the teaching of values clarification in primary schools?'

In research, in order to obtain reasonable answers, we need to ask the right sort of questions. The questions need to be:

1. worth asking in the first place
2. capable of being answered.

There are many questions or issues which are eminently capable of being researched, but which may not be worth asking. For example, it would be technically feasible to determine the number of Spanish interpreters who wear designer jeans, or the relationship between the wearing of rubber thongs and academic achievement. However, it is highly dubious whether these questions are worth asking. Unfortunately, often the questions which are easiest to answer are not worth asking.

On the other hand, there are many questions worth asking which cannot, in any practical sense, be answered. So in formulating a research question we need to strike a balance between the value of the question and our ability to develop a research proposal we are capable of carrying out.

213

Research questions can come from many different places. Usually they result from our reading around in an area that is of interest to us. If we are lucky, we may find a piece of published research which we can either take one step further or apply to a different context. For example, we may come across a study demonstrating that background cultural knowledge has a significant effect on reading comprehension. This may prompt us to ask, 'What is the effect of background knowledge on listening comprehension?' Or, we may come across research which shows that the order in which German morphosyntax is acquired is relatively fixed, impervious to instruction, and determined by speech processing constraints. This may prompt us to ask whether the same constraints exist for English.

Having identified a general area, such as listening comprehension, or morphosyntactic development, we need to refine our question so that it is worthwhile and doable. We may start out with a worthwhile question such as: 'Is there an impermeable order of morphosyntactic acquisition for English, which can be accounted for in terms of speech processing constraints?' Such a question, however, could occupy a team of postdoctoral researchers for several years.

Recognising the breadth of the issue, we may decide to chip away at a small piece of the puzzle. After thinking and reading around the area, we may decide that we will restrict our attention to the acquisition of question forms. Our new question might read: 'What is the order of acquisition of question forms in English? Can this order of acquisition be accounted for in terms of speech processing constraints?'

At this point there are two things to note. In the first place, the question has been derived from the literature, and in the second place, it is theoretically motivated. In other words, it is underpinned by a theory of language acquisition, which is itself based on a broader cognitivist view of learning.

Our next step is to begin thinking about the data we might collect to explore our questions. In order to do this, we need to develop a research proposal. The proposal needs to take into consideration the issues of validity and reliability. Will we collect our data in a laboratory setting, thus guarding against threats to internal validity but possibly weakening our ability to generalise the results, or will we collect the data in the field? In coming to our decision, we might consider Beretta's (1986a) comments on the tension created when we try to deal with threats to the internal and external validity of our research. (You will recall Beretta's assertion, reported in Chapter 1, that strengthening internal validity by collecting our data through some sort of controlled experiment may lead to a situation in which outcomes can not be generalised to non-experimental contexts.)

In addition to internal/external reliability/validity, we need to operationalise the constructs we are working with. In other words, we need to describe their characteristics in a way which would enable an outsider to identify them if they came across them. If researchers fail to provide 'up front' definitions, then we need to read between the lines. For example, if a study investigates 'listening comprehension', and the dependent variable is a written cloze test, then the default definition of 'listening comprehension' is 'the ability to complete a written cloze passage'. If we were to find such a definition unacceptable, we would be questioning the *construct validity* of the study. Construct validity has to do with the question: Is the study actually investigating what it is supposed to be investigating?

In developing a research problem or question, Wiersma (1986) suggests that the problem be broadly stated in the first instance and then progressively refined and restricted through a review of the literature. He provides the following examples of how an initial broad area can be reformulated, either as a problem statement or question.

Original	Achievement and teaching techniques
Restatement	A study of the effects of three teaching techniques on science achievement of junior high school students
Question	Do three different teaching techniques have differing effects on science achievement scores of junior high school students?

Original	Bilingual education
Restatement	A study of the nature and characteristics of bilingual education in the elementary schools of City A
Question	What are the nature and characteristics of bilingual education as it is implemented in the elementary schools of City A?

Original	The role of the guidance counselor
Restatement	A survey of the practices of the guidance counselors in the high schools of City B
Questions	What proportion of guidance counselors' working day is taken up with nonguidance activities?
	What are the major strengths of guidance counselors' practices as perceived by the students?
	What are the major weaknesses of guidance counselors' practices as perceived by the students?
	What practices are perceived by guidance counselors as most effective in advising students about college selection?

(Wiersma 1986: 31–32)

Seliger and Shohamy (1989) suggest that the preparatory stage of any research project should consist of four phases:

Phase 1: Formulating the general question (this may emerge from the experience and interests of the researcher, other research in language, or sources outside second language acquisition)

Phase 2: Focusing the question (here the researcher decides on the importance and feasibility of the question)

General area:
Research question(s):
Key constructs:
Justification:
Subjects:
Procedure and methods:
Type of data:
Type of analysis:
Outcome(s):
Anticipated problems:
Possible solutions:
Resources required:

Figure 10.1   A research outline to guide in the development of a research project

Phase 3: Deciding on an objective
Phase 4: Formulating the research plan or objective.

I have found that the creation of a research outline at the beginning of the project can greatly facilitate the planning process. The outline in Figure 10.1 is one used by my graduate students, who add a short statement under each heading as they develop and refine their project.

The literature review

An essential step in any research project is the literature review. The function of the literature review is to provide background information on the research question, and to identify what others have said and/or discovered about the question. It may well be that in the course of carrying out the literature review, you come across a study which answers the very question you are proposing to investigate. The literature review, if carried out systematically, will acquaint you with previous work in the field, and should also alert you to problems and potential pitfalls in the chosen area.

A good way to begin a literature review is to prepare an annotated bibliography. As the name suggests, an annotated bibliography contains a list of relevant studies relating to the research question or issue. These may range from brief research reports to books. Each entry contains a summary or abstract of the particular work. The following sample extract from a commercially published literature review provides some idea of the length and detail of the annotations.

Kennedy, C. 1987. Innovation for a change: teacher development and innovation. *ELT Journal, 41,* 3: 163–170.

Author describes a university level ESP project in Tunisia where the aim was to further teacher education. Teachers were involved with materials production. They were required to produce a materials blueprint taking into consideration questions of approach and design, which make them aware of gaps in their theoretical knowledge about language and learning. Kennedy believes that this approach, i.e. creating a situation which generates a demand for theory arising from a questioning of practice, is the best way to influence deep seated value and belief systems and thus to have a lasting effect on teacher behaviour.

(Dallas 1990)

Abstracts such as these can be either kept on index cards or entered into a word processing or computer database to be drawn upon in the creation of a literature review. A literature review differs from an annotated bibliography in that the researcher extracts and syntheses the main points, issues, findings, and research methods which emerge from a critical review of the readings. Merriam (1988) suggests that, in carrying out a literature review, it is a good idea to differentiate between data-based research and non–data-based writings. As the name suggests, data-based literature is based on empirical information collected by the researcher. Non–data-based writings, on the other hand, 'reflect the writer's experiences or opinions and can range from the highly theoretical to popular testimonials' (Merriam 1988: 61).

Wiersma (1986) provides the following practical advice for carrying out a literature review:

1. Select studies that relate most directly to the problem at hand.
2. Tie together the results of the studies so that their relevance is clear. Do not simply provide a compendium of seemingly unrelated references in paragraph form.
3. When conflicting findings are reported across studies – and this is quite common in educational research – carefully examine the variations in the findings and possible explanations for them. Ignoring variation and simply averaging effects loses information and fails to recognize the complexity of the problem.
4. Make the case that the research area reviewed is incomplete or requires extension. This establishes the need for research in this area. (Note: This does not make the case that the proposed research is going to meet the need or is of significance.)
5. Although information from the literature must be properly referenced, do not make the review a series of quotations.
6. The review should be organized according to the major points relevant to the problem. Do not force the review into a chronological organization, for example, which may confuse the relevance and continuity among the studies reviewed.
7. Give the reader some indication of the relative importance of results from studies reviewed. Some results have more bearing on the problem than others, and this should be indicated.
8. Provide closure for the section. Do not terminate with comments from the final

study reviewed. Provide a summary and pull together the most important points.

(pp. 376–377)

Numerous resources exist to facilitate the literature review process, and most of these can be found in university and college libraries. If one has only a vague idea of the general area one wishes to investigate, it is a good idea to consult an educational encyclopedia to obtain a general overview of the area in question. The library subject catalogue can also provide information on relevant books and periodicals. In order to obtain references to journals it is best to start with a periodical index such as ERIC *(Educational Resources Information Centre)* or the *Reader's Guide to Periodical Literature.* The *ERIC Thesaurus* provides descriptors of concepts. Subject indexes such as the *Current Index to Journals in Education* (CIJE) and *Resources in Education* (RIE) will give you lists of resources. Finally, there are the specialised abstracting journals such as *Language Teaching,* which provide summaries of recently published journal articles.

Implementing the research project

Most of this book has been devoted to an analysis of different methods of collecting and analysing data, and in this section, I should like to summarise some of the main points which have been made in greater detail in the body of the book.

In Chapter 1, we looked at different traditions in research, and I contrasted psychometric with interpretive research. While the distinction between these traditions is, in many ways, oversimplistic, I argued that the distinction was a real one, and that different conceptions of reality and the nature of evidence underlay the different traditions. I also took pains to point out that, despite the impression which is sometimes conveyed by proponents of the different approaches, there is no intrinsic superiority in one rather than the other. In selecting a general orientation, it is important to match one's data collection methods and methods of analysis to the question one is asking. Some questions, particularly those positing a strong causal relationship between variables, suggest some form of experimental research design and the use of statistical tools to analyse the data and make inferences from one's sample to the larger population. Other questions, particularly those concerned with investigating behaviour in context, suggest descriptive and interpretive research.

In addition to ensuring consistency, and to ensure that the data collection and analysis are going to answer your question(s) (and not some other question), there are several other key considerations to be borne in mind during the data collection and analysis phases of the research. In particular, one needs to ensure that adequate care has been taken over the constructs under-

218

lying the research and the way in which these have been operationalised. You will recall that this involved defining the constructs and developing operational measures of the constructs which are accessible to the outside observer. It is also important, not only during the planning but also during the implementation phases of the project, to be aware of possible threats to the validity and reliability of the research, and ways in which these threats might be dealt with.

In moving from a general consideration of the research process to the practicalities of planning and implementing a research project, it is a good idea to try and anticipate the practical problems likely to be encountered, and some of the potential solutions to the problems. Problems encountered by graduate students, teachers, and others carrying out action-based research include the following:

1. Lack of time (this is a particular problem for those who are working full-time)
2. Lack of expertise, particularly with critical phases of the research, such as formulating the research question and determining the appropriate research design and statistical tools
3. Difficulty in identifying subjects
4. Problems in negotiating access to research sites
5. Issues of confidentiality
6. Ethical questions relating to collecting data (these arise when one wants to collect oral language without alerting subjects to the fact that they are being observed – recall Labov's 'observer's paradox')
7. Problems flowing from the growth of the project after initiation
8. Sensitivity of reporting negative findings, particularly if these relate to worksites of individuals with whom one is associated
9. Preparation of a written report of the research.

Lack of time is, without doubt, the most frequently reported problem from researchers. Walker (1985), writing in the context of collaborative, action-based research in educational settings, suggests the following strategies for the time constraint.

adapt standard methods
be flexible
convince authority of need for more resources
clarification of task in small group/team discussion before whole staff work
    together
check on present use of time
timetable for research and support activities
try to delegate some of your responsibilities
use resources of students, university, college, etc.
a proper meeting calendar
use parents

term in which research undertaken – autumn most favourable

management team undertaken structured servicing of research, implementing action etc.

close school early on one day a term

second staff

release staff using INSET (in-service education and training) money

be judicious in collecting data

seek co-operation of colleagues

team teaching

don't transcribe everything

reappraisal of professional priorities

(p. 193)

An insightful and eloquent testimonial to the practical and conceptual difficulties of doing research is provided by Dingwall (1984). She contrasts the messiness of the research process with the 'hygienic' appearance of the research as it actually appears in written reports and accounts.

It may be too strong to suggest that there is a 'conspiracy of silence' among academics about the problems, the possibilities, the limitations, and the pressures of research practice; but certainly for most graduate researchers working in comparative isolation, it is painful to discover the extent of compromise and ambiguity inherent in their work. (1984: 1)

Bogdan and Biklen (1982: 147–154, cited in Merriam 1988), although working within a more general research field, provide nine practical suggestions for facilitating the research process which are applicable to language research and can help to obviate some of the pitfalls of doing research. These are set out in Table 10.2.

In a recent survey, a group of graduate students of applied linguistics at Macquarie University were asked to nominate the problems they had encountered in the course of carrying out their research, and the solutions they had found to these problems. The results of this survey, which are set out in Table 10.3, illustrate the typical concerns of graduate-level investigations.

Presenting the research

There are many ways of presenting research. The traditional way is in the form of paper presentations at conferences and, in written mode, as theses, journal articles, or monographs. In the case of research carried out as part of a formal tertiary award, there is a requirement that the research be presented in writing. I have found that many students have a great deal of difficulty when it comes to writing up their research. The process itself is greatly facilitated if one has a clear idea of the audience for whom one is writing. In some

TABLE 10.2 IDENTIFYING AND REFINING A RESEARCH AREA

Area	Strategy
1. Research focus	You must discipline yourself not to pursue everything . . . or else you are likely to wind up with data too diffuse and inappropriate for what you want to do.
2. Type of study	You should try to make clear in your own mind . . . whether you want to do a full description of a setting or whether you are interested in generating theory about a particular aspect of it.
3. Developing questions	Some researchers bring general questions to a study. These are important because they give focus to data collection and help organize it as you proceed. . . . We suggest that shortly after you enter the field, you assess which questions you brought with you are relevant and which ones should be reformulated to direct your work.
4. Ongoing data collection	In light of what you find when you periodically review your fieldnotes, plan to pursue specific leads in your next data collection session.
5. Observer's comments	Write observer's comments as you go to stimulate critical thinking about what you see and to become more than a 'recording machine'.
6. Memos	Write memos to yourself about what you are learning which can provide a time to reflect on issues raised in the setting and how they relate to large theoretical, methodological, and substantive issues.
7. Feedback	Try out ideas and themes on subjects. While not everyone should be asked, and while not all you hear may be helpful, key informants, under the appropriate circumstances, can help advance your analysis, especially to fill in the holes of description.
8. Explanation	Experiment with metaphors, analogies, and concepts. Nearsightedness plagues most research . . . Ask the question, 'What does this remind me of?' Another way to expand analytic horizons is to try to raise concrete relations and happenings observed in a particular setting to a higher level of abstraction.

Source: Adapted from Bogdan and Biklen (1982: 147–154).

TABLE 10.3 PROBLEMS ENCOUNTERED AND SOLUTIONS FOUND BY GRADUATE
STUDENTS IN CONDUCTING RESEARCH

Research area	Problems encountered	Solutions
Identifying a research area	– Narrowing the area sufficiently – Identifying an area in which I can get help – Ensuring adequate subjects for area selected – Having several competing areas – Coming from a non-teaching background – Constraints imposed by sponsor – Identifying an area that is practical – Matching needs with interests – Being pulled between different interests	– Get advice from supervisor – Get advice from former students – Do extensive reading – Spend time in field – Talk to practitioners
Developing a question	– Refining question so it is doable – Formulating operational questions – Identifying which competing question to do – Being too ambitious – Avoiding vagueness – Deciding if one question is sufficient	– Get advice from supervisor – Study existing research – Go to outside agencies – Rank order questions – Make preliminary data analysis – Match questions and interests
Conducting a literature review	– Finding inaccessible articles and reports – Identifying the steps involved/ how to do it – Lack of literature in chosen area – Having too much literature in chosen area – Lack of non-English literature – Being unfamiliar with library – Lack of time – Knowing what to exclude/ include – Covering the cost of photocopying – Finding relevant studies	– Use library reader services – Get help from supervisor – Find specialist library – Learn to use ERIC – Use interlibrary loan – Use vacation time to do review – Access other literature reviews
Determining data collection methods	– Lack of time – Lack of expertise in questionnaire design – Matching method to question	– Get help from supervisor – Get help from practitioners – Replicate published study

TABLE 10.3 *(cont.)*

Research area	Problems encountered	Solutions
	– Deciding whether to use ethnography or experiment – Ensuring reliability and validity – Finding enough appropriate subjects – Negotiating release of data – Collecting data before doing research methods course – Determining own role within research site – Choosing between multiple types of relevant data – Lack of confidence over statistics – Dealing with the unexpected – Managing data that keep changing	– Consult statistician
Analysing data	– Identifying equipment – Doing statistical analysis – Making reliable and valid interpretation – Drawing conclusions from data – Collecting too much data – Determining whether to quantify qualitative data – Lack of time – Being objective – 'Seeing' what is there – Lack of confidence	– Apply for a grant – Have supervisor code part of data – Learn to use computer
Drawing conclusions	– Identifying population to which findings apply – Coming to definite conclusions – Interpreting statistical data – Knowing how far to go – Being relevant – Overgeneralising from data	– Don't draw definite conclusions – Get help from supervisor – Take care not to generalise
Writing up research	– Determining appropriate structure – Lack of time – Being unable to type – Covering the cost of binding	– Study other dissertations – Take annual leave – Find book on how to write research report – Consult supervisor

(continued)

TABLE 10.3 *(cont.)*

Research area	Problems encountered	Solutions
	– Meeting requirements of thesis writing – Knowing where to start – Making report logical and relevant – Identifying overall layout – Finding style appropriate to both linguistics and sociolinguistics – Being concise – Being a non-native speaker	– Do a small amount at a time – Have fellow students check draft

cases there may be more than one audience – for example, one's supervisor and one's colleagues/peers – in which case more than one version of a report may be called for.

The writing process can also be greatly facilitated if one works out a structure for the report before beginning. Figure 10.2 illustrates the structure of one comprehensive research report. It can be seen that the report falls naturally into several sections. It begins with an introduction, purpose, and rationale, including an indication of the limitations and delimitations of the research. This is followed by several chapters summarising the literature review. The study itself is then described, and the results are presented and discussed. The report concludes with a discussion of the theoretical and practical implications of the research.

While research reports will vary, I have included Figure 10.2 as a model because it contains all of the essential elements of a good report. While it has been taken from a psychometric investigation, it can also be used for interpretive research. Once one has identified one's research area, identified the research question, and begun the literature review, it is a good idea to create a word processing file with the heading and subheadings one wishes to use. As the research project proceeds, data can then be inserted into the report under the appropriate heading, and by the end of the project, you will have a draft report. Admittedly, this will need editing, but a great deal of the work of writing up the report will already be done.

Shaw (1983), cited in Chaudron (1988), provides a summary of the staging and sequencing of a research project (a doctoral investigation of the language of engineering professors). The process distinguishes between 'on-site' and

Title: Discourse processing by first language, second phase[a] and second language learners

List of tables
List of figures
Summary
Acknowledgments
Chapter 1   Introduction
                    The problem
                    Purpose of the study
                    Significance of the study
                    Background to the study
                    The aims and justification of the study
                    Limitations and delimitations
                    What this study proposes
Chapter 2   Literature review: the reading process
Chapter 3   Literature review: cohesion and coherence
Chapter 4   Literature review: the assessment of discourse processing
Chapter 5   Literature review: comparing first and second language learning
Chapter 6   Experimental design
                    The research questions
                    Definitions of terms
                    The research hypotheses
                    Subjects used in the study
                    Test materials
                    Scoring procedures
                    Design and administration
                    Statistical analysis
                    Summary
Chapter 7   Presentation and discussion of results
Chapter 8   Theoretical and pedagogical implications
Chapter 9   Summary and conclusions
                    Major aims
                    Minor aims
                    An evaluation
                    Further research
References
Appendix   Test materials

[a]'Second phase' learners are learners who have been in the target language community long enough to acquire oral fluency and general communication skills, but who may have problems with the academic language encountered in school.

Figure 10.2   The structure of a research report: an example

TABLE 10.4   SEQUENCE OF OUTCOMES AND ACTIVITIES IN RESEARCH

Stage in research sequence	*Research outcome*	*Research activity*	
		Off-site	*On-site*
I	Conditions and limits of study established; sites selected	Literature reviewed	Pilot study (ethnography and audio recording)
II			Longitudinal ethnography begins
III	Class for audiotaping selected	Initial professor interviews	Cross-sectional ethnography begins
IV			Audio-recording Videotape recording
V	'General picture' emerges	Transcription begins Professors debriefed	Cross-sectional ethnography ends
VI	Hypotheses generated from transcript review	Fieldnotes completed and reviewed	Longitudinal ethnography ends
VII	Data matched against hypotheses generated in VI	Transcripts complete Transcripts reviewed and analysed	
VIII	'General model' emerges	Final data analysis (integrated analysis)	

'off-site' research activity, and illustrates the range of data and data collection methods, as well as the interaction between data collection, hypothesis formation, and data analysis. Table 10.4 summarises the activities and outcomes in a research project.

Conclusion

In this chapter, I have related the key issues and concerns from the book as a whole to the practical concerns of carrying out research. In Table 10.5, these issues and concerns are formulated as a set of questions to be used as a guide in the design of a research project.

TABLE 10.5   CHECKLIST OF QUESTIONS TO GUIDE THE DESIGN OF A RESEARCH PROJECT

Area	Questions
Question	Is the question worth investigating?
	Is the question feasible?
	Does my research question imply a strong causal relationship between two or more variables?
	What are the constructs underlying my question?
	How are these to be operationalised?
Design	Does the question suggest an experimental or non-experimental design?
Method	What methods are available for investigating the question?
	Which of these are feasible, given available resources and expertise?
	Is it possible to utilise more than one data collection method?
	Given my chosen data collection methods, what threats are there to the internal and external reliability of the study?
	Given my chosen data collection methods, what threats are there to the internal and external validity of the study?
Analysis	Does my research entail statistical or interpretive analysis or both?
	Do I have the necessary skills to carry out the statistical analysis?
	Is it necessary or desirable for me to quantify qualitative data, and if so, what means suggest themselves?
Presentation	How can the research best be presented?
Results	What are the outcomes of the research?
	Does the investigation answer the question I originally asked?
	Does it answer other questions?
	Are my results consistent with the findings of similar studies?
	Are there any contradictory findings? How can these be accounted for?
	What additional questions and suggestions for further research are thrown up by the research?

Questions and tasks

1. Prepare a detailed research plan for a project of your choice. Include information on the following:

I. Background
General area:
Title:
The problem, question, or issue:
Purpose of the study:

      Significance of the study:
      Background to the study:
      The aims and justification of the study:
      Limitations and deliminations:
      What this study proposes:
  II. A statement relating to the literature review, e.g., resources, journals to be consulted
 III. Experimental design
      The research questions:
      Definitions of terms:
      The research hypotheses:
      Subjects used in the study:
      Data collection methods:
      Data analysis procedures:
 IV. Statement on how results will be presented

2. Evaluate the proposal against the set of questions in Table 10.4. (It may not be possible to provide a response to every question.)

3. What problems do you anticipate or have you experienced in planning and implementing research? Can you think of possible solutions?

Further reading

Seliger and Shohamy (1989) contains a number of practical suggestions on doing research. An excellent publication which deals at length with the planning, implementation, and reporting of qualitative research is Merriam (1988). Additional useful suggestions can be found in Nunan (1989), Walker (1985), and Wiersma (1986).

Glossary of key terms in research

action research   A form of self-reflective inquiry carried out by practitioners, aimed at solving problems, improving practice, or enhancing understanding. It is often collaborative.

analysis of covariance (ANCOVA)   A more sophisticated version of ANOVA (see below) which enables the researcher to statistically control for the effect on the dependent variable of variables other than the independent variable.

analysis of variance (ANOVA)   A statistical procedure for testing the difference between two or more means. It is used for estimating the probability that the means have been drawn from the same or different populations.

applied linguistics   A broad field of inquiry concerned with the study of language use, language acquisition/learning, and language disability utilising models and concepts from a range of disciplines including theoretical linguistics, anthropology, education, sociology, and psychology. It has many applications, including language pedagogy, speech pathology, deafness education, translation, lexicography, computational linguistics, and stylistics.

case study   The investigation of the way a single instance or phenomenon ... ntext. In applied linguistics, it usually involves the investi- ... behaviour of a single individual or limited number ... riod of time.

central tendency ... endency of a set of scores to cluster around a par- ... ual measures of central tendency are the mean, ...

chi square ... istical procedure for comparing the frequencies of ... es.

construct ... ological attribute such as intelligence, aptitude, or motivation w... to account for observable behaviour.

correlation   A set of statistical procedures for testing the strength of association between sets of scores.

deductivism   The testing of a theory through the collection of data. Deductivism contrasts with inductivism, where theory is derived from data.

diary   In language education, a first person account of the experience of language learning or teaching.

dispersion   The tendency for a set of scores to spread out or depart from the average or 'typical' values in the set of scores. Dispersion is usually mea-

229

sured through the range, the mean deviation, the variance, and the standard deviation of the scores.

distribution   The representation of a set of scores according to their frequency of occurrence (see, for example, Figure 2.1).

elicitation   A range of procedures for obtaining speech samples and other data from subjects. Such procedures may range from the administration of standardised tests through to questionnaires and interviews.

ethnographic techniques   Techniques such as participant observation, non-participant observation, interviews, diaries, and journals for documenting sociocultural aspects of behaviour in the natural settings in which those behaviours occur.

ethnography   A non-manipulative study of the cultural characteristics of a group in real-world rather than laboratory settings, utilising ethnographic techniques and providing a sociocultural interpretation of the research data.

experiment   A procedure for testing an hypothesis by setting up a situation in which the strength of the relationship between variables can be tested. A true experiment consists of control and experiment groups to which subjects have been randomly assigned, and in which all subjects are tested before and after the intervention or treatment under investigation has been administered to the experiment group. A pre-experiment may have pre- and posttreatment tests, but lacks a control group. A quasi-experiment has both pre- and posttests, and experiment and control groups, but no random assignment of subjects.

factor analysis   A number of techniques for studying the correlations between a number of variables simultaneously in order to identify patterns of relationships among the variables.

frequency table   A table showing the number of times different scores occur.

grounded theory   The practice of deriving theory from data rather than collecting data with the aim of supporting or refuting a theory. The term refers to the fact that theory is grounded in descriptive data from real life situations.

hypothesis   A formal statement about an expected relationship between two or more variables which can be tested through an experiment. For example: 'Field-independent learners will learn grammar more effectively through a deductive approach than through an inductive approach'.

inductivism   The development of theories and principles from data collected through observation.

inferential statistics   Statistics designed to enable the researcher to make generalisations about a population from data derived from a sample.

interaction analysis   A family of procedures for analysing and interpreting recorded speech data.

interpretive research   Research based on discursive rather than statistical analysis.

interview   The elicitation of data by one person from another through person-to-person encounters.

introspection   The process of observing and reflecting on one's thoughts, feelings, motives, reasoning processes, and mental states with a view to determining the ways in which these processes and states determine or influence behaviour.

literature review   A written summary and critique of research relating to a particular issue or question.

mean ($\overline{X}$)   The average of a set of scores, obtained by adding the scores together and dividing by the total number of scores.

median   That value of a set of scores which has the same number of observations above and below it when the observations are ranked from highest to lowest.

mode   The value which occurs most frequently in a set of scores.

naturalistic-ecological hypothesis   The belief that the context in which behaviour occurs will have a significant effect on that behaviour.

population   All cases, situations, or individuals who share one or more characteristics.

pre-experiment   See *experiment.*

program evaluation   The systematic collection and interpretation of data about one or more aspects of a program with a view to improving practice.

protocol   A written record of a subject's data, usually obtained through some form of elicitation.

psychometric research   Research carried out by the collection of data through an experiment, and the analysis of that data through the use of inferential statistics.

qualitative data   Data which are recorded in non-numerical form, such as transcripts of classroom interactions.

qualitative-phenomenological hypothesis   The belief that there is no objective reality that is separate from the observer.

quantitative data   Data which are recorded in numerical form.

quasi-experiment   See *experiment.*

questionnaire   An instrument for the collection of data, usually in written form, consisting of open and/or closed questions and other probes requiring a response from subjects.

range   The difference between the highest and lowest values in a set of scores.

reliability   The extent to which (a) an independent researcher, on analysing one's data, would reach the same conclusions and (b) a replication of one's study would yield similar results. *Internal reliability* refers to the consistency of the results obtained from a piece of research. *External reliability* refers to the extent to which independent researchers can reproduce a study and obtain results similar to those obtained in the original study.

research   A systematic process of inquiry consisting of three elements or components: (1) a question, problem, or hypothesis, (2) data, and (3) analysis and interpretation of data.

sample   A subset of individuals or cases from within a population.

second language acquisition (SLA)   The processes through which individuals develop skills in a second or foreign language in tutored or untutored environments.

single case research   The investigation of a single subject in which the experimenter intervenes and tests the effect of this intervention on the subject's behaviour.

standard deviation (SD)   A measure of the dispersion of a set of scores from the mean of the scores. It is calculated by obtaining the square root of the variance of a set of scores.

standard error (SE)   The standard deviation of sample means. For a given sample, it can be calculated by dividing the standard deviation of the sample by the square root of the number of observations in the sample.

statistical inference   The process of making judgments about the characteristics of an entire population based on data from a subset or sample of that population.

statistics   Sets of mathematical procedures for collecting, classifying, and analysing quantitative data.

stimulated recall   A technique in which the researcher records behaviour, usually on video- or audiotape, and then gets the subject to comment on the behaviour, using the recording as an aid to memory.

survey   The collection of data (usually related to attitudes, beliefs, or intentions) from subjects without attempting to manipulate the phenomena/variables under investigation.

think aloud   A data collection technique in which subjects verbalise their thought processes as they complete a task or solve a problem.

true experiment   See *experiment*.

***t*-test**   A statistical procedure for testing the difference between two or more means. It is used for estimating the probability that the means have been drawn from the same or different populations.

validity   The extent to which one has really observed what one set out to observe, and the extent to which one can generalise one's findings from the subjects and situations to other subjects and situations.

variable   A property or characteristic which may differ from individual to individual or from group to group. A great deal of research is carried out in order to identify or test the strength of relationships between variables. When one variable influences or affects a second variable, the first variable is called an *independent variable,* and the second is called a *dependent variable.*

variance   A measure of dispersion, calculated for a set of scores by subtracting each score from the mean, squaring the resulting values, adding these together, and dividing by the remainder of the number of scores minus 1.

References

Adelman, C., D. Jenkins, and S. Kemmis. 1976. Rethinking case study: notes from the second Cambridge conference. *Cambridge Journal of Education, 6,* 3, 139–150.

Airasian, P. 1974. Designing summative evaluation studies at the local level. In W. J. Popham (ed.), *Evaluation in Education: Current Applications.* Berkeley: McCutchan.

Akst, G., and M. Hecht. 1980. Program evaluation. In A. S. Trillin and associates, *Teaching Basic Skills in College.* San Francisco: Jossey-Bass.

Alderson, J. C. 1983. The cloze procedure and proficiency in English as a foreign language. In J. Oller (ed.), *Issues in Language Testing Research.* Rowley, Mass.: Newbury House.

1992. Guidelines for the evaluation of language education. In J. C. Alderson and A. Beretta (eds.), *Evaluating Second Language Education.* Cambridge: Cambridge University Press.

Alderson, J. C., and A. Beretta (eds.). 1992. *Evaluating Second Language Education.* Cambridge: Cambridge University Press.

Allen, P., M. Fröhlich, and N. Spada. 1984. The communicative orientation of language teaching: an observation scheme. In J. Handscombe, R. Orem, and B. Taylor (eds.), *On TESOL '83.* Washington, D.C.: TESOL.

Allwright, D. 1988. *Observation in the Language Classroom.* London: Longman.

1991. A critique of action research. Paper presented in the colloquium on the diffusion of innovation. TESOL Convention, New York, April 1991.

Allwright, D., and K. M. Bailey. 1991. *Focus on the Language Classroom: An Introduction to Classroom Research for Language Teachers.* Cambridge: Cambridge University Press.

Anderson, A., and T. Lynch. 1988. *Listening.* Oxford: Oxford University Press.

Asher, J. 1972. Children's first language as a model for second language learning. *Modern Language Journal, 56,* 133–139.

1977. *Learning Another Language Through Actions: The Complete Teacher's Guide Book.* Los Gatos, Calif.: Sky Oaks Productions.

Asher, J., J. Kusudo, and R. de la Torre. 1974. Learning a second language through commands: the second field test. *Modern Language Journal, 58,* 24–32.

Aslanian, Y. 1985. Investigating the reading problems of ESL students: an alternative. *ELT Journal, 39,* 1, 20–27.

Aston, G. 1986. What's a public service encounter anyway? Paper presented at the PIXI Seminar, Bagni di Luca, October 1986.

Atkinson, J. M., and J. Heritage (eds.). 1984. *Structures of Social Action: Studies in Conversational Analysis.* Cambridge: Cambridge University Press.

Au, K. H.-P., and C. Jordan. 1981. Teaching reading to Hawaiian children: finding a culturally appropriate solution. In H. T. Trueba, G. P. Guthrie, and K. H.-P. Au (eds.), *Culture and the Bilingual Classroom: Studies in Classroom Ethnography.* Rowley, Mass.: Newbury House.

Bachman, L. 1989. The development and use of criterion-referenced tests of language ability in language program evaluation. In R. K. Johnson (ed.), *The Second Language Curriculum.* Cambridge: Cambridge University Press.

Bailey, K. M. 1983. Competitiveness and anxiety in adult second language learning: looking at and through the diary studies. In H. Seliger and M. Long (eds.), *Classroom Oriented Research in Second Language Acquisition.* Rowley, Mass.: Newbury House.

1990. The use of diary studies in teacher education programs. In J. C. Richards and D. Nunan (eds.), *Second Language Teacher Education.* New York: Cambridge University Press.

Bailey, K. M., and R. Ochsner. 1983. A methodological review of the diary studies: windmill tilting or social science? In K. M. Bailey, M. H. Long, and S. Peck (eds.), *Second Language Acquisition Studies.* Rowley, Mass.: Newbury House.

Bailey, N., C. Madden, and S. Krashen. 1974. Is there a 'natural' sequence in adult second language learning? *Language Learning, 21,* 235–243.

Barlow, D. H., and M. Hersen. 1984. *Single Case Experimental Designs: Strategies for Studying Behavior Change.* New York: Pergamon Press.

Bartlett, L., S. Kemmis, and G. Gillard (eds.). 1982. *Perspectives on Case Study.* Geelong, Australia: Deakin University Press.

Bell, J. 1987. *Doing Your Research Project.* Milton Keynes, England: Open University Press.

Bellack, A. S., M. Hersen, and S. M. Turner. 1978. Role play tests for assessing social skills: are they valid? *Behavior Therapy, 9,* 448–461.

Bennett-Kastor, T. 1988. *Analyzing Children's Language: Methods and Theories.* London: Blackwell.

Beretta, A. 1986a. A case for field experimentation in program evaluation. *Language Learning, 36,* 3, 295–309.

1986b. Program-fair language teaching evaluation. *TESOL Quarterly, 20,* 3, 431–444.

1992. Evaluation of language education: an overview. In J. C. Alderson and A. Beretta (eds.), *Evaluating Second Language Education.* Cambridge: Cambridge University Press.

Beretta, A., and A. Davies. 1985. Evaluation of the Bangalore Project. *English Language Teaching Journal, 39,* 121–127.

Bogdan, R. C., and S. K. Biklen. 1982. *Qualitative Research for Education: An Introduction to Theory and Methods.* Newton, Mass.: Allyn and Bacon.

Briggs, C. 1986. *Learning How to Ask.* Cambridge: Cambridge University Press.

Brindley, G. 1990. Interviews. In D. Nunan (ed.), *Action Research in Language Study: Study Guide.* Sydney: National Centre for English Language Teaching and Research.

Brislin, R. W., W. J. Lonner, and R. M. Thorndike. 1973. *Cross-Cultural Research Methods.* New York: Wiley.

Brown, G., and G. Yule. 1983. *Discourse Analysis.* Cambridge: Cambridge University Press.

Brown, J. D. 1988. *Understanding Research in Second Language Learning: A Teach-*

er's Guide to Statistics and Research Design. New York: Cambridge University Press.

1989. Language program evaluation: a synthesis of existing possibilities. In R. K. Johnson (ed.), *The Second Language Curriculum*. Cambridge: Cambridge University Press.

Brown, R. 1973. *A First Language: The Early Stages*. London: Allen and Unwin.

Brumfit, C., and R. Mitchell (eds.). 1990. *Research in the Language Classroom*. London: Modern English Publications.

Buhler, K. 1951. On thought connections. In D. Rapaport (ed.), *Organization and Pathology of Thought*. New York: Columbia University Press.

Campbell, D., and J. Stanley. 1963. Experimental and quasi-experimental designs for research on teaching. In N. Gage (ed.), *Handbook of Research on Teaching*. Chicago: Rand-McNally.

Canale, M. 1981. On some dimensions of language proficiency. In J. Oller (ed.), *Current Issues in Language Testing Research*. Rowley, Mass.: Newbury House.

Candlin, C., H. Coleman, and J. Burton. 1983. Dentist-patient communication: communicating complaint. In N. Wolfson and E. Judd (eds.), *Sociolinguistics and Language Acquisition*. Rowley, Mass.: Newbury House.

Carrasco, R. L. 1981. Expanded awareness of student performance: a case in applied ethnographic monitoring in a bilingual classroom. In H. T. Trueba, G. P. Guthrie, and K. H.-P. Au (eds.), *Cultural and the Bilingual Classroom: Studies in Classroom Ethnography*. Rowley, Mass.: Newbury House.

Chalmers, A. 1982. *What Is This Thing Called Science?* Brisbane, Australia: University of Queensland Press.

1990. *Science and Its Fabrication*. Milton Keynes, England: Open University Press.

Chaudron, C. 1988. *Second Language Classrooms: Research on Teaching and Learning*. New York: Cambridge University Press.

Chaudron, C., and J. Richards. 1986. The effect of discourse markers on the comprehension of lectures. *Applied Linguistics, 7, 2,* 112–127.

Clark, J. L. 1969. The Pennsylvania Project and the 'Audio-Lingual' vs. "Traditional" question. *Modern Language Journal, 53,* 388–396.

Cleghorn, A., and F. Genesse. 1984. Languages in contact: an ethnographic study of interaction in an immersion school. *TESOL Quarterly, 18,* 595–625.

Cohen, A., and E. Olshtain. 1981. Developing a measure of sociocultural competence: the case of apology. *Language Learning, 31, 1,* 113–134.

Cohen, L., and L. Manion. 1985. *Research Methods in Education*. London: Croom Helm.

Coleman, H. 1992. Moving the goalposts: project evaluation in practice. In J. C. Alderson and A. Beretta (eds.), *Evaluating Second Language Education*. Cambridge: Cambridge University Press.

Cook, G. 1989. *Discourse*. Oxford: Oxford University Press.

Dallas, S. 1990. *NCELTR Bibliographic Series No. 2: ELT and Management*. Sydney: National Centre for English Language Teaching and Research.

Davidson, J. 1984. Subsequent versions of invitations, offers, requests, and proposals dealing with potential or actual rejection. In J. M. Atkinson and J. Heritage (eds.), *Structures of Social Action: Studies in Conversational Analysis*. Cambridge: Cambridge University Press.

Denny, T. 1978. Story-telling and educational understanding. No. 12, Occasional

Paper Series, College of Education, Western Michigan University. Reprinted in L. Bartlett, S. Kemmis, and G. Gillard (eds.), 1982, *Perspectives on Case Study*, Geelong, Australia: Deakin University Press.

Dingwall, S. 1984. Critical self-reflection and decisions in doing research: the case of a questionnaire survey of EFL teachers. In S. Dingwall and S. Mann (eds.), *Methods and Problems in Doing Research*. Lancaster, England: Department of Linguistics and Modern English Language, University of Lancaster.

Dobson, C. B., M. Hardy, S. Heyes, A. Humphreys, and P. Humphreys. 1981. *Understanding Psychology*. London: Weidenfeld and Nicolson.

Dowsett, G. 1986. Interaction in the semi-structured interview. In M. Emery (ed.), *Qualitative Research*. Canberra: Australian Association of Adult Education.

Duff, P. 1990. Developments in the case study approach to SLA research. In T. Hayes and K. Yoshioka (eds.), *Proceedings of the 1st Conference on Second Language Acquisition and Teaching*. Tokyo: International University of Japan.

Dulay, H., and Burt, M. 1973. Should we teach children syntax? *Language Learning, 23*, 245–258.

1974. Natural sequences in child second language acquisition. *Language Learning, 24*, 37–53.

Edelsky, C. 1981. Who's got the floor? *Language in Society, 10*, 383–421.

Eisenstein, M., N. Bailey, and C. Madden. 1982. It takes two: contrasting tasks and contrasting structures. *TESOL Quarterly, 16*, 381–393.

Ellis, R. 1985. *Understanding Second Language Acquisition*. Oxford: Oxford University Press.

1988. *Classroom Second Language Development*. London: Prentice Hall.

1990a. Researching classroom language learning. In C. Brumfit and R. Mitchell (eds.), *Research in the Language Classroom*. London: Modern English Publications.

1990b. *Instructed Second Language Development*. Oxford: Blackwell.

Ericsson, K. A., and H. A. Simon. 1984. *Protocol Analysis: Verbal Reports as Data*. Cambridge, Mass.: MIT Press.

1987. Verbal reports on thinking. In C. Faerch and G. Kasper (eds.), *Introspection in Second Language Research*. Clevedon Avon, England: Multilingual Matters.

Faerch, C., and G. Kasper (eds.). 1987. *Introspection in Second Language Research*. Clevedon Avon, England: Multilingual Matters.

Feldmann, U., and B. Stemmer. 1987. Thin__ a_____ and retrospective da_____ in C-te_____ taking: diffe_____ languages – diff_____ learners – sa_____ approaches? In C. Faerch and G. Kasper (eds.), *Introspection in Second Language Research*. Clevedon Avon, England: Multilingual Matters.

Fletcher, P. 1985. *A Child's Learning of English*. London: Blackwell.

Fletcher, P., and M. Garman (eds.). 1986. *Language Acquisition*. Cambridge: Cambridge University Press.

Foster, S. H. 1990. *The Communicative Competence of Young Children*. London: Longman.

Fowler, F. 1988. *Survey Research Methods*. Newbury Park, Calif.: Sage Publications.

Fraser, B. 1979. Research in pragmatics in second language acquisition: the state of the art. Paper presented at the 13th Annual TESOL Convention, Boston, March 1979.

Freed, B. 1984. Proficiency in context: the Pennsylvania experience. In S. Savignon and M. Berns (eds.), *Initiatives in Communicative Language Teaching.* Reading, Mass.: Addison-Wesley.

Freeman, D. 1992. Collaboration and co-constructing a shared understanding of the foreign language classroom. In D. Nunan (ed.), *Collaborative Language Learning and Teaching.* Cambridge: Cambridge University Press.

Frölich, M., N. Spada, and P. Allen. 1985. Differences in the communicative orientation of L2 classrooms. *TESOL Quarterly, 19,* 27–57.

Garfinkel, H. 1967. *Studies in Ethnomethodology.* Englewood Cliffs, N.J.: Prentice Hall.

Glaser, B. G., and A. L. Strauss. 1967. *The Discovery of Grounded Theory.* Chicago: Aldine.

Goodson, I., and R. Walker. 1983. Telling tales. In L. Bartlett, S. Kemmis, and G. Gillard (eds.), *Perspectives on Case Study 3: Story Telling.* Geelong, Australia: Deakin University Press.

Green, J. L., and J. O. Harker (eds.). 1988. *Multiple Perspectives on the Analyses of Classroom Discourse.* Norwood, N.J.: Ablex.

Gregg, K. 1989. Second language acquisition theory: the case for a generative perspective. In S. Gass and J. Schachter (eds.), *Linguistic Perspectives on Second Language Acquisition.* New York: Cambridge University Press.

Griffin, P. 1986. *The Development of an Interview Test for Adult Migrants.* Melbourne, Australia: Ministry of Education.

Gronlund, N. 1981. *Measurement and Evaluation in Teaching,* 4th ed. New York: Macmillan.

Grotjahn, R. 1987. On the methodological basis of introspective methods. In C. Faerch and G. Kasper (eds.), *Introspection in Second Language Research.* Clevedon Avon, England: Multilingual Matters.

Guba, E. G., and Y. S. Lincoln. 1981. *Effective Evaluation.* San Francisco: Jossey-Bass.

Haastrup, K. 1987. Using thinking aloud and retrospection to uncover learners' lexical inferencing procedures. In C. Faerch and G. Kasper (eds.), *Introspection in Second Language Research.* Clevedon Avon, England: Multilingual Matters.

Halliday, M. A. K. 1975. *Learning How to Mean: Explorations in the Development of Language.* London: Edward Arnold.

Hargreaves, P. 1989. DES-IMPL-EVALU-IGN: an evaluator's checklist. In R. K. Johnson (ed.), *The Second Language Curriculum.* Cambridge: Cambridge University Press.

Hatch, E. (ed.). 1978. *Second Language Acquisition: A Book of Readings.* Rowley, Mass.: Newbury House.

1992. *Discourse and Language Education.* New York: Cambridge University Press.

Hatch, E., and A. Lazaraton, 1991. *The Research Manual: Design and Statistics for Applied Linguistics.* New York: Newbury House.

Hatch, E., J. Wagner Gough, and S. Peck, 1985. What case studies reveal about system, sequence, and variation in second language acquisition. In M. Celce-Murcia (ed.), *Beyond Basics: Issues and Research in TESOL.* Rowley, Mass.: Newbury House.

Heath, S. B. 1983. *Ways with Words: Language, Life, and Work in Communities and Classrooms.* Cambridge: Cambridge University Press.

Hudson, T. 1989. Mastery decisions in program evaluation. In R. K. Johnson (ed.), *The Second Language Curriculum.* Cambridge: Cambridge University Press.

Ingram, D. 1984. *The Australian Second Language Proficiency Rating Scale.* Canberra: Department of Immigration and Ethnic Affairs.

Jaeger, R. M. 1988. Survey research methods in education. In R. M. Jaeger (ed.), *Complementary Methods For Research in Education.* Washington, D.C.: American Educational Research Association.

Johnson, R. K. (ed.). 1989. *The Second Language Curriculum.* Cambridge: Cambridge University Press.

Johnston, M. 1985. *Syntactic and Morphological Progressions in Learner English.* Canberra: Department of Immigration and Ethnic Affairs.

1987. The case of -ing for the beginning learner. *Prospect, 3,* 1, 91–102.

Jung, K. 1910. The association method. *American Journal of Psychology, 21,* 219–269.

Kazdin, A. E. 1982. *Single-Case Research Designs.* New York: Oxford University Press.

Kemmis, S., and R. McTaggart (eds.). 1988. *The Action Research Planner.* 3rd ed. Geelong, Australia: Deakin University Press.

Krashen, S. 1981. *Second Language Acquisition and Second Language Learning.* Oxford: Pergamon.

1982. *Principles and Practice in Second Language Acquisition.* Oxford: Pergamon.

Labov, W. 1972. *Sociolinguistic Patterns.* Philadelphia: University of Pennsylvania Press.

Larsen-Freeman, D., and M. H. Long. 1991. *An Introduction to Second Language Acquisition Research.* London: Longman.

LeCompte, M., and J. Goetz. 1982. Problems of reliability and validity in ethnographic research. *Review of Educational Research, 52,* 1.

Lemke, J. L. 1985. *Using Language in the Classroom.* Geelong, Australia: Deakin University Press.

Levinson, S. 1983. *Pragmatics.* Cambridge: Cambridge University Press.

Lincoln, Y. S., and E. G. Guba. 1985. *Naturalistic Inquiry.* Newbury Park, Calif.: Sage Publications.

Lomax, P. (ed.). 1989. *The Management of Change.* Clevedon Avon, England: Multilingual Matters.

Long, M. H. 1980. Inside the 'black box': methodological issues in classroom research on language learning. *Language Learning, 30,* 1–42.

1984. Process and product in ESL program evaluation. *TESOL Quarterly, 18,* 3, 409–425.

1986. Theory building in applied linguistics. Paper presented at the Applied Linguistics Association of Australia Annual Conference, Adelaide, 1986.

1990. The design and psycholinguistic motivation of research on foreign language learning. Honolulu: Center for Second Language Classroom Research, University of Hawaii.

Martin, P., and P. Bateson. 1986. *Measuring Behaviour: An Introductory Guide.* Cambridge: Cambridge University Press.

McCarthy, M. 1991. *Discourse Analysis for Language Teachers.* Cambridge: Cambridge University Press.

McLaughlin, B. 1987. *Theories of Second Language Learning.* London: Arnold.

Medawar, P. 1984. *Pluto's Republic.* Oxford: Oxford University Press.

Meisel, J., H. Clahsen, and M. Pienemann. 1981. On determining developmental stages in second language acquisition. *Studies in Second Language Acquisition, 3,* 109–135.

Merriam, S. B. 1988. *Case Study Research in Education: A Qualitative Approach.* San Francisco: Jossey-Bass.

Merritt, M. 1976. On questions following requests. *Language in Society, 5,* 315–257.

Mitchell, R. 1992. The independent evaluation of bilingual primary education: a narrative account. In J. C. Alderson and A. Beretta (eds.), *Evaluating Second Language Education.* Cambridge: Cambridge University Press.

Nisbett, R., and T. Wilson. 1977. Telling more than we can know: verbal reports on mental processes. *Psychological Review, 84,* 231–59.

Nunan, D. (ed.). 1987. *Applying Second Language Acquisition Research.* Adelaide: National Curriculum Resource Centre.

1988. *The Learner-Centred Curriculum.* Cambridge: Cambridge University Press.

1989. *Understanding Language Classrooms.* London: Prentice Hall.

1991a. *Classroom Interaction.* Sydney: National Centre for English Language Teaching and Research.

1991b. Methods in second language classroom oriented research. *Studies in Second Language Acquisition, 13,* 2, 249–274.

(ed.) 1992. *Collaborative Language Learning and Teaching.* Cambridge: Cambridge University Press.

O'Malley, J. M., and A. U. Chamot. 1990. *Learning Strategies in Second Language Acquisition.* New York: Cambridge University Press.

Oxford, R. 1990. *Language Learning Strategies: What Every Teacher Should Know.* New York: Newbury House.

Palmer, A. 1992. Issues in evaluating input-based language teaching programs. In J. C. Alderson and A. Beretta (eds.), *Evaluating Second Language Education.* Cambridge: Cambridge University Press.

Perkins, K., and P. Angelis. 1985. Some considerations for ESL program evaluation. *RELC Journal, 16,* 2, 72–93.

Pienemann, M., and M. Johnston. 1987. Factors influencing the development of language proficiency. In D. Nunan (ed.), *Applying Second Language Acquisition Research.* Adelaide: National Curriculum Resource Centre.

Popper, K. 1968. *The Logic of Scientific Discovery.* London: Hutchinson.

1972. *Objective Knowledge.* Oxford: Oxford University Press.

Porter, P. A., L. M. Goldstein, J. Leatherman, and S. Conrad. 1990. An ongoing dialogue: learning logs for teacher preparation. In J. Richards and D. Nunan (eds.), *Second Language Teacher Education.* New York: Cambridge University Press.

Reich, P. 1988. *Language Development.* Englewood Cliffs, N.J.: Prentice Hall.

Reichardt, C., and T. Cook. 1979. Beyond qualitative versus quantitative methods. In T. Cook and C. Reichardt (eds.), *Qualitative and Quantitative Methods in Evaluation Research.* Beverly Hills, Calif.: Sage Publications.

Richards, J. 1985. Planning for proficiency. *Prospect, 1,* 2.

Richards, J., J. Platt, and H. Weber. 1985. *Longman Dictionary of Applied Linguistics.* London: Longman.

Rist, R. 1977. On the relations among educational research paradigms: from disdain to détente. *Anthropology and Education Quarterly, 8,* 42–49.

Rivers, W. M. 1983. *Communicating Naturally in a Second Language: Theory and Practice in Language Teaching.* New York: Cambridge University Press.

Robson, C. 1973. *Experiment, Design and Statistics in Psychology.* Harmondsworth: Penguin.

Roger, D., and P. Bull. 1989. *Conversation.* Clevedon Avon, England: Multilingual Matters.

Ross, S. 1992. Program-defining evaluation in a decade of eclecticism. In J. C. Alderson and A. Beretta (eds.), *Evaluating Second Language Education.* Cambridge: Cambridge University Press.

Rost, M. 1990. *Listening in Language Learning.* London: Longman.

Rowntree, D. 1981. *Statistics Without Tears.* Harmondsworth: Penguin.

Sato, C. 1985. Task variation in interlanguage phonology. In S. Gass and C. Madden (eds.), *Input in Second Language Acquisition.* Rowley, Mass.: Newbury House.

Schegloff, E. A. 1984. On some questions and ambiguities in conversation. In J. M. Atkinson and J. Heritage (eds.), *Structures of Social Action: Studies in Conversational Analysis.* Cambridge: Cambridge University Press.

Schmidt, R. 1983. Interaction, acculturation and the acquisition of communicative competence: a case study of an adult. In N. Wolfson and E. Judd (eds.), *Sociolinguistics and Language Acquisition.* Rowley, Mass.: Newbury House.

Schmidt, R., and S. Frota. 1985. Developing basic conversational ability in a second language: a case study of an adult learner of Portuguese. In R. Day (ed.), *Talking to Learn.* Rowley, Mass.: Newbury House.

Schramm, W. 1971. *Notes on Case Studies of Instructional Media Projects.* Washington, D.C.: Academy for Educational Development.

Schumann, J. 1978. *The Pidginization Process: A Model for Second Language Acquisition.* Rowley, Mass.: Newbury House.

Seliger, H., and M. H. Long (eds.). 1983. *Classroom Oriented Research.* Rowley, Mass.: Newbury House.

Seliger, H. W., and E. Shohamy. 1989. *Second Language Research Methods.* Oxford: Oxford University Press.

Shaughnessy, J. J., and E. B. Zeichmeister. 1985. *Research Methods in Psychology.* New York: Knopf.

Shaw, P. 1983. The language of engineering professors: a discourse and registral analysis of a speech event. Unpublished Ph.D. dissertation, University of Southern California, Los Angeles.

Shuy, R. 1973. What is the study of variation useful for? In R. Fasold and R. Shuy (eds.), *Analyzing Variation in Language.* Washington, D.C.: Georgetown University Press.

Slimani, A. 1992. Evaluation of classroom interaction. In J. C. Alderson and A. Beretta (eds.), *Evaluating Second Language Education.* Cambridge: Cambridge University Press.

Smith, L., and W. Geoffrey. 1968. *The Complexities of an Urban Classroom.* New York: Holt, Rinehart and Winston.

Snow, C., and C. Ferguson (eds.). 1977. *Talking to Children: Language Input and Acquisition.* Cambridge: Cambridge University Press.

Spada, N. 1990. Observing classroom behaviors and learning outcomes in different second language programs. In J. Richards and D. Nunan (eds.), *Second Language Teacher Education.* New York: Cambridge University Press.

Spradley, C. 1979. *The Ethnographic Interview.* New York: Holt, Rinehart and Winston.

References

Stake, R. 1988. Case study methods in educational research: seeking sweet water. In R. M. Jaeger (ed.), *Complementary Methods for Research in Education.* Washington, D.C.: American Educational Research Association.

Stenhouse, L. 1975. *An Introduction to Curriculum Research and Development.* London: Heinemann.

1983. Case study in educational research and evaluation. In L. Bartlett, S. Kemmis, and G. Gillard (eds.), *Case Study: An Overview.* Geelong, Australia: Deakin University Press.

Strauss, A. 1988. Teaching qualitative research methods courses: a conversation with Anselm Strauss. *Qualitative Studies in Education, 1,* 1, 91–99.

Strong, M. (ed.). 1988. *Language Learning and Deafness.* New York: Cambridge University Press.

Stufflebeam, D. (ed.). 1971. *Educational Evaluation and Decision-Making.* Itasca, Ill.: Peacock.

Swaffar, J., K. Arens, and M. Morgan. 1982. Teacher classroom practices: redefining method as task hierarchy. *Modern Language Journal, 66,* 24–33.

Valette, R. 1970. Some conclusions to be drawn from the Pennsylvania study. In P. D. Smith (ed.), *A Comparison of the Cognitive and Audiolingual Approaches to Foreign Language Instruction. The Pennsylvania Foreign Language Project.* Philadelphia: The Center for Curriculum Development.

van Lier, L. 1988. *The Classroom and the Language Learner.* London: Longman.

1989. Reeling, writhing, drawling, stretching, and fainting in coils: oral proficiency interviews as conversation. *TESOL Quarterly, 23,* 489–508.

1990. Ethnography: Bandaid, bandwagon, or contraband. In C. Brumfit and R. Mitchell (eds.), *Research in the Language Classroom.* London: Modern English Publications.

Walker, R. 1985. *Doing Research: A Handbook for Teachers.* London: Methuen.

Walshe, J., J. Hammond, G. Brindley, and D. Nunan. 1990. *Evaluation of the Disadvantaged Schools Writing Project.* Sydney: National Centre for English Language Teaching and Research.

Watson-Gegeo, K., and P. Ulichny. 1988. Ethnographic inquiry into second language acquisition and instruction. *University of Hawaii Working Papers in ESL, 7,* 2.

Wells, G. 1981. *Learning Through Interaction.* Cambridge: Cambridge University Press.

Wiersma, W. 1986. *Research Methods in Education: An Introduction.* Boston: Allyn and Bacon.

Willing, K. 1988. *Learning Styles in Adult Migrant Education.* Adelaide: National Curriculum Resource Centre.

1990. *Problem-Solving Communication in the Professional Workplace.* Sydney: National Centre for English Language Teaching and Research.

Wilson, S. 1982. The use of ethnographic techniques in educational research. *Review of Educational Research, 47,* 1, 245–265.

Winograd, T., and F. Flores. 1986. *Understanding Computers and Cognition: A New Foundation for Design.* Norwood, N.J.: Ablex.

Wolcott, H. 1988. A case study using an ethnographic approach. In R. M. Jaeger (ed.), *Complementary Methods for Research in Education.* Washington, D.C.: American Educational Research Association.

Woods, D. 1989. Studying ESL teachers' decision-making: rationale, methodological issues and initial results. *Carleton Papers in Applied Language Studies,* 6, 107–123.

Yin, R. 1984. *Case Study Research.* Beverly Hills, Calif.: Sage Publications.

Index